Thunder's
Glory

Thunder's Glory

LORYN KRAMER STALEY

ARCHWAY
PUBLISHING

Archway Publishing books may be ordered through booksellers or by contacting:

Archway Publishing
1663 Liberty Drive
Bloomington, IN 47403
www.archwaypublishing.com
1 (888) 242-5904

ISBN: 978-1-4808-2181-1 (sc)
ISBN: 978-1-4808-2182-8 (hc)
ISBN: 978-1-4808-2183-5 (e)

Library of Congress Control Number: 2015951926

Print information available on the last page.

Archway Publishing rev. date: 12/2/2015

Dedicated to the memory of Cory Scott Horton and his family, Gina Horton Cheatham, Jill Horton Carpenter, and Kirby Horton. Through you, Cory's love of life and family will be forever present. He will always live in the hearts of those blessed with the honor and privilege of calling him friend. In spirit and love, we are forever on his team.

Also by Loryn Kramer Staley

The Righteous Enemy

1230 North Garfield

PROLOGUE

Four-year-old Cory Horton struggled to remain in bed. Too young to tell time on the old, analog clock, he stepped to the window. Dawn had not yet broken. *Surely, the sun was out there somewhere.* Returning to the twin bed he often rolled out of and onto the cold, hard floor beneath, he settled deep into the warm sheets, turned toward the window, and looked to the open sea.

Beyond the dock, running lights from a passing trawler lit up the Caribbean's calm water. Pulling a thin, elastic strap over his mop of red hair, he covered his left eye with the pirate patch he received on his birthday. He already decided next year he would ask for a telescope.

Hoping to catch sight of a real pirate wearing an eye patch like his and a heavy steel hook at the end of his arm, he peeked through the binoculars he had forgotten to return to his father. Pressing his face against the glass, he caught sight of Spitty, his neighbor.

Standing with one foot on the dock, Spitty used the other to anchor *On the Fly,* a seventeen-foot Cobia fishing boat. Minutes earlier, when his flashlight went dark, he became tangled up in a mess of grapey seaweed. Before he could steady his feet, he fell face first into the cold, wet sand. Crawling along the beach, he muttered words he once read in a bathroom stall. Each time he tapped the temperamental flashlight against the palm of his hand, a quick flash lit up the shore.

Mesmerized by the light show, Cory threw the aluminum blinds over his shoulder. He pulled a sleeve over his hand and wiped at the gray fog his breath left behind. Tossing the heavy binoculars to the floor, he jumped across the bed. Grabbing a flashlight from the bedside table, he hurried to return to his post. Eager to join in Spitty's game, he held the tubular flashlight to the window. Letting go a laugh, he slid the silver power switch up and down until his thumb grew tired.

Minutes away from pulling anchor and casting off for a morning of fishing the island's best-kept-secret reef, Spitty was drawn to the flash of lights. Expecting Cory to be at his side in the coming minutes, he felt a pull at his heart. It was one of the many times he regretted not settling down and having children.

Watching Fenndus, an aging spaniel Spitty often described as long in the chassis, race across the sand, Cory was ready to dart. But rules were rules, and the first on his father's list was to be followed. *Wait for the morning sun.*

Settling back into bed, he plopped down on his pillow. Humming a tune he learned while watching Saturday morning cartoons, he glanced around the room. Stacked on his bedside table was his prize collection of comic books. A vendor working near his father's construction job traded these for cheap booze and cigarettes. On the cover of each magazine was an action picture of The Incredible Hulk—his favorite super hero. Having not yet learned to read, he flipped through the colored pages so many times, the smudged drawings had begun to blur. Strategically placed on the wall opposite his bed was a poster of The Hulk. Clad in torn and tattered clothing, the gargantuan hero bolted down busy streets, tossing matchbox cars against tall buildings, while stomping others into the concrete pavement. A determined look upon his green face let the reader know their hero was on a mission to right yet another villain's wrongdoings.

Restless and bored, and having lost interest in playing flashlight tag with Spitty, he cracked his knuckles, a habit his father gave up trying to break, and then picked at a stubborn scab a slip on a bed of rocks had left behind. Looking toward the window, he was thrilled when a hint of morning finally shone through a slim crack in the blinds.

No longer able to ignore the ocean's call, he rubbed sleep, a name his sisters called the crusty boogers that caked his long lashes, from the corners of his eyes. He tossed the lightweight blanket aside, jumped to the floor, and balancing on one leg, slipped out of his Dallas Cowboy pajamas and into the faded drawstring trunks his brother had outgrown years earlier. Tiptoeing through the sleeping house, he grabbed the yellow floaty wings he was required to wear every time he went near the water. Worried the day would start without him, he raced out the door so fast he nearly tripped over his growing feet.

A lazy sun created a halo around him as he sprinted barefoot over the white, sandy beach. Kicking a cloud of sand off his heels, he sank deep into the otter puddles low tide left behind. Forgetting his hurry, he stopped to gather washed up seashells and pieces of smooth sea glass, examine bits of broken coral, and looking over his shoulder to make certain no one was watching, trample the sand castles the tides left standing. Squinting from the sun, he worked the inflated water wings up his arms and over his elbows. Stepping onto the pier, he scanned the water's surface for sharks. Finding the coast clear, he skipped along the weathered planks. Taking his usual place at the edge of the dock, he wrapped an arm around a post before stretching his big toe into the cool water.

On this morning, he shared the pier with Spitty, the only name he knew to call his island neighbor who always wore sunbaked skin and greasy lip balm. Each time Spitty spoke, saliva spewed from a widening gap between his front teeth.

"Good morning, young man," Spitty greeted with a welcoming wave. "Tell me how it is you know Morse code?"

He ignored Spitty's question. Instead, he grew interested in a raised bump a bite from a no-see-um had left on his leg.

In his hurry to set out on the water, Spitty appreciated Cory's silence. "Anywho, Morse code was once a popular dot and dash form of communication."

Eyeing the fishing rod and recalling the small gray and black fish Spitty caught off the dock and oftentimes returned to the water, he shot off the question he asked each morning. "What are you fishing for today, Spitty?"

"Reef donkeys."

Twisting a floaty wing in a barrel motion, he forced a doubting frown. "That's silly, Spitty. Donkeys don't live in the ocean. Everybody knows donkeys can't swim."

"That's another name for amberjacks. They call them that because they stay near the reefs. Don't bother asking why."

Growing quiet, a habit Spitty wished he would perfect, he ran his hand over the flashlight's recently acquired dents. "I liked playing flashlight tag."

Having once caught Spitty without a shirt, Cory's eyes had grown wide when he saw the scars on his chest. "What happened, Spitty?" He asked not out of concern, but a child's curiosity.

Forgetting the scars a charged defibrillator left behind, Spitty assumed he was asking about the letters tattooed on his chest. Just as he was about to answer, he looked toward Robert, Cory's father. Locking eyes, he understood Robert didn't want to reveal the raised scars remained after his heart needed a jump start, or that the tattoos were meant to inform first responders and emergency crews his wish not to be resuscitated.

"This here D stands for dream; something I think keeps me young." Searching for words to describe the letter in the middle had Spitty at a loss. When an answer came to him, a smile crossed his tanned face. "The N stands for knowledge." Pausing, he enjoyed a laugh. "Back in the day, I was a wide receiver for the Nebraska Huskers. This here R at the end reminds me to relax. That's what I do each morning on this old fishing boat."

While he continued with his line of questioning, Spitty filled the narrow boat with provisions he would need out on the water. A small cooler protected a bag of potato chips, a canister of salted nuts, and a ceviche sandwich made with a land crab he caught the night before. Wearing battle scars it had earned over the years, a larger cooler held a school of nervous minnows he would use to bait his dinner.

Running along the beach, Fenndus chased balls that existed only in his head. Each time he caught a mouthful of sea air, he put his nose to the sand. Rolling forward, his bottom tumbled over his head, bringing with it a crooked tail and a playful growl. Giving up the chase, Fenndus claimed a spot on the pier. Stretched out on his freckled tummy with a tangled ear flipped over his head, he kept watch over the sea.

———

Rubbing at his unshaven face and fidgeting with tortoise shell eyeglasses, Robert Horton filled the coffee maker with tepid water and a generous scoop of Caribbean Blend, an island favorite among the locals and visiting snowbirds. Keeping a watchful eye out the window, he did not worry his youngest child would enter the water, only that he might fall in. Always moving about like desert tumbleweed caught up in a tornado, Cory's unsteady feet and constant clumsiness kept him covered in bruises and bandages. An active child, whose wild imagination encouraged him to explore under rocks and conquer sea monsters, he lived with nicks and cuts, bruised shins, and raw and tender elbows. Unlike his older siblings, Cory had not expressed an interest in learning to swim. Preferring to hold onto fear, he learned early on to respect the water.

The three-bedroom rental, along the coastal region of Schooner Bay, had provided a comfortable life for Robert and his family. The bungalow in St. Croix's Christiansted's high-rent district afforded breathtaking views, peace and tranquility, and miles of Caribbean waters and sugary-white sandy beaches for Cory and Jill to enjoy. Building sandcastles and tie-dying T-shirts helped keep their minds off their mother and her unexpected death. In the evenings, long after the children had settled into their beds, he took a seat on the same pier where Cory had greeted the day. Inhaling a salty sea mist, he strummed his guitar until tired eyes sent him indoors.

Sipping a mug of medium roast, he made his way out the door. "Cory! It's time for breakfast!"

Hearing his father's voice, Cory glanced over his shoulder. Waving, he gave him a tender smile. Turning back toward the water, he saluted a sailor and his crew. Turning on his heels, he sprinted back to the house, stepping in the prints his tiny feet left behind minutes earlier.

Catching Spitty's eye and Fenndus' ear, he shouted a morning greeting. "I hope they're biting today!"

Spitty waved a fishing rod overhead, and keeping with the greeting they fell into when they first met, yelled back in a speak-easy voice. "Lately, it seems I'm doing more fishing than catching."

Back in the house, he went to work in the kitchen, causing a clatter when a cast iron skillet slipped from his hand.

Awakened by the crash outside her door and the familiar smell of fried bacon, Jill forced herself to breakfast. Shuffling into the kitchen, her haggard face and yesterday's hair warned she needed less hullabaloo and more sleep.

Fearing what was sure to come, he stood with his hands on Cory's narrow and bony shoulders. He shifted his weight and cleared his throat. Ignored, he forced a cough. "Kids, I need you to listen up." Before continuing, he waited for Jill to settle down, and Gina and Kirby to turn their attention from the television. When their tired eyes turned to him, he threw out the news. "I've been offered a job back in Springfield."

Looking up from the table, Jill's head swiveled so fast he worried she suffered whiplash.

"Springfield, Missouri? We can't move again. It's not fair, Dad. I'm just starting to make friends here."

Scooting to Jill's side, Cory patted her on the back. "You'll make friends wherever you go."

"I'm not going, Dad. I like it here." Pulling Cory to her side, she evened the playing field. "I bet I can talk him into staying with me."

As a proud man, shame and embarrassment prevented him from apologizing, especially to Jill. She had begged to stay behind in Springfield when a friend offered him a construction job and the opportunity to get away for a while just weeks after Wanda, his wife and the mother of their children, passed. Now that the building project was days away from completion, it was time to return home, replant his roots, and allow his children to plant theirs. He would not share with his children that he was done running. Perhaps, with the passing of time, he would find the words to help them understand the reasons for his actions.

"I know you've enjoyed living here, and I have, too." Looking toward the patio, he paused to admire St. Croix and the beauty of island living. Hummingbirds fluttered near the mango and papaya trees, pelicans and bull-legged grebes waddled along the shore, and a coconut palm made the perfect backdrop for the yellow allamanda and pink hibiscus. "Mark my words. I have a feeling we'll be back here someday."

Rolling her eyes, Jill forked a slim slice of bacon.

C H A P T E R 1

The Dallas Cowboys and the Pittsburgh Steelers exited the field, and Diana Ross was making her grand entry onto the center stage of Tempe's Sun Devil Stadium to perform the halftime show, when Cory eyed the empty shelf under the television. Ignoring a thick layer of dust and a kernel of popcorn, he prayed the video recording he meant to hide earlier had fallen behind the television and not into the hands of his buddies. Fearing what would surely come if his friends were in possession of the hour-long movie, his face turned fiery red, matching his hair and the back of his neck. Hearing a commotion, he knew their attention was not on the music entertainer but focused on him.

"Here's to Corky—wrestling's best bodyguard!" His friends toasted with plastic tumblers they had rushed to refill after the game's heated second quarter.

Always a good sport, he raised his cup and laughed. Experience taught him that sooner rather than later, he would get a turn to poke fun at their silliness.

"Next thing you know, Barnum and Bailey will want to shoot him out of a cannon!" Rubbing a hand over his flattop, Kenny found humor in everything and was quick to share it with everyone within earshot. "To Corky, the human rocket!"

Days after he returned to Memphis, he met Kenny at a cookout. They had little in common, but what they shared was always followed by a hearty laugh.

Under his breath, he cursed his sisters for sharing with his friends the nickname they tagged on him when he was a young boy. Thinking back about the song they would sing each time he dodged their kisses made him smile. *"Corky Scott is a snot, and he stinks up everywhere!"* Upset with their teasing, he chased after them, shouting his name, over and over again.

Tucked around the backside of an old building, where cockroaches the size of Cuban cigars and river rats often mistaken for house cats frolicked year-round in Memphis' four distinct seasons, his apartment was on the second floor of a three-story walk-up. Exposed bricks were slurried with water and mud, and the nylon carpet was below average grade. Window screens violated by burglars and unknown no-gooders, along with metal latches that failed to live up to their warranty, begged to be retired. A poor imitation of the Mona Lisa hung on the paneled wall opposite the double-hung window. The popcorn ceilings were water stained, and the dull, pink walls were the color of Pepto-Bismol. Months earlier, when he leased the apartment, he asked the agent if they had been painted with sidewalk chalk. Open windows, and generous gaps in the original weather stripping, conditioned the air. In the winter months, very little heat came from the hard-working radiator. His nights were spent wrapped in an electric blanket he purchased at a half-price sale.

Years earlier, the landlord covered the fireplace with painted tile samples he picked up at building-supply stores. The fireplace in his apartment provided a montage of themes: autumn vegetables, Dutch flowers, and wild birds of Canada. His bedroom held very little in the way of furniture. In the cramped room, which the landlord promised measured two square feet more than the actual space, he slept on a twin bed without a headboard or box spring. A bed of concrete cinder blocks placed under the mattress prevented him from falling through to the floor. A small bureau held a framed picture of his mother, and its shallow drawers stored the folded clothes the narrow closet could not. The Dallas Cowboys poster he moved from one home to the next, was taped to the wall opposite the window. Already seven months into a year long lease, he shared the small two-bedroom unit, dubbed "The Hobo," with Bill Hoffman, who, waving a movie video in the air, now held everyone's attention, including his.

Leaving Bill to struggle with the stubborn recorder he purchased with pocket change at a Saturday garage sale, the teasing and joshing continued. "Dude, are you serious? A wrestling movie?"

Reaching into a roasting pan filled with over-salted popcorn, he lined up his ammunition. Taking aim at his friends, he flicked popcorn their direction. "That's what I've been trying to tell you for months. It's really more like a show than a movie, and listen to this—they paid me. Thirty big ones." When they laughed, he again bombed his friends with his favorite snack.

"Did you wrestle Jerry *"The King"* Lawler?" Ignoring the five-second rule and the old carpet's dust-filled piles, Kenny raked his fingers across the floor, scooping up the puffed treat he flicked at the back of his head. "And what is that awful smell? Are you burning poop candles in here?"

He returned a pinched face. "The dumpster is under our balcony." Turning away, he glanced at the television. Diana Ross was still on the fifty-yard line. Until Dick Enberg, Phil Simms, and Paul Maguire returned to the commentators' box, he would be forced to endure their abuse.

A smile crossed his face when he recalled the prank he played last month on this same group of friends. It was Sunday, December 17. Lunching on wet ribs, fried onion loaves, and a creamy slaw topped with fresh jalapenos, they were parked in front of the television watching the Cowboys and the New York Giants play at Texas Stadium. During a commercial break, he stepped away for ice cream. Standing in the galley kitchen, out of sight from the guys, he reached into the cupboard for chocolate syrup, a topping he liked over vanilla ice cream. When he pushed aside a tub of Crisco shortening, he recalled a trick his sisters once played on him. Taking a quick peek to make certain his friends were still engrossed in the game, he put into play a prank he knew his friends would never forget. Setting his bowl aside, he scooped heaping spoons of the white lard into small bowls, topping each scoop with a swirl of creamy chocolate. Placing a spoon in the lard's center, he returned to his friends, who eagerly accepted the frozen treat he offered. Focused on the close scoring game, they forced loaded spoons into their mouths. It was only after they swallowed the greasy lard they threatened to get even.

Another time, when warm weather forced the windows to be left open, Kenny and his date, Tonya, were so wrapped up in a thriller they rented, they were unaware he had sneaked out of the apartment and into the night. Making his way around to the back of the building, he kept a watchful eye for the alley's long-tailed rodents and feral cats he had been warned were aggressively territorial. Dark and shoddy, the alley shed little light to the paltry walking path and slim balconies where damp towels hung at sunset often came up missing. Using a flashlight to guide him, he shimmied up the side of the dumpster. Careful not to make a noise or call attention to his questionable activity, he scaled the brick wall. Trusting weak biceps, he climbed his way onto his apartment's balcony.

Sneaking a peek through the glass, he was pumped to find Kenny and Tonya facing the television. Quiet as a mouse, he waited and watched until the thriller's chilling scene. Having already seen the movie, he pounded on the glass at the exact moment the door to the old and abandoned crypt flew open. Stepping back into the shadows, he listened and laughed at Tonya's high-pitched screams. Sitting on the edge of their seats, Kenny and Tonya argued about who should check the balcony for the mysterious noise—which, within seconds, was repeated. Losing a round of rock, paper, scissors, Tonya crept to the balcony. Waiting until her face was inches from the window, he popped up and rushed the glass. Holding the flashlight under his chin, he bared his teeth and let out a deep, guttural howl. Fearing for her life, Tonya turned to run, only to find Kenny had already dashed from the apartment, closing the door behind him. Later, when Kenny returned, he laughed at the mischief while promising to get even. As for Tonya, she was not seen or heard from again.

"Aw, man, *The King* could take you down with his pinky finger." Imitating the moves he had seen on television, Bill held his hands shoulder-width apart and stomped his bare feet on the shag carpet. "I bet it's a commercial, 'cause with you in the ring, it would be the shortest fight in history."

Rolling his eyes at his roommate's childish behavior, he took to the floor. "I play a bodyguard. I go into the ring and break up a fight. And I don't recall hearing anything about *The King.*" Demonstrating the moves he was taught by a middle-aged, balding man with a scar over his left eyebrow and acupuncture needles fanned out on his earlobes, he walked the rug. Painting a serious look on his face and placing a hand on Bill's shoulder, he hiked over the sofa.

Jerry "*The King*" Lawler often participated in wrestling events throughout Memphis and the mid-South, but in this brief performance, he had not seen him or heard his name mentioned. Given his friend's teasing nature, he did not share that his small role required him to be thrown out of the ring. All too soon, they would see for themselves.

"How did you get the job?"

Gloating over the look of envy he recognized on his best friend's smug face, he crossed his beefy arms over his chest, forcing the extra weight he recently packed on to protrude over his belted khaki shorts. Days earlier, he declared his body fatter than an island tick on the Fourth of July. "Someone at Tigers knew somebody who knew somebody." He was referring to the swim team, for which he was an assistant coach.

Starry-eyed, Bill looked at his famous roommate. At this moment, he would have given anything to trade places with him. For as long as they had been roommates, they watched *WWF*, the World Wrestling Federation program. Catching his eye, Bill gave a proud smile.

While he watched Bill search under sofa cushions and chairs for the remote control, he spoke of building his own swim team, and with it, adopting the WWF's introduction. "I want the same thunderous roar and loud cheers when my team enters the natatorium, ready to kill and destroy any swim team that dares to challenge them." Expecting laughter and more teasing from his friends, he offered a pause. Surprised by their silence, he continued. This time, pride supported him. "I'm going to call my team Thunder, and the logo will look just like that." He pointed to the fierce gray bolt on the television's screen. "Every time we step up to the starting block, all the other teams will fear our thunder and lightning."

"You can't use that, buddy. It's their wrestling logo. Seriously, I'm not sure you should go there," Bill suggested.

He was well aware he might encounter a legal battle, but determined to use the name and the logo. "If I get busted, so what? The worst they will do is sue me." Inviting his friends to scan the apartment's few pieces of furniture and bare walls, he gave a cat's grin. "They won't get much."

"Why your own team? And why swimming?" his friend asked.

He wished he could ponder the question, but the answer had always been with him. "I want to make a difference." If time permitted, and the half-time clock was not ticking, he would have shared with his friends that he wished to help each child he coached reach their potential. He wanted to watch those who stood in the shadows step into the light. His dream was to see the look on their faces when the scoreboard cheered their victory. He wanted to shout their names when he congratulated their hard work. What he did not wish to share with his friends was that these were accolades he once craved and desired. Brushing an orphaned ringlet aside, he welcomed the attention. "When I was swimming out in San Diego, I studied the swimmers in the class I took at the university. I observed and learned. One morning, I was getting ready to get into the water, and for whatever reason, I stopped to watch this guy who swam for his college team. He moved through the water with a confidence I'd never seen before. Later, when I thought no one was watching, I tried to copy his strokes. I could visually see the technique, but as hard as I tried, I couldn't apply it to my own strokes. There was this one day I suggested to a guy in the next lane that he should try extending his arm on the pull. He let go of the wall, played with the stroke in his head for a few minutes, and when he was ready, he took off. He looked stronger and his form was better. He thanked me later. The guy coaching the master's program came over and told me I had a good eye. After that, I toyed with the idea of coaching, so when I came back to Memphis, I went for it."

"I hear you're pretty good. If I ever have kids, and they want to swim, I'd want you to coach them. However, right now, I'm interested in your acting skills. What's the name of the television show again?" Kenny asked.

He had been waiting for this question. He loved nothing more than wrestling. Landing a role where he rubbed elbows with his favorite WWF guys was a slice of heaven. "*WWF Monday Night Raw.*"

When the tape finally played, and his friends settled down, he watched along. This time, though, he watched through his friend's eyes. Unlike the many times he watched the video alone, this time he accepted the role he played was not critical to the movie's success. His pale legs were way too skinny to be threatening and the shirt he wore made his shoulders fall into his armpits. The gel the make-up girl rubbed through his curls made him look as if he had seen the ghost of Christmas past.

Later that evening, long after the Cowboys won the Super Bowl and his friends, who had grown tired of ribbing him about his fifteen seconds of fame had gone home, he faded in and out of sleep on the worn, green sofa he rescued some time ago from a neighboring dumpster. In the apartment's small living room, he dreamed of his future.

"*Someday, my sweet baby boy, people will call your name. Their cheers will rock the earth like unleashed thunder.*"

Sometime after midnight, when he was pulled from a deep sleep, he shot up. Tucking the Dallas Cowboys blanket he had slept with since third grade under his chin, he took several deep breaths. A desperate search of the apartment let him know the dream—the same one he dreamed every night—was once again over.

C H A P T E R 2

On the far side of the university's Olympic-size pool, the announcer called the 50 fly, the three-day meet's next event. Knowing they were about to go up against the strongest swimmer in their age group, Silvie Mercer's competition stood with their shoulders slumped and a burning sensation in their chests. Lowering their heads, several chewed nervously at their fingernails, while others fidgeted with their goggles. None of the girls who waited in the bullpen or paced the deck wore the face of a winner—*only Silvie.*

Swinging pink goggles in one hand, nine-year-old Silvie used her free hand to tap her coach's shoulder. "Coach Cory, wish me luck!"

"You don't need luck, just do your best, and remember to keep your eyes on the finish line." Patting her on the head, he pulled a permanent marker from his pocket. Holding her chin steady, and oblivious to the inquisitive stares from swimmers and coaches who stood nearby, he drew the coveted monkey on her forehead. Giggling, she made her way to her assigned lane. She knew he would use the same black marker to give her the most desired mark of all—*the mark of excellence*—when the event was over. She did not give any thought to the significance of the lane she was assigned, but eagerly accepted Cory's excitement when he learned she would swim in the middle lane, away from the backwash the outside lanes coughed up and spit out.

Taking her place behind the starting block, she caught a glimpse of Gabrielle Rose, her idol. Making eye contact, Gabrielle pumped her fist in the air and she returned a thumbs-up, an exchange they started the previous year when Gabrielle visited her old team during the long-course season. Stepping onto the steel block, she looked to the coach's table. When Cory waved the heat sheet overhead, she knew it was time to buckle down and put on her game face.

Before crouching into a diver's stance, she secured her goggles and circled her arms in a windmill pattern, a ritual she performed each time she prepared to enter the water. Rocking back and forth, she closed her eyes. Unlike the other swimmers who waited nearby, she imagined the race in her head. Envisioning the stroke, she turned her thoughts to the dive she hoped to execute and the flip turn that almost always pushed her ahead of the competition.

When the announcer called her name, a ground-shaking roar filled the natatorium. Spectators cheered and coaches from other teams, along with their roster of swimmers, gathered to witness what they already knew would soon be a new pool record for the host team and another victory for the young Memphis Tigers swimmer. She sprang off the starting block like a world-class sprinter. Kicking through the water like Flipper, she never looked back. The first to touch the time pad, she did not disappoint the crowd of onlookers. She climbed out of the water and serpentined the deck, taking a victory lap around the pool before returning to Cory's side. While she listened to his suggestions and instructions, he placed the earned checkmark on her cheek.

———

Cory's assistant coaching position had allowed him to work with Gabrielle Rose, a strong butterfly, freestyle, and individual medley swimmer. Years later, she would compete for Brazil in the Summer Olympics held in

Atlanta, Georgia, and in 2000, for the United States in Sydney. Displaying an admirable work ethic and constant discipline, it was easy to see great things awaited her.

In addition to his coaching responsibilities, he was placed with the *Guppy's,* the youngest swimmers on the team's after-school program. Encouraging the kids to participate, he opened every practice with a cheer. *We are the guppies, and we're here to swim. When Coach Cory speaks, we zip our lips and listen to him.* This always brought a chuckle from the older swimmers who often repeated the cheer when the guppies played Marco Polo, Captain Crunch, and other popular pool games.

Before he received his first paycheck, he had separated his guppies into two mini-teams he lovingly called his tadpoles and pollywogs. Each team was assigned a leader whose job was to line up her team behind the starting blocks. Goggles in hand and kickboards at their feet, they stood ready in their assigned positions. Placing sensitive and delicate feelings ahead of those who exhibited a future puffed with exaggerated egos, he did not share with them that he arranged their placement based upon speed. Encouraging the slower swimmers to keep up with the pace, the faster swimmers were placed in the lead. Laps later, when the leaders grew exhausted, they were moved to the end of the line, forcing the second in command to take the lead and continue the pace. The mini-teams allowed him an opportunity to evaluate each swimmer's strength and identify where instruction was needed.

Occasionally, Cory would mix things up. Placing the team's fastest swimmers bumper-to-bumper in the same lane, it did not take long for each team member to push harder, better their speed, and perfect their strokes. While most excelled in the stroke of freestyle, he was quick to identify those who showed potential in the breaststroke, butterfly, and backstroke, the other necessary strokes. This helped in arranging strong relay teams and individual medleys for upcoming meets.

He coached the guppies for nearly a year when Silvie's parents arrived on the pool deck just as morning practice was coming to a close. The troubled looks on their faces beckoned him in their direction. Instructing his team to continue the assigned cool-down drill, he made his way across the deck.

"Cory, we hate to do this, but we have to take Silvie off the team," her mother apologized. Rolling tired eyes, she narrowed the space between them. "Randy lost his job...we don't have the extra money right now. Don't even get me started. We're already months behind on fees and expenses."

At her young age, Silvie had the potential to be the team's next Gabrielle Rose. Like Gabrielle, she never missed practice, rarely complained of being tired or having to miss birthday parties or sleepovers, and at the end of each practice, she always asked to swim, *just one more lap.* In between scheduled practices, when he entered the results of previous meets on the computer, he was never surprised to learn she was faster than many of her older teammates. Her diving skills needed little improvement, and her perfectly timed flip turns shaved seconds off her already impressive times. Always a leader in the Guppy events, he believed her fellow age-group swimmers encouraged her success, including Margo, who was always one stroke shy of taking the lead.

Months younger, Margo McCawley was already showing promise. In the Southeastern Conference, she went unchallenged in both the butterfly and backstroke events, and usually beat the times of the older girls who swam the age group above her. Coaches wanted to train her, and envious and less talented swimmers wanted to be her. Graceful as a ballerina, she moved effortlessly through the water, and like Silvie, never missed or skipped practice.

His mind raced with a myriad of plans, but each required the Mercer's to pay swim fees. Asking Silvie to cut her practice schedule in half would only serve to hurt her. "I really think she needs to continue swimming. I can't make any promises, but let me see what I can do."

As her parents turned to leave, he took the first step toward his vision. If he wanted to keep her in the pool and coach her from the deck, he would have to do two things. First, he must call his father for advice, and then he would have to build a team to support her training and his living expenses.

CHAPTER 3

"Your own team? Are you sure about this?"

"Dad, I'm already running on empty. Deli meats are a luxury I hope to afford at the end of the month when the bills are paid. When I need something fancy to wear, I'm buying my clothes at estate sales. This is not a time to remind me they were once worn by dead people."

"They weren't dead when they wore them," his father laughed. "At least I hope not."

"You know what I mean. I can't even bring myself to search the pockets of my slacks." Just the thought made him shiver. "I'm ready to roll the dice, even if it means I'll have to forage for food and live like a pauper for the rest of my life." A quick glance around his apartment reminded him he was already living paycheck to paycheck. Always held back by life's circumstances, Cory was ready to go after what he wanted. "Silvie's good, Dad. She's as good as Gabrielle was at this age. Maybe even better."

Being a part of the team that coached Gabrielle Rose had put him on the map. *Was it possible he would have the chance to coach a second Olympic hopeful?* Although they were miles apart, he heard his father's deep sigh. Pressing the telephone to his ear, he imagined his face. Living in the islands and fishing for dinner off the dock left him with a farmer's tan and sun-bleached hair, that in recent years, worked in his favor, especially among the widowed ladies who wanted a reason to flirt or an occasional dinner companion.

"She's mastered all four strokes and has that competitive drive it takes to succeed. She doesn't need discipline. She needs direction." He used these same words days earlier when talking about Margo. "I feel really good about this. She might be young, but she's as good as, if not stronger than, any high school swimmer. When she walks the deck, she exudes a confidence I would expect to see in a world-class athlete." Thinking about Olympic talent, his thoughts drifted to the articles he once read about Mark Spitz.

In his youth, he spent hours reading the dog-eared and yellowed pages of the 1970s *Sports Illustrated* and *Rolling Stone* magazines his father could not bring himself to throw away. Reading about *Mark the Shark*, a nickname his teammates had given him, and Doc Counsilman, Spitz's coach, made him wonder if coaching was in his future.

"I truly believe I can coach Silvie to Olympic level, and I know Katie Siegal will follow me. She's a tough little athlete. She amazes me with the amount of strength she has. She powers through the water like a cigarette boat."

"Cigarette boat? That must be one fast swimmer you have there. What's your gut telling you?"

"When it's not tied up in knots, it's telling me to go for it. Dad, these girls are unstoppable. I don't want to lose this opportunity to regret."

"Son, you are given only one life. Give it meaning and purpose. I'm sure you've been told this before, but what you put in your life basket will carry with you forever. If you need your own team to take you to a better place, the girls included, then I'm your biggest supporter. With this comes my blessing. I'm not sure what I can do financially, but I'll help where I can. You know you have your work cut out for you, and you can be sure it won't always be easy. Don't be discouraged when you find some of the roads you might be forced to travel aren't sanded. You're going to need a roster of swimmers and parents willing to pay monthly fees to cover your overhead. You also need to take into consideration your own monthly expenses. You have rent to pay, utilities, groceries, gas, and insurance. What about your car?"

"Come on, Dad. You know it's paid for."

"Oh, that's right. Best I recall, you paid cash. How about car insurance?"

"I'll shop around for a lower premium. Lately, I've been thinking I can get it cheaper from someone who isn't a friend."

Recalling a similar situation when he paid out the kazootie for a used car his cousin promised he would sell him at "the family discount," had Robert rolling his eyes. "We've all been there. Hold on a second. Give me a minute to work the numbers in my head." Their conversation hung in silence until Robert cleared his throat. "I'm thinking you'll need at least thirty kids on your team, but more importantly, you're going to need a pool. That's going to be your big ticket item."

Holding the phone next to his ear, he half-listened to his father. His thoughts were already racing through the few training pools Memphis had to offer. It was a given that once he gave notice he intended to develop and build his own team, the university's pool would not be available to him. Country club pools were small, typically twenty-five meters, and his experience had been that training a competitive team was allowed, but only if the club's lesser swimmers were permitted to join the team.

"Maybe I can work something out with the Shrine Building. They have an Olympic-size pool in the basement." He was quick to share with his father that in recent months, he and a tenant in the building had taken advantage of the private pool after cycling alongside the Mississippi River and Riverside Drive. "It's a haul downtown, especially on Union Avenue during rush-hour traffic."

"The Shrine Building? Is that the high-rise on Monroe?" Rubbing tired temples, Robert recalled working construction nearby.

"It's at the corner of Monroe and Front. It's a nice pool, and I would only use it until I secure a permanent base. It goes without saying, I have to have a pool if I'm going to coach my team."

His thoughts turned to the men who had coached him in elementary school, and in later years, during high school. Hired by the school district, they taught auto mechanics, woodworking, and physical education classes during the day. When the dismissal bell rang, they coached basketball, football, wrestling, or track. In his years in Halfway, Missouri, and during his brief time in Memphis, he was never provided an opportunity to learn the sports of golf, tennis, lacrosse, or his sport of choice, cycling.

"My belief is in your determination. You're going to muddle through some tough times, but you of all people, know faith will lead you to the right place. If nothing else, swim in the adventure."

"Nice pun."

"Thank you. First and foremost, keep things right with Coach Fadgen. He's a good man who not only saw the best in you, but also laid the groundwork for your future."

"Of course. He's a great guy. I owe my future to his faith in me. He didn't push me to do better—he celebrated my success. By the way, how's island life treating you?"

"I'm busier in my retirement than I was when I was working construction. I've played every night this week and I'm scheduled to play next week over at the marina." Looking across the room, Robert admired his old guitar.

"All that fame and fortune without a single lesson. I'm happy for you, Dad."

—

Sipping a soda and picking at the toppings on a pepperoni pizza he brought home days earlier, Cory combed the yellow pages. Using a marker, he circled the apartments with listings mentioning a pool. The Hobo lacked not only the southern charm one expected to find in midtown Memphis, but it also lacked the usual amenities most developments offered. At The Hobo, there were no tennis courts or a fitness facility filled with the latest machines and free weights, and just thinking about swimming circles in the round pool made him dizzy.

Research revealed that the fitness facilities with indoor pools were already committed to coaches and swim teams, and a phone call to a YMCA let him know he and his swimmers were required to be members. That was not going to happen—a look in his thinning wallet reminded him his cash flow was slipping away. However, one thing was certain. His new team needed a pool and it was his job to find it.

Soon after indigestion set in, he placed a call to his friend who lived in the Shrine Building. Minutes later, he cleared the first hurdle. Thunder had a practice pool.

CHAPTER 4

"I'd like to coach Silvie."

"Cory, we've been over this, and believe me when I tell you it sickens us to do this, but we can't afford to keep her on the team." Mrs. Mercer's weak voice was saddled with exhaustion.

His brief pause went unnoticed. He had already spoken with Katie Siegal, who, in a single breath, had committed to his team. She had taken it upon herself to call him when she learned he was leaving the Tigers. "Coach Cory, I want to be on your team," she said in her little voice. Hoping she would follow him, he proudly proclaimed her the team's first official member. In the background, he heard Lori, Katie's older sister, asking for the phone. "I want to talk to Cory," she repeated over and over until the telephone was placed in her outstretched hand. Tagging alongside her sister, Lori was always quick to search the pool deck. When she would catch sight of Cory, she would run to him with her tiny arms wide open, calling his name over and over as the distance between them grew shorter. In the passing minutes, she would tell him about her day at school. On the days when she and the Company D Dance Troupe, the team she performed with, learned a new routine, she danced for him and the swimmers who stood nearby. When she insisted upon teaching him a new step, he took to the floor. Together, they laughed each time he tripped over his feet. "I've been told I have three left feet," he joked.

"I'm leaving Tigers and starting my own team. Nothing against Coach Fadgen or the Memphis Tigers—he's a great coach and a good man—and the swim program is to be commended, but I'm just ready to move on. I'll cover Silvie's expenses until you're back on your feet. You won't have to pay a penny."

On the other end of the phone, Silvie's parents exchanged a puzzled look. "How can you afford this? What about meet fees? They add up quickly. Thirty dollars here, twenty dollars there, and if she attends an away meet, there are hotel stays."

Having forgotten about hotel costs, he wanted to kick himself. He had not given any thought to the many out-of-town meets he would expect Silvie to attend. The added expense of hotel rooms would eat away at the revenue he had yet to secure. Pushing worry aside, his only concern was coaching Silvie. "I'll cover meet fees and her USS swim dues, and I'll take care of your travel expenses, including hotel stays."

Wearing out the rug, he paced the carpeted floor while adding numbers in his head and on his fingers. His heart quickened, and wearing layers of stress on his shoulders, he was relieved the Mercers could not see the beads of sweat on his forehead.

While he searched for answers, Mrs. Mercer continued to fire off questions. "Where will you train? Will you be taking other swimmers with you?"

Caught without answers, he circled the floor. As panic tried to worm its way in, he acted quickly to kick it to the curb. Feeling his stomach cramp, he worried he might lose control of agitated and irritated bowels. Now was not the time to show doubt or concern, and reneging on his offer to the Mercers never entered his mind. "I won't recruit swimmers from existing teams, but if someone wants to try out for Thunder, I'll welcome the opportunity. Until I have a pool, we'll be practicing at the Shrine Building. As to the team, I'll build one."

"Cory, forgive me for asking, but why are you taking such a risk for Silvie?"

"Mrs. Mercer, I believe your daughter has gold medal potential. She already shows great promise. All I'm asking is for you to take this leap of faith with me."

"Thunder, huh? I like the name. Sounds like a force to be reckoned with."

Although his heart was beating fast, he appreciated the smile that warmed his face. "Full name is Memphis Thunder. I'll either make Silvie a medaled swimmer or die trying. You have my word."

—

Days later, when the Tigers practice was coming to a close, Cory asked his team to take a seat on the deck. While tiny eyes focused on him, he announced his departure. "I have truly enjoyed coaching you and having the opportunity to watch each of you become a better swimmer." Looking to the team's weakest swimmer, he raised an eyebrow. "Keep doing what you're doing. I see great things in your future."

Shouting over one another, the young guppies blasted him with questions they wanted answered. Standing at a distance, Terie, an attractive young woman who visited the pool area several days each week, listened as he spoke of his departure. Believing no one would notice, she flirted with her eyes, a tactic she knew worked well for her. Finding her thin as a dime and a dead ringer for a young Lauren Bacall, he had taken notice of her months earlier when she threw a curve ball at his concentration. In passing, they shared a smile. He wanted to know more about her, but her confidence dwarfed his enthusiasm. When she swam alone in the dive well at the far end of the pool, he presumed she was a college student. Later, when he asked about her, he learned her name and that she was a triathlete. When he heard she was single, his heart skipped a beat.

"Where are you going?" A young guppy asked.

"Are you coming back?" Margo questioned with concern in her voice.

"Who will coach us, Cory?" Another swimmer asked.

"Hush, my little puppies." Aware of Terie's continued presence, he searched the deck. Standing at the edge of the observation deck's upper level, she had a bird's-eye view of the center's two pools and his every move. When she turned to meet his gaze, his arms broke out with goose bumps. Blushing, he turned back to the curious faces that waited for an answer. Unable to get her off his mind, he wondered if she, too, waited to hear his response. Catching her eye a third time, he thought she appeared interested in him. Before she stepped away, she gave a gentle wave. He was so flustered, he thought he would melt right then and there. It was not until he heard a giggle that his thoughts returned to his team.

"I'm sorry, my little gupsters. Now, where was I?" Always considerate of their feelings, he explained to the young children gathered around him that having his own team had always been his dream. Accepting his words, they stood in line to give him a hug. Watching as they forced damp towels, wet goggles, and blue and yellow training fins into their canvas swim bags, it pained him to overhear their whispered voices questioning who would coach them. Just as he was about to explain they would be in good hands, Coach Fadgen called out his name.

"I just want you to know I've enjoyed working with you and I wish you the best of luck in your new endeavor."

"Thank you, Coach. Coming from you, that means a lot. I hope I can be half the coach you are. Listen, I appreciate all you've done for me. I arrived here without a degree and zero experience in coaching. I expected to be turned away, but you welcomed me with open arms." Following a genuine handshake and a sincere hug, he gave a heartfelt smile. "It's been an honor working with you."

Navigating the center's crowded parking lot, he was surprised to find Tripp, a swimmer with great talent and determination, leaning against his car.

"Hey, buddy. You need a ride?"

Brushing a large hand through brittle hair the color of mustard, Tripp snorted a laugh. "Not unless you have another set of wheels."

"It may not be the nicest car, but it's paid for and gets me where I need to go…most of the time."

"Listen, I heard you in there talking about starting your own team. I want to go with you."

He worried this would happen. Breaking pool records and holding onto new ones, Tripp was the team's star swimmer. He did not want to cause a riff in the swimming community by recruiting the area's best swimmers. "I appreciate it, Tripp, but as with any team, there will be a tryout period. I'm sure you're aware that when you join a new team, you swim unattached, which means you can't post times or score points for the team. This could hurt you if you're hoping for a scholarship."

Surprised, Tripp returned a constipated face. "How long is this unattached period?"

"A hundred plus days from the day of your last competition."

A beefy guy who often displayed a condescending attitude and little respect for rules or authority, Tripp shrugged his shoulders. "Whatever." Grabbing his swim bag, he pushed off the car. Before falling out of sight, he threw an open hand over his shoulder. Having witnessed such behavior in recent weeks, Cory was not surprised by the brush-off.

Later that evening, long after thoughts of Tripp floated off in a fog, he received the call he prayed Margo's parents would make. "She cried all the way home from practice. She couldn't tell me where you're going, but wherever it is, she wants to go with you. Please tell us you're staying in Memphis."

"Are you telling me Alaska is a deal breaker?" When Margo's mother did not laugh at his humor, he grew embarrassed. "I'm staying in Memphis. And I'm happy to hear Margo is interested in my new team. I've always been envious of her gracious spirit. She has incredible potential."

"You know, Cory, it doesn't matter where she swims as long as you're coaching her."

Relieved to have Margo on board, his excitement grew as he spoke of the training pool and goals he had not only for Katie, Silvie, and Margo, but also for Thunder. "I'm designing the team suit and swim cap, and I have a guy working on the logo. I've spoken with a guy in Birmingham about a discount on bags, and I'm hoping to have Thunder towels and swim parkas." He wanted to shout that someday, his team—their team—would be recognized as an elite team whose members would be known and respected and that their hard work would be richly rewarded with scholarships and opportunities. Instead, he chose to keep his vision quiet and guarded. There would be time later to share with the world the Olympic dreams he planned for his team.

"First practice will be at four o'clock tomorrow."

CHAPTER 5

"There it is, on the left." Cory pointed to a tall building at the corner. Pulling cat-eye sunglasses to the tip of her nose, Silvie's mother worked to grab a stray hair caught on the back of an earring as she weaved through slow-moving traffic. "I've lived in Memphis my whole life and I never knew this building had a pool."

Excited to get underway, he nodded. "Yeah, and it's heated. By the way, Monroe's a one-way street, so you can let us off in front."

Turning left onto Monroe, Mrs. Mercer pulled to the curb. Throwing the car into park, she surveyed her surroundings. "I'll be waiting right here after practice."

Hustling Silvie and Margo from the car, he wedged his foot in the building's door. Twice, while herding them inside, he asked the girls to carry their swim bags instead of dragging them across the sidewalk. Turning back, he waved to Silvie's mother as she waited to merge into traffic.

Inside the building's lobby, a triple-tiered chandelier hung from the tiled ceiling, and rich, marble floors echoed their footsteps and resonated their voices. Admiring their reflections, the girls asked if the large doors on the far side of the vestibule were made of gold.

He gave a teasing grin. "Solid gold, from what I've been told."

Encouraging Margo to laugh with her, Silvie pointed to him. "Hey, you're a poet and didn't know it."

Laughing along, he pointed a finger at her nose. "Well, your face is funny and your nose is runny. So there. And I've heard that everyone who lives in the building gets a set of gold doors, just like those." Relieved to find the reception area empty and the building's manager away from the desk, he counted heads before stepping into the waiting elevator. "…and mine makes three," he added, placing a hand on his own.

"Cory, can we go to the rooftop?" Silvie asked, eyeing the elevator's brass panel.

Catching Silvie's outstretched finger as she reached to press the button, he reminded his team that if they acted like monkeys, he would force them to swim at the zoo. "In with the alligators and crocodiles."

"They don't have alligators and crocodiles at the zoo. They live in an aquarium with sharks and whales," Silvie sassed matter-of-factly.

"Au, contraire, mon frère. My friend, who works at the zoo, called me last night to ask if we wanted to train in their pool. They have this new training technique I think you'll like. As soon as you dive into the water, they release baby crocs and gators right behind you. They haven't been fed in weeks. He told me they get mean when they're hungry. Anyway, it trains you to swim faster, especially when they chomp down on your feet. He told me you could lose a toe that way. He also said that if one does grab on, the worst thing you can do is try to pull away. One itsy-bitsy jerk and they'll rip off your foot. I hear they gnaw on the bones for days." Thinking it possible, the girls grew quiet. Seeing he had them, hook, line, and sinker, he carried on. "I told my friend we might swim there next week." *Hopefully, he would remember to tell them after practice he was teasing.*

The Shrine Building's two-story basement was lit up with rows of canister lights. The walls were windowless and the constant hum of rotating air vents drowned out the street's rush-hour traffic.

"Where do we change?" Silvie asked, dragging out each word into two syllables.

"See that door down there? On the far side of the rescue equipment? That's the girls' locker room." Turning toward the door, they heard a familiar voice call out his name. Trailing behind with her mother, Katie followed Lori, her sister, as she journeyed across the deck.

"Hey, Lor!" he shouted.

"What's up, Cor?" Lori asked with a big smile. "I have a new song for you." Taking a deep breath, Lori hurried to serenade him with a Shania Twain song. Proud of the new dance routine she learned, she moved about the deck as she sang out, *Whose Bed Have Your Boots Been Under?* When it came time to leave, she circled the deck announcing in a booming voice she was going to marry him someday. "My name will be Mrs. Lori Cory Horton."

Turning red as a radish, he laughed along. Theirs was a special relationship filled with mutual love and respect. Both he and his young friend saw the best in people. When they met a challenge, they did not let the outcome define them.

When the girls scampered off to change into their swimsuits, he headed to the far end of the pool, with Lori and her mother following suit. It was, once again, time to focus on his team. Noticing the deck did not have starting blocks, he would instruct the girls to jump in feet first. This would do nothing to help their diving technique, but it eliminated a possible injury. Knowing his team was without insurance, this was not only the safest option but also the only one.

Once his team returned, he proudly announced Thunder's first practice was underway. "Never forget this moment. We're not walking on the moon here, but believe me when I say this is one giant step for Memphis Thunder. We have arrived." Smiling at his team, his heart grew large and full. Pretending to have something in his eye, he wiped away a tear. "If I had looked into a crystal ball, I would never have believed this is what I'd see in my future."

Staying true to a warm-up routine he established at Tiger's, he positioned Silvie, Margo, and Katie in a single lane. Since Katie had a slight advantage in the freestyle and would keep a steady pace, he placed her in the lead.

"Warm-up is a 200 free. After that, we'll practice touch turns. Remember, this is history we're making here today. Oh, and one more thing, I don't want to see any flip turns."

"Why can't we do flip turns?" Margo questioned in a whiney voice.

"When I'm comfortable you're familiar with the pool, we'll do flip turns. Until then, I want you to touch the wall." Having come to expect it, he ignored the eye rolling he witnessed from his team. "Now, let's get to it."

—

By the end of the first week, flip turns replaced touch turns, and Thunder added another swimmer to its roster. Larger in number and louder than before, it did not take long for his team to raise eyebrows among the building's residents. It also came as no surprise when, weeks later, a tenant in the building interrupted practice.

"Excuse me, do you live here? In the building?" Her voice was loud and rough—a coupling of New Jersey and Boston dialects.

Embarrassed he would be thrown to the curb, Cory stepped away from his team. "No, I live in midtown." Unsure if he should mention his friend lived in the pricey corner apartment on the fifth floor, he remained silent. No sense getting his friend into trouble, too.

"Well, unfortunately, this pool is for tenants and their invited guests only. Because there are no children in the building, I'm assuming they don't live here, either." Turning away, she faced off with the girls who now stood with their arms crossed over their chests. They wore deep frowns she was expected to understand meant business.

Losing the stare-down, the woman turned her frosty exterior back to him. Putting her hands together and interlocking slender fingers, she sucked the air from her cheeks. "You can finish up here today, but if I see you down here again, I'm hoping I'll be able to welcome you to the building."

Forgetting their stance, the girls cheered. "Cory, you'll get gold doors!"

"Gold doors?" the woman asked.

Embarrassed, Cory looked away. *How could he possibly explain such childish nonsense?*

Suddenly, Silvie was standing at his side. Aware she held the woman's interest, she slid her hand into Cory's. "Is she going to swim with us?" she asked, giving his hand a forceful squeeze.

"She's welcome to swim with us anytime she'd like," he squeaked.

Looking fit and athletic in her two-piece Speedo, the young woman replaced her curious look with a warm smile. "I might just take you up on that once you've moved in."

Balancing on one leg, Silvie pirouetted in a full circle before planting her feet. "Coach Cory isn't married."

Caught off guard, he stood motionless. Silvie always spoke her mind, and in doing so, she often got into trouble. Most of the time he found her innocence admirable, but because she put the focus on him, he grew embarrassed. While his team watched on, his pale cheeks turned bright red. *Is she playing matchmaker?* Struggling for something to say, he turned his attention to Katie and Margo, who were now giggling and blowing air kisses in his direction. Always by their side, coaching and encouraging, he watched in surprise as their individual personalities unfolded. "Please excuse us for a minute," he said, pulling Silvie aside.

"What are you doing?"

"She has a crush on you."

Lowering his voice, he asked the same of her. "She can probably hear you. What do you mean a crush? What are you talking about?"

"She's looking at you the same way Allie looks at Cameron. You know, all smiley and everything." Waving him close, she whispered in his ear. "Did you see her foot?"

Unfamiliar with the name, he scratched his head. "Who is Allie? And what about her foot?"

"That lady doesn't have a big toe, and Allie goes to my school."

"Silvie, your school only goes to the eighth grade," he said, sneaking a peek at the foot with a missing digit.

Placing her hands on her hips, Silvie bobbed her head. "See, I told you so, and Allie's in the sixth grade."

"Kids have crushes in sixth grade? Never mind. Let's forget about Allie for a minute. Just stop with the nonsense and ballyhoo." Returning to his team, he again apologized. "Sometimes, it's like I'm coaching cats."

This time, when the woman spoke, her low voice was sweet as sugar. "This is your swim team? Three swimmers? Where I come from we call this a trio."

Still red in the face, he pointed to Margo, Katie, and Silvie, who now hopped around on one foot. Rolling his eyes, he made a mental note to talk with them later about better ways to utilize their energy. "Yep. These little snotchkins make up my team. Oh, and one other," counting Kelli, who was absent from practice. "That makes my little team a quartet."

Planting her feet, she waived a finger in the air. "Just so you know, I've been to Coney Island, and I'm thinking they might just be a quartet of yellow-bellied monkeys chained to an organ grinder. No offense. Either way, if you're going to coach these little *snotchkins*, as you call them, the least you could do, as my invited guest, is help me with my butterfly stroke. My paws weren't made for the dolphin kick, and my breathing goes haywire every time I break the surface."

Quick to jump at the mention of paws, Silvie pointed to the woman's four-toed foot. "Do you swim at the zoo?"

Finding the question odd, the woman did not answer. Arching her brows, she turned on her heels and returned to the pool.

In the passing days, many of the building's tenants joined in Cory's practice. Not wanting to take coaching time away from his team, he arrived an hour early to work with a handful of the recreational swimmers who begged him to correct mistimed flip turns, better their breathing, or improve wayward windmill strokes.

It was late April when he came face-to-face with the property manager. Standing behind Margo, he was moving her arms through the butterfly technique when he looked up to find a simple woman with a serious face walking in his direction.

"I'm sorry to have to say this, but I've had some complaints about allowing you to train here. I know many of our tenants have invited you, but I'm being reminded of the rules."

Nodding his understanding, he quickly apologized. "I'm sorry if we caused any problems. I've tried to keep our noise to a minimum. If we've disturbed anyone's pool time, I apologize."

"The tenants haven't complained about noise, the girls, or poor behavior, they just want their pool to remain private. It's the only pool in downtown Memphis, except for the one over at The Peabody."

He had never seen The Peabody's pool but heard from friends the hotel's spa offered a small pool designed for comfort, not competitive swimming. Unless he wanted to add synchronized swimming to Thunder's repertoire, the pool was of no help to him.

"To be fair, you're welcome to come by and work with the tenants, but we can't have a team practicing here." Turning to walk away, she looked back over her shoulder. "By the way, those swimmers over there," she pointed to a group of capped swimmers in the far lanes, "are serious triathletes. I know a few of them could benefit from your coaching." Across the pool, a young woman with a warm smile and shapely calves, waved in their direction. "Oh, I believe you've met Terie."

Returning a wave and a sheepish grin, he hoped his interest was not obvious.

CHAPTER 6

As hard as he tried, Cory could never escape the outcome of his first attempts at competing in the sport of triathlon. The events of the competition in San Diego played over in his head, leaving him with memories he wished only to forget. During the triathlon's swim portion, race officials stayed by his side. Insisting he grab onto their lifeboats, they worried he would sink out of sight, drift out to sea, or worse, drown in knee-deep water.

Years later, in the spring of 1995, he entered a second triathlon. Once again, he struggled to get through the swim portion. As he had been instructed to do in his earlier attempt, he held onto the ropes just to stay afloat. Never one to give up, he was ready to give the sport another shot.

The opportunity came days later when Bill, his roommate, invited him to come along on a group ride. "You'll be fine. No doubt some of the cyclists are in serious training, but we'll be able to keep up with the majority. Plus, after the ride, we're going to the Blue Plate."

Recalling the café's blueberry pancakes and thick slices of smoked bacon made his mouth water. "Well, if we're going to the Blue Plate, count me in."

He enjoyed the camaraderie and looked forward to the weekend rides. He made new friends and reconnected with old ones. When asked about the upcoming Memphis in May triathlon, he was surprised to find he was looking forward to competing. He enjoyed nothing more than joining in the conversation's excitement. Having participated in group rides, he was now in better shape. He quickly committed to the bike portion and hurried to recruit a swimmer and a runner. He would not repeat his previous failed attempts. Hoping to convince his relay team to compete in the triathlon's shorter sprint distances, he was a little nervous when they talked him into signing up for the Olympic distance, which included a forty-kilometer bike ride. "That's a lot of mileage on my bottom."

When the day of the triathlon finally arrived, he felt rested and up to the course's challenge. Soon after his teammate took to Navy Lake, he hurried to the bike station. Hanging his helmet from the bike's handlebars, he checked to make certain the water bottles were filled and secured. He pinned his race bib to his jersey, and glancing at his watch, learned he had plenty of time until the ride. Returning to the water's edge, he cheered for his teammate. When she reached the moored buoy, the swim portion's turnaround point, he hurried to take his place in the bike station. When he spotted his teammate in the chute, he pulled his bike from the rack. Aware race officials were watching, he threw on his race helmet and buckled the chinstrap. He was set to go.

Pedaling the old Schwinn, he passed several cyclists, each time taking notice of the numbers written on their legs. The digits represented the age group in which they were competing. He took satisfaction each time he swooshed by a younger competitor. The same could not be said when a cyclist sporting a higher number raced by him like a guided missile. Fueled by the competition, the chase was on. Energized, he rode his old bike at record speeds. He turned the pedals so fast he feared they might fall off.

Catching up with the cyclist he knew only by the number on his leg, he gave a deserving smile before picking up his speed. It was not long before the older cyclist was hot on his tail. Looking over his shoulder to gauge the distance between them had seemed like a good idea at the time, but it allowed Walt Rider, a seasoned triathlete and bike enthusiast, to once again overtake him.

Jockeying back and forth, he gained on him. Thrilled to have overtaken the lead, he was surprised when Walt passed on his left. When the flat course began to climb, Walt took off, leaving him in his dust. The harder he pushed to catch up, the further he fell behind. Short of breath and his lungs ablaze, he cursed the old Le Tour. Minutes later, when he entered the bike chute, he spotted Walt on the running course. Their race was over.

Exhausted and in need of sustenance, he met up with several of Memphis' finest triathletes, including Walt, at the Blue Plate. Seated at a round table in the café's back room, Lesley Brainard, Katie Siegal, Jimmy Reed, and others whose names were unknown to him, ribbed one another about their performances. When he complained of muscle fatigue and a sore bottom, they were merciless in their teasing. "You're falling short here, Cory. You only had to complete *one leg* of a three-member relay." It was Walt who cheered his effort, and thinking back on the course, suggested he upgrade his ride. "You put up a good fight out there today. Just imagine what you could do with a lightweight frame and race wheels. Mark my words, you'll narrow the gap the next time. For what it's worth, I welcome and enjoy the competition. That little game of bike tag we played out there bettered my time."

CHAPTER 7

Having lost their privileges at the Shrine Building, it came as a relief when the Mercers offered their pool for Thunder's daily practice.

"There's plenty of parking out front and you're welcome to use the bathroom off the kitchen."

Listening to Mrs. Mercer give directions, Cory was quick with the hand to put pen to paper. Driving along Sweetbriar until he spotted the English Tudor she had gone to great lengths to describe, he turned left at the next mailbox. Staying the course until the two-lane road narrowed to one, he finally eyed the small sign he was twice reminded not to miss.

Located in a cul-de-sac off Sunday Bridge Road, the Mercer's stucco home was framed with sweet bay magnolias, cascades of fragrant wisteria, and aged wrought iron, that over time had turned Verde in color. Mature boxwoods lined the gravel drive and a circular fountain sputtered recycled water on an enclosed terrace the Mercers swore they would use when they justified the added expense. Since losing his job, Silvie's father spent his days cutting the lawn's zoysia grass, pulling weeds from flower beds and raised berms, and pruning unsightly suckers from the crepe myrtles he planted years earlier when the house was under construction.

Repeatedly giving thanks to Silvie's mother, Cory made it understood he appreciated the pool, while promising to continue in his search for a training facility that would allow year-round training.

The Mercer's spacious backyard spread out over a quarter of an acre. A gas grill and a spare propane tank hugged the side of the house, and matching chaise lounge chairs faced east to capture the afternoon sun. A glance at Mrs. Mercer's dark tan told him she spent her afternoons outdoors. Anchoring the far end of the rectangular pool, colorful clay pots offered a display of artificial ferns and plastic flowers Mrs. Mercer placed in topsoil she shoveled from a barren spot behind the garage. Taking his place near the pool's tiled entry, he announced practice was underway.

"The rules are the same as those we followed at the Shrine Building. No running, no splashing, and no yelling. Do your best to act civilized. That said, let's get started."

In the weeks that followed, he was bombarded with telephone calls from parents who learned of Thunder and wanted to add their swimmers to the team. Building a team that would financially support the training his team deserved required more income. It was time to expand the roster.

Within one month's time, he added four swimmers, including Will, Margo's younger brother, to the team.

Training at the Mercer's home went smoothly until the arrival of September's cool temperatures. Because the swimming pool did not have a heating system, the kids often complained that the pool was too cold. Soon, with recruiting ramping up, they would outgrow the residential pool. Having already grown tired of moving from pool to pool, he was desperate to find an adequate facility, one that would allow him to focus on coaching instead of real estate.

One afternoon, while driving home to his apartment, he decided to avoid Poplar Avenue's bumper-to-bumper traffic and its montage of vicious potholes and take the side roads leading away from Sunday Bridge Road instead. Turning off White Station, he took the little-known and less-traveled Helene, the shortcut through Colonial Acres, an established neighborhood with ranch-style homes built in the 1950s. The drive soon placed him in front of an unkempt one-story building.

Overgrown grasses, mangy weeds sprouting from cracks in the uneven asphalt, and aged signage, had him believing the old building was once a thriving neighborhood club. A 1984 four-door Buick Skyhawk parked under a light post added to his curiosity.

Drawn to the old building, he pulled his aging car to the side of the torn up road. Hearing the car's cat whiskers scrape against the curb, he hoped he had not lost another hubcap—two had already rolled away, leaving behind an ill-matched pair he was willing to let escape. Careful to avoid broken glass and expansive puddles, he crept along, holding the steering wheel with one hand and pushing at the falling ceiling with the other. Staples and pushpins no longer secured the sagging fabric, and the overhead dome light hung from curled electrical tape he earlier hoped would be a quick fix. Moving along at a snail's pace, he studied the old building. Looking through a weathered gate, he spotted a diving board. Eager to learn if there was a pool under it, he turned into the wide driveway.

Exiting the car and its lingering odors, he was quick to recognize and appreciate the sweet fragrance of wild honeysuckle. A rotted fence, buried under a marriage of leggy vines and healthy weeds, reminded him of the small garden his stepmother tended to when he was a young boy. A shameless smile swept over his face when he recalled the many times he sprinted through newly planted annuals and garden vegetables, stomping under his feet the infant plants she lovingly adored.

Weaving through the parking lot's cracked concrete and deep ruts filled with stagnant water, he arrived at the building's entrance. He stepped around the rickety screen door and observed the large room he guessed, by the aged sofa and candy wrappers that peppered the thick piled floor, was the club's game room. Sitting center stage in the middle of the room was a crippled foosball table. A closer inspection revealed the table had not been played in recent times. The playing field's exposed corkboard had peeled away in three of its four corners and several of the team's plastic players had exited the field. A tangled ball of fur rested in one of the goal chutes alongside a water beetle that, in recent months, had succumbed to death after losing its way. A disfigured chunk of chewed gum displaying an obvious overbite, and nuggets of hardened mud, littered the cracked linoleum floor. A handwritten sign on a closed door suggested to anyone in need of a bathroom they should use the outdoor toilets in the pool's changing area. Reading this, he gave a two-thumbs up. Changing rooms with working toilets was a bonus for his team. His nose was pressed against a window overlooking the pool deck when he heard footsteps and a low growl behind him.

"Are you with Mary Kay?"

Turning around, he gave a puzzled look. "Who?"

"Mary Kay, the cosmetic company. You know, their employees drive those pink cars." Stretching her neck, the woman looked around the low wall and out to the parking lot. "That's not a Cadillac, is it?"

Having been teased about the old car more times than he cared to remember, he was surprised when his cheeks turned tomato-red. "It's a Jetta and it's red."

Years earlier, while biking along Grandview Avenue on his way to afternoon practice, he noticed a painted sign offering the car for sale. The older model Jetta had allowed the homeowner's housekeeper to take their children on field trips to the Pink Palace, the zoo, and Mother's Day outings at a church blocks away along Memphis' busy Poplar corridor. Now, suffering from bouts of blurred and failing vision, the housekeeper could no longer drive. Yards shy of 100,000 miles on the original engine and almost as many on the elderly housekeeper, the car's asking price was well within his limited budget. Interested in the car and finding himself without a cell phone, he made his way to the door.

The car's title holder, a thirty-something man dressed in tasseled leather loafers, straight-leg trousers, and a cable-knit sweater he thought was too bulky for the mild temperatures, offered information about the car and the purpose for its sale. In his desperate state, he found details about the tire's worn treads, the average fuel mileage in the city, and the *hardly noticeable* glitch on the driver's side windshield wiper, interesting but irrelevant. When Dabney, the name the man offered, learned his fish-on-the-line coached at the university, his alma mater, the car's asking price fell ten percent.

Pointing to the car's bumper, he asked about the "I Beat Lapides" sticker. "Is that a disease?"

Dabney chuckled and shook his head. "George Lapides. He is a sports commentator. He challenges his listeners to beat him at predicting college football scores. Behind doors, the paper's editor tells him he should accept that more than half the playing public beats him on a weekly basis. There was this guy in my old neighborhood, a young stud with his ear always pressed to the sports station, who woke up one morning with fifteen stickers on his windshield. Lapides was his hero. What I took away from that was this George guy knows sports."

Splitting hairs right down to the penny, the two men shook hands. Pushing his shoulders back and holding his head high, he threw the old Schwinn into the car's spacious trunk and made his way to The Hobo.

"If you say so, but it sure looks pink to me." Staring at his red hair, a look of pity covered the woman's face. She wondered what color he used to describe it. "What can I do you for, young man? And don't worry about Miss Kitty. She won't bite until I give her the signal."

Afraid to ask about the signal, he asked about the Rottweiler's name.

"I was a huge fan of *Gunsmoke*. Oh, in case you're wondering what those cloudy smears are on the glass, she's been boogering up the windows."

Turning toward the window, he made an empty observation. He had no idea what it was she expected him to see. "What's boogering?"

Giving a spirited laugh, the woman threw her head back. "Nose yuck. And don't worry about her bark. Sometimes I think I should have named her Michelin. She acts likes she's been kicked a few times."

The woman's adenoidal voice had him staring at *her* nose. Expecting something far worse than warm air to escape her nostrils, he stepped out of the line of fire. Beneath a three-button cardigan, she wore a plaid skirt with deep pockets that accentuated her wide hips. On her wrist was a double strand of snow-white pearls. A recent experiment with a wrinkle filler had left her with a droopy eyelid, and the wart on her ear told him she was comfortable with the skin tag. Years of smoking had left a cross-shaped wrinkle above her upper lip, and when she shifted her weight, he spotted a paperback tucked into her armpit. The surprised look on her face had him thinking she rarely had visitors.

"I'm Cory. Cory Horton. Is there someone I can talk with about the pool?"

With any threat of danger having passed, the woman relaxed her broad shoulders and removed her eyeglasses. The deep sigh she gave had him wondering if she was practicing Lamaze. "What is it you want to know?"

When the woman scrunched her face, he was reminded of Mr. Potato Head, a piece-together toy his sisters had played with when they were young girls growing up in Halfway. "I'm a swim coach and I'm looking for a training pool for my team."

The woman's laugh sounded like a crow caught in the crosswinds. "Swim coach, that pool hasn't been used in years, except to collect leaves and wayward critters. You know, like garden snakes and raccoons." Thinking about the rat she had seen out back a few days ago gave her the shivers. "By the way, I'm Donna."

He was tempted to ask about the wayward critters, but nodded toward the diving board, instead. "Would it be okay if I walked back there to take a look?"

"Suit yourself. Just be sure to keep an eye out for the homeless guy." Holding his attention, Donna gave a wink with the droopy lid.

Unsure how to respond, he remained silent. Unlocking the door leading out to the deck, he made his way outside. In the distance, a dog let out a threatening growl. He hoped it was behind a fence.

A few feet from the gate was a small building. Not seeing another building on the property, he assumed the flat-roofed, windowless building had a working bathroom.

A rusted gas pump and an overturned kayak claimed a grassy patch near the fence. Empty chlorine buckets, paint cans freckled with splatter, and plastic pails he recognized as paint primer littered the rectangular pool. Plastic lawn chairs sat stacked under a metal awning, and bird poop peppered the threadbare artificial turf. A neglected baby pool sat off to the side.

A thick layer of shriveled leaves, snapped twigs, and food wrappers from fast-food joints blanketed the pool's deep end. Inhaling a repulsive odor, he pinched his nose. There was no doubt sewage water awaited at the bottom. Broken and discolored tiles that once stood proud against the gunite now peeked out from the murky water. Roofing shingles weighed down old newspapers exposed to nature's elements and faded some time ago.

In the shallow end, a three-prong extension cord held a weathered sweatshirt hostage to a laundry basket. Scratching his head, he wondered how the basket came to rest at the bottom of the pool. Hanging by a single hinge, the diving board turned away in shame.

Standing at the pool's edge, he was in full agreement with Donna. The pool was old and in need of repair, but when he heard the hum of the old pump, hope replaced doubt.

Turning to head back indoors, he was startled to come face-to-face with an odorous creature. *Could this be man's missing link?* Wrapped in a burro blanket and sporting a head of matted hair that looked as though a cat coughed it up and spit it out, the hunched-over vagrant wreaked of human feces and the sour stench of urine. His breath smelled like he had been gnawing on road kill, and his scarred and boney fingers were orange in color. Dark circles under his eyes rested against his haggard face. Eyeing flakes of dried blood on his chin and peeking out from the crevices of his aging neck, he wondered if the man had scurvy. Over his shoulder hung a plastic garbage bag that smelled of rotten flesh and three-day-old-fish.

"Peace, man," the drifter grunted as he sidestepped around him and into loose gravel.

Staring into his eyes, the man turned his dry and cracked lips into a smile. An unexpected twitch in his cheek put him on alert. When the vagrant winked through a clouded eye, he stumbled backward. Unfazed by his appearance, the old man shuffled to an iron gate and slowly made his way to a shopping cart filled with tree branches, packing quilts, and soda cans.

Fearing head lice and fleas had jumped onto him, he hurried to rake his fingers through his hair. Eyeing the laundry basket, he wondered if the man washed his clothes in the pool. Glancing back at him, he dismissed the idea. Passing by the changing rooms, a rancid odor had him choosing to forgo a tour. Satisfied he had seen enough, he returned to the clubhouse.

"I see you met Down on His Luck Chuck."

Covering his nose with his fingers, he wondered if Chuck was the man's real name. "I think Chuck's been skipping bath time for quite a while. Does he live out there?"

"I believe so, but I'm not sure. He's like a toot. You won't always see him, but you know he's nearby." When she parted the blinds, he worried Chucky was making his way back to the clubhouse, but when Donna rested a chubby elbow on the sill, he gathered Chuck was a safe distance away. Throwing a hand to her head, she circled the air with a pointed finger. "I hear he has squirrels in the attic."

He snorted a giggle. "I believe the expression is, he has bats in the belfry."

"I'm sure he has those, too." Cackling, she slapped a hand against her thigh. "Sometimes he moseys on down the tracks toward Poplar Pike. You know, at the intersection there by Park Place Mall. I'm guessing he gets more handouts down that way." Glancing at her nails, Donna paused to bite at a torn cuticle. "He won't be hanging out around here once the remodel gets underway. Oh, by any chance did you see a polecat out there? That little critter keeps dodging our traps."

Hearing remodel and polecat made him squirm. "What's a polecat?"

"It's the offspring of a ferret and a skunk. Darn thing stinks to high heaven. He showed up here a few months ago. He most likely got away from his owner or maybe got dumped here. Anyway, judging by the scat piles, I'd say he's well fed."

He was desperate for a training facility and because the club was only a handful of miles away from the schools his swimmers attended, its location was perfect. *Except for Chuck and the I-240 overpass he lived under.* Having no clue what scat is, he had little concern about the unwanted pet. "Do you know when the work will begin?"

Displaying a chipped fingernail, Donna gave a wave with her hand. "The plans aren't even drawn up yet."

Frustrated, he gave an obvious sigh. "Who would I need to talk with about leasing the pool?"

"You really want to rent that pool?" A snort and a hiccup followed Donna's laugh. "Like I said earlier, that old pool hasn't been used in years."

"Well, the pump still works and that gives me hope."

This time, when Donna looked at him, she leaned against the door-frame, tilted her head, and crossed thick arms over her chest. "It's Cory, right? Listen, give me a telephone number where we can reach you and I'll ask someone to give you a call. It'll be sometime next week. By the way, what's the name of your team?"

Standing taller than he had in his entire life, he invited confidence to support him. "We are Memphis Thunder."

CHAPTER 8

Saturday morning found the clubhouse in Colonial Acres buzzing with activity. The kids pushed mops and wiped down walls and windows while their parents swept brooms across the deck and vacuumed the fake grass and carpeted floors. Surfaces were cleaned with soap and disinfectants, and plastic bags were filled with garbage waiting to be dragged to the curb. Wearing fishing waders he borrowed from a neighbor and a gardening mask he picked up at a local garden store, Cory shoveled muck and debris from the pool's deep end. The odor was toxic and he worried about the creatures he was sure to unearth. When his friends arrived with a power washer, he gave a broad smile. Holding his hand in the air and pressing a finger to his thumb, he gave an okay sign.

By mid-afternoon, he recruited a handful of friends to help shuck the pool with pitchforks and load a flatbed truck with heavy garbage bags and worthless junk. Hearing of his project, several neighbors stopped by to lend a hand. Taking in the eyesore, they did not have to ask what needed to be done. Missing pool tiles were replaced, and those that managed to survive abandonment and vandalism received a thorough cleaning with toothbrushes and good old elbow grease. Secondhand starting blocks he purchased at an auction in nearby Arkansas were bolted to the concrete. After a good rinsing, the baby pool sparkled like new.

When his crew grew hungry, they wrapped up the day with hot pizza and cold sodas. After the last slice of pie was devoured, Cory thanked his team and friends as they took to the parking lot.

Alone and resting in a plastic lawn chair with a full moon lighting up the night, he kept watch over the rubber garden hoses used to fill the eight-foot deep pool. Giving in to exhaustion, he closed his eyes. Comforted by the water's rhythmic purr, his thoughts turned to his childhood and the stories he often heard.

CHAPTER 9

It was the fall of 1969, months before Wanda Horton expected to give birth to her fourth child. Because it was the weekend, her older children were away at church camp. She wanted only to rest at the home she shared with her husband and their three children on the west side of Rogersville, Missouri. Like most homes in the 1960s, windows were open and doors were left unlocked, theirs included. Living in a small town, it was likely they would know their burglar.

When the children were underfoot, including Jill who was still just a toddler, moments of respite were few and far between. Minutes earlier, Wanda had pulled wet sheets from the washing machine. After taking a quick peek to make certain Jill was still napping, she made her way through the house, all the while creeping along on tiptoes. Hoping to return to her Bible reading once the laundry was finished, she prayed her footsteps would not disturb her sleeping child. Not hearing a peep, she made her way outdoors.

Keeping a safe distance from the mulberry trees, a lesson she learned the hard way when a bird resting on a branch above her lightened his load, she took a moment to enjoy the afternoon's gentle breeze and the sun's warm rays. She lifted her face to the sky, and pushing aside a throbbing headache, praised the Lord for the glorious weather. In recent days, temperatures had soared to triple digits, bringing with it biting horseflies, bloodthirsty mosquitoes, and nights filled with restless sleep. Tossing and turning, and oftentimes removing the socks she wore each night, she struggled to ward off the stifling heat.

Glancing at the crops her neighbors farmed, she wished for them a healthy harvest. Placing her hands on widened hips, she frowned at the pathetic garden she tended until last month when allergies and headaches kept her indoors. Next year, if time permitted, she would grow fat radishes and the long reddish-orange tomatoes she thought were called Indian River. These were vegetables she had come to crave in recent weeks. Because they were the children's favorites, she also hoped to plant sweet corn and snapping green beans.

Feeling the wind at her face, she knew the laundry would dry in no time at all. Once the wet linens were hung, she ventured out to the garbage. As much as she disliked burning the trash the city's sanitation workers did not collect, she knew Robert, her husband, would appreciate the help, especially since he was busy with the many construction projects he worked, not only in Rogersville but also in neighboring counties.

Keeping a watchful eye on the screen door for any sign of Jill, she hurried to fill the old barrels with empty soda cans, month-old newspapers, and the plastic milk jugs she had forgotten to rinse. Trained eyes told her there was room in the larger barrel for the cardboard box a baby gift arrived in days earlier. Breaking it down along the creases of its once-folded sides, she forced the box into the slow burning fire. Twice she stopped to push her wind-blown hair behind her ears. The third time she paused was to stretch her tired body. Standing tall, she arched her back and rolled her shoulders. Rubbing a hand over her pregnant belly, she used the other to shield her eyes from the blinding sun. A faint kick to her tummy reminded her that although she was only five months along in her pregnancy, the baby she carried was an active one.

Pulling strands of stray hair away from her face, she was suddenly aware the gentle breeze she expected to dry towels and bed sheets was fast becoming an unexpected northern wind. Swirling about, it lifted the fire's red-hot embers into a tornadic cyclone. Checking to make sure the fire was burning below the barrel's rim, she did not feel its threat. She poked and prodded at the fire with a garden rake she found near the trash until a burning vein ran through the box. When a gust of wind knocked her off balance, she stepped away from the barrel. Caught in the path of a dangerous storm, she had no way of knowing these same winds that now taunted the burning trash had already downed power lines and uprooted trees in neighboring Green County and were headed toward Rogersville's Webster County at damaging speeds.

Stacked in thick piles a stone's throw from the burning barrels were grass clippings, dry leaves a recent rain had plucked from nearby trees, and fallen branches Robert had gathered days earlier when he worried the children would poke out an eye. Now, frightfully aware of the possible danger high winds could create, she decided to hold off burning the pile of yard debris.

Startled by a loud bang, she looked up at the house. A second thud let her know a window shutter had fallen victim to an unsuspecting burst of wind. Sparks floated about, and when she felt a pinching sting, she worried another migraine was coming on. Brushing a hand behind her ear, she let out a yelp when she felt a fiery ember. Touching raw skin, she let out a cry. Bending at the waist, she shook out her hair.

As she hurried to throw metal screens over the burning barrels, violent winds whipped about, taking with it empty cans, tattered plastic, and funnels of leaves whose edges burned a fiery red. Feeling a burning sensation on her back, she pulled at her blouse. Carried on a gust of wind and spreading like water over the blouse's polyester fabric, raging flames took hold of the sleeves. A plume of gray smoke filled the air. Dropping to the ground, she let out a howling scream.

Inside the house, young Jill opened her weary eyes. Hearing a cry, she had been pulled from sleep. Hopping from the bed she usually shared with Gina, her older sister, she ran through the house, frantically searching the rooms as she called out for her mother. Her eyes grew wide with fear as she reached the screen door. Afraid to step outside, she watched in horror as wild flames jumped from her mother's flailing arms to her dark hair. Within seconds, Wanda was buried under a bed of fire. Overhead, tree branches blazed and sparks flew from ravaged power lines.

Hearing an explosion, Jill watched as a mushroom of dark smoke rushed the sky. When a burning branch fell to the roof, she covered her eyes.

Neighbors passing by the Horton's home noticed the thick smoke. Until they heard the cries for help, they thought Robert was burning trash. Shoving the truck into park, Mrs. Mathews raced through the deep ditch to the Horton's backyard while Mr. Mathews hurried to call for help. Eyeing Jill on the porch and the house that was now an inferno, he shouted for her to make a run for the truck. Rushing to Wanda's side, Mrs. Mathews promised her neighbor she would be okay. "Help is on the way."

Moving quickly, Mrs. Mathews pulled damp linens from the clothesline. Dragging them across the yard, she positioned herself upwind of the growing fire. Praying for a miracle, she threw the sheets over Wanda's head and back, and with no time to consider the risks she was taking with the unborn child, she pulled at her feet until she was out of harm's way. Holding Wanda in her arms, they waited for the paramedics to arrive.

Fortunate to be alive, she suffered third-degree burns to her face, arms, chest, and back. What little hair remained was singed, and her scalp suffered minor burns. Emergency crews were able to save her and her unborn child, but because the fire department was not alerted to the emergency, the Horton's lost their home and everything in it.

While she remained in the hospital, the Horton family moved to a new home in nearby Springfield. The house, which Robert helped construct, was white brick and a shade of brown not found on any color chart. Black shutters framed the first-floor windows. Unlike their home in Rogersville, the house was located in an established neighborhood with streetlights and sidewalks. Suffering nightmares and intense pain, she was relieved to learn fire hydrants were close by.

Months later, on a bitter wintry December day that left parts of Missouri with intermittent outages, miles of unplowed roads, and below-freezing temperatures, Wanda held her head in her hands. Fearing it might explode, she prayed the pain would go away. Finding the headache more stubborn than the others she suffered, she was unable to leave the bed. The table next to her was littered with half-filled water glasses, prescription medication, and empty aspirin bottles. A sleep mask peeked out from an open drawer. Needing the space the small table offered, she had pushed the lamp to the floor.

In past weeks, she missed daily mass, the many women's luncheons she was asked to host, and the mentor program she, along with dear friends, had founded. With strong Christian values, she wanted only to serve as a moral compass for her friends, family, and community, but an increase in migraines kept her exhausted and homebound.

Outside the bedroom window, bitter winds uprooted several trees while others were left saddled with thick ice. Drooping low, their tender branches kissed the frozen crystals newly fallen snow left behind. While the northeaster continued to deliver a wind chill far below zero and blanket rural Springfield, a growing drift nestled against the north side of their single-story house. Several of the shutters, now buried under heavy snow, held on by hinges that promised in their burdened state, would not weather another storm. Iridescent icicles not yet yellowed by ill-mannered squirrels hung from the gutters, and a thin cloud of smoke escaped the fireplace's hardworking chimney.

Discouraged by the weather and her unrelenting headaches, she could no longer ignore the tightening she felt in her abdomen.

As the evening hours fell on December 27, 1969, and during one of the worst winter storms to pound the Midwest, she and Robert welcomed their fourth child. When Robert learned he had been blessed with another son, he burst with pride. Although she often expressed an interest in the tradition of passing along family names, her ancestors had lost to the trendy names she came across in the newspaper and in the church bulletin.

Weighing in at seven pounds, Cory Scott Horton won the hearts of the nurses who cared for him and the friends who, risking icy roads, came to visit. Resembling his sisters, he was born with sapphire eyes, rosy cheeks, and a full head of bright red hair his siblings called orange each time they were asked about the family's new addition. Like a trained pianist, his fingers were long and slender, and his vocal chords would most certainly be the envy of every tenor. Wrapped in a warm blanket, he was passed from one family member to the next, each teasing Wanda that the wildfire she battled months earlier had caused his hair to turn its fiery color.

Taking his first step at thirteen months, Cory followed his sisters from room to room, learning from them along the way. Standing at Jill's side, he was fascinated with the view the living room's large picture window offered of the outside world. When the neighbor's golden retriever barked at squirrels and passers-by, he pressed his button nose against the screen. Cupping his mouth the way Kirby taught him, he barked in return. When he giggled, his full cheeks turned cherry red. In the afternoons when their mother napped, a routine that lessened the intensity of the migraines she continued to suffer, his older siblings took turns reading to him the books their mother checked out from the local library, along with those she borrowed from church.

Although he was not allowed to ride the horses Gina saddled and groomed each day after school, he enjoyed playing in the barn. Seated on an old wooden bench their father made from scraps he salvaged from construction sites, he clapped his hands together each time Gina took to the arena. Pointing to Pepper, a Fox Trotter she rode in competitions, he shrilled with excitement. Wanting to ride the buckskin mare, he shouted his sister's name. Each time Gina responded with a frown, he squeezed his eyes shut and pushed out his bottom lip.

Unlike his sisters, he avoided the damp and dark waters located along the southernmost border of the acreage's tule patch. When Gina chased wild rabbits and slow-moving beetles into the tufted and tall grasses, willow-leaved sunflowers, and the grass he feared the most—the rattlesnake master—he took to the porch. One day, when a ball he kicked rolled into the thick and spiky blades, he raced into the house, never stopping to look over his shoulder for fear angry weeds were on his tail.

———

Four months after Cory celebrated his second birthday, Wanda visited with her doctor a fifth time. "My headaches are worsening and now my vision is a little blurred, especially early in the mornings when I'm trying to read my Bible. Just this morning I couldn't get through 3 John without giving my eyes a rest."

"I feel certain before long you'll be zipping through Genesis." Offering a gentle smile, her doctor opened the thick file the nurse had left for him. Canvasing the pages, he repeated the same words he spoke each time they visited. "Wanda, it's just allergies."

Concerned about his wife's health, Robert encouraged her to make an appointment with a specialist. The five-week wait seemed far longer, and soon Wanda found herself burdened with worry. She had watched her brother, a practicing minister, suffer from headaches, nausea, and vomiting, and as his body weakened, loss of hearing and balance that forced him to resign from his leadership position at his house of worship. Eventually, he lost the battle and his life to an aggressive and malignant brain tumor.

When the day of the appointment finally arrived, she walked unsteadily through the building's automatic doors. Several times, she considered turning around and going back home, but the pounding in her head forced her to seek relief and answers. Shielding her family from the fears that raced through her aching head, she eased their concerns when she pretended the appointment was routine. "When we leave here, we're going to eat ice cream and donuts until the cows come home."

Worried about his wife, Robert reached for her hand. A single tear on his cheek let her know he admired her courage. "Chocolate with sprinkles," he lovingly added.

The elevator ride left her nervous and mildly nauseous. Afraid of what she might learn in the coming hours, she pulled her children close.

Wrapping her weak and scarred arms around Cory, she pressed him against her breast. "Everything's going to be okay," she whispered reassuringly. As the words escaped her lips, she was brought to tears. The words were not meant to ease their fears or disguise her own. She had hoped they would convince her the fears that burdened her were misguided.

In the passing hours, while her family worked to keep their minds busy, the nurses put her through a myriad of medical tests and drew several vials of blood. When a nurse told her more tests were necessary, her worry turned to panic.

—

The Horton family's greatest fears were confirmed the following day when Wanda received a telephone call from the neurologist. "The tumor is about the size of a small orange, but at this point I'm not concerned." Pausing, he read through the report. "I suggest we hold steady for a few months and see what happens."

Unable to bite back tears, she rubbed a hand over her scalp. Searching for a bump or tender spot, her fingers moved over the scars the burns she suffered years earlier had left behind. Trembling, she worried for her future. "I want it removed."

Before responding, the doctor gave an audible sigh. "It's really not necessary at this time."

Raising her voice, she shouted into the phone. "I want it removed—now."

Resigned, the doctor agreed. "Of course."

Ending the call, she made her way to the bathroom. Burdened and consumed with worry, she stepped over wet towels the kids had been instructed to hang on the row of hooks on the porch. Taking a washcloth from the sink, she locked eyes with the reflection in the mirror. Staring back at her was a woman zapped of energy and filled with worry. Having recently celebrated her thirty-fifth birthday, she was taken aback by the dark circles under her eyes and the lifeless skin she expected to see not now, but decades later. Feeling a chill come over her, she rubbed her arms with hands she no longer recognized. *When had they grown so pale and thin?* Easing her shoulders, she swept nervous fingers through her hair, and catching a tangle with her wedding ring, her thoughts turned to her family. Robert was a good father, but she worried he would not be able to care for their children if something happened to her. The thought of another woman raising her children brought on a hammering headache. *No one would ever love them enough.* She rubbed her throbbing temples, knowing surgery was her only hope. She could not continue to live like this.

She pulled her dark hair into a tight ponytail. Pulling a scarf from a drawer, she wrapped it around her head, and with unsure hands, clipped earrings to her lobes. Taking a step back, she again looked into the mirror. This time, it was fear that stared back at her.

Coming up behind, Robert took her in his arms. "It's not your hair that makes you beautiful, Wanda. It's your forgiving heart, your love of life, and the way you love our children and me. I'm constantly amazed and awed by your love of the Lord and your servant's spirit."

"Luke 22:27. Am I wrong to trust this doctor with my life? And what about our children? Who will care for them if…"

Cutting her off, Robert held her face in his hands. "Wanda, nothing is going to happen to you. When you get out of surgery, you'll be better than new. The neurologist is well known and highly respected. The wall plaques, awards, and certificates displayed in his office tell me he's a capable and qualified surgeon. Honey, he's on staff at a nationally recognized hospital."

The following Tuesday, the day before her scheduled surgery, she called her children to her side. "Kirby, you're the oldest and I'm trusting you to help your father with your sisters and Cory. I'm not sure when I'll be up and about, or when my hair will grow back, so there might be times I'll need you to help me, especially when your dad is away at work. Gina, your father will wash the laundry, but it would be a big help if you could fold and put it away. I want you to promise you'll help with Jill and Cory."

Gina wiped at her cheeks with the sleeve of her blouse. "I will, Mom. I'll get books from the library, and every night before bedtime, I'll come right here and sit next to you and read from the Bible."

"I'll help, too," Jill promised. "And when your hair grows back, I'll brush it for you."

Concerned for their mother, the children grew quiet. Too young to understand, Cory searched their faces. Dragging Chimpa, a stuffed toy with a mop of red hair much like his own, he toddled over the cold floor to his mother's outstretched arms.

Placing Cory on her lap, she rocked back and forth. "I love all of you with all my heart. When this is over and my headaches are long gone, we'll do things as a family again. As for you, my little man, I'll take you to the park, snuggle up with you at night, and read bedtime stories. And when you get a little older, I'll teach you how to ride a bike."

Reacting to her excitement, Cory placed a kiss on her wet cheek.

Later that night, while Robert tossed and turned in the bed they shared since their wedding night, she whispered in the dark. "If I don't survive this, please take good care of our children. I want you to promise you will not allow them to forget me."

Fighting back tears, Robert moved to her side. "God knows your fears, and He will place his loving hand on you. All He asks of you is that you have faith." When Robert was certain she had fallen asleep, he reached for his Bible.

—

The following morning, Wanda's family sat in silence in the hospital's waiting area. Nervous and concerned, Robert bit at his lip and tapped at the tile under his feet. Glancing at the big clock above the television, he was reminded he checked it minutes earlier.

When Cory grew restless, Gina pulled him up to her lap. When he continued to fuss, Jill read a story of superheroes and evil ogres. Taking advantage of his sisters' youth, Kirby challenged them repeatedly to a game of tic-tac-toe. When Jill grew frustrated, Kirby allowed her to win at a game of thumb war.

In the mid-morning hours on May 3, 1972, thirty-seven minutes into surgery and eleven days shy of Mother's Day, Wanda Horton did not succumb to a brain tumor, but instead lost her life when the surgeon she placed not only her faith in, but also her future, accidentally severed an artery.

For the Hortons, the days ahead dragged on. Mother's Day was acknowledged with a visit to the cemetery where the children placed bright orange lilies they picked from the backyard on their mother's grave.

When Robert lost interest in work and his children suffered at school, he sold the house and moved to St. Croix. Years later, when his heart began to heal, he moved his family back home to Springfield.

—

Before the refrigerator had time to chill and Robert had a chance to stock the pantry, another woman claimed his fragile heart. Rushing first their relationship and then their vows before a justice of the peace at the Christian County Courthouse, where he wore a tweed suit and she walked the carpeted aisle in a silk gown the color of grilled eggplant, the mother of two teenage daughters moved in while he was away razing houses. Before they could catch their breath, his children were forced to acknowledge the many changes taking place, including Barbara, their new stepmother, and the young girls whose presence forced Gina and Jill to share a bedroom.

"Where did you meet her?" Gina asked once she was alone with him.

"Oh, here and there," he answered off the cuff.

"What is she? A stray?"

"I know you meant that to be funny, and it is, but you are to be kind."

—

In late December, just days after Christmas, the family, including Barbara and her daughters, gathered in the kitchen. After dinner dishes were washed and put away, Robert announced it was time to celebrate Cory's birthday. In the middle of the table, next to an acrylic napkin holder and matching salt and pepper shakers, sat a cake with four candles. Earlier in the day, a bucket of vanilla ice cream had been scratched off the shopping list, but forgotten in the grocery store's freezer.

Placing his small hands on the table's edge, Cory looked quizzically at his father. Receiving a smile and a nodding approval, he pushed back in the chair, filled his cherub cheeks with air, and while his family watched on, blew out the cake's blue and white striped candles. Digging into the slice his stepmother served on paper plates left over from the Thanksgiving holiday, it did not matter the cake was stale, the yellow icing was hard as rock, or that his name was misspelled.

Retreating to the kitchen, Barbara questioned her presence and position in the Horton family. Having moved in with Robert and his children so soon, she worried they acted in haste. With his children underfoot, and her daughters at her side, she and her new husband were not always able to sneak away for a romantic dinner for two, entertain friends at their home, or take a Sunday drive to explore the countryside. Instead, she spent her days making the Horton's house her new home.

An avid gardener with a green thumb to be admired, she planted a variety of vegetable seeds in the garden she asked Robert to till one afternoon when he came home during his scheduled lunch hour. Unable to nurture her tender garden and keep a watchful eye on Cory, she insisted he stay at her side.

In the early days of their relationship, which were few in number, she told curious friends and acquaintances she was over the moon in love with him. Holding hands, the lovebirds enjoyed long walks, often discussing plans for their future. Sharing her dream, she spoke of wanting a lake house in the boot heel of Missouri. A simple man with realistic dreams, Robert wanted guitar lessons from Wendell Fike, an elderly gentleman who often played on the weekends at local cafes, and when requested, in the evenings at well-lit diners. When time and money permitted, she hoped to tour Europe's many castles, while he looked forward to exploring

Missouri's century-old cemeteries. Sharing a hobby they both enjoyed, they looked forward to the weekends when they would meet up with friends at a popular bowling alley on Gorier Street, some thirty miles away from the county line.

In the early morning hours, while the house was quiet, Robert often enjoyed word search games, playing solitaire while sipping a strong brew of Turkish coffee, scribbling notes he would later forget to send to the paper's editor, and whistling along with the mockingbirds that gathered in the branches of the hardy pecan trees outside the window. Although his life was not perfect, it was at best, simple.

The above-ground pool he purchased from an elderly neighbor who up and moved to Applesfield, a one-horse town south of Halfway, kept the children entertained from late April until school resumed in August. While Kirby and Gina splashed around and raced in circles, Jill balanced on her hands with her legs shooting out of the water and straight up in the air. When this grew tiresome, she would sit Indian style on the bottom, counting the seconds on her pickled fingers until survival forced her to the surface for a breath of air. Embarrassed to admit he was afraid of the water, Cory kept a safe distance from the edge, often complaining his tummy hurt or grumbling that his siblings' splashing hurt his tender skin.

One afternoon, when the family sat around the pool, a swarm of yellow jackets hovered over the water and near the chair where Cory sat reading a comic book. Fearing their poisonous stingers, he jumped away. Catching his foot on the chair, he fell face first into the waist-deep water. While his family watched on, he thrashed about as he slowly sank out of sight. Gina, the family's better swimmer, jumped in to save her baby brother. Pulled from the shallow water, his face turned red as a raspberry while his pride shriveled like an aging prune. Spitting pool water and crying alligator tears, he raced into the house. Later, when his family teased him, he called the fall into the pool a near-drowning experience.

Long before Cory entered elementary school, Robert and Barbara were having problems. Their fighting, which included screaming, slamming of doors, and weeks of silence and cold stares, left the family in turmoil. He often worried his new mother would not return home each time she threatened to leave the house. Before his kindergarten year came to a close, his father and Barbara divorced. Noticing his struggles at school and his pattern of poor attendance, school officials suggested he repeat kindergarten when the new school year arrived the following fall.

Before summer's end, Kirby enlisted in the navy, Gina moved in with a friend from school, and Barbara and her daughters returned to the house in Springfield. Although hesitant, Robert opened his heart and his home, hoping this time he and Barbara could hold on to love and respect. His children needed a caregiver, and he needed the love of a good woman. Exchanging vows a second time, and wanting to live near Barbara's parents in Halfway, Robert uprooted his family, moving them to Hominy Creek, a farming community located near Bolivar, the county seat.

Gray in color, the old wood and stone house was located at the end of a gravel road miles away from the nearest paved road in rural Halfway. When asked to give directions, Robert would say, "Drive 'til you get to nowhere, then keep going. We live in the heart of Nowheresville."

Heated by three wood-burning fireplaces, the large home had a finished basement, which provided a bedroom for the children. Although the house appeared a single story, the wooded backyard afforded a view of the two stories and the pasture where the Horton's raised calves and kept horses.

Built in the 1920s, the house was without indoor plumbing, a problem Robert found odd and promised to fix. Drawing water from a well on the back porch, the children took turns pulling up five-gallon buckets to be stored under the kitchen sink. The sink did not have pipes, only a plug and a hole the home's original owner hammered into the cast iron for proper drainage. After dishes had been washed, the plug was pulled. Placed under the hole, a second bucket collected the dirty water. Those times when the filled bucket was forgotten, the next washing flooded the floors.

When nature called, the family found relief on a portable toilet tucked behind a shower curtain in the far end of the living room. Cory's father called the small, windowless corner his library. Shelves were not required, as there were not any books to fill them. The only reading material was a Montgomery Ward catalog someone left behind. When a visit to the curtained corner involved a two-zy, the television's volume was turned up and the windows pushed open. It was not unusual for the thin, two-ply tissue to roll across the floor, under the curtain, and out of arm's reach, requiring the library's occupant to sing out, *"What'll I Do,"* a song written by Irving Berlin in the 1920s and popular among the Horton family.

Once a week, usually on Sundays, Barbara herded her daughters and Robert's two youngest children out to the car and to her parent's home. Filling the home's only bathtub, the children formed an assembly line, each holding a threadbare towel they carried from home. After Barbara's daughters had finished bathing, each having had their time in a tub of fresh water, the tub was wiped down and refilled. Because she was older than Cory, Jill was next in line. When she was squeaky clean, she turned the lukewarm bath over to Cory. By the time he stepped into the tub, the water was cold and cloudy.

During the summer months, when the air was warm, the children bathed in a galvanized cattle trough their father dragged up to the house from the pasture. Placing it near Barbara's garden, Robert filled the fifteen-gallon, oval-shaped tub with buckets of well water. Experience reminded the children to hold off on bathing until the afternoon sun warmed the cool water.

On those days when their father was away on business, Jill and Cory took over the chore of caring for and feeding the calves. Like puppies, they followed behind, oftentimes nipping at their heels. Expected to meet the school bus when it stopped at the mailbox, they were out of bed before sunrise, rubbing sleep from their tired eyes as they threw on the clothes they set out the night before.

Mixing the milky formula in five-gallon buckets, they filled nursing bottles, fed the hungry calves, and before heading back to the house to have their own breakfast, washed the empty bottles so they would be clean for the next scheduled feeding.

After losing his job with the county's only homebuilder, Robert joined a team of out-of-work construction workers who hoped to find employment in Alaska. Learning he would be away for three months, Barbara insisted upon traveling with him. Leaving her daughters with their grandparents, the now eleven-year-old Jill and little Cory were left to fend for themselves. Without their father to help and guide them, they tackled the daily task of caring for the young livestock—and also each other—a task neither was able to do well. Often exhausted after morning chores, Jill convinced Cory the days ahead were school holidays. Skipping school, they return to the comfort their warm beds offered where they would sleep until grumbling tummies and hunger pangs awakened them.

Halfway did not offer much in the way of entertainment, the art of fine dining, or boutique shopping. However, it did provide a full-service gas station where an oil change could be done in an hour—if a local farmer's combine or plow did not require immediate attention—and an attendant who pumped free air into your tires. A single-employee post office promised a timely delivery, and a windowless van offered library books to those readers who did not mind reading books that failed to make *The New York Times* best seller's list. In the heart of the town, known to the locals as Halfway's Circle, sat the school. The building's six classrooms surrounded the gymnasium, the school's apex when state funds were approved a decade earlier. Kindergarten through sixth grade shared overworked teachers, as well as a small playground outfitted with the usual merry-go-round, a relaxed metal slide, and a steel climbing dome the kids called monkey bars. The upper school shared a split-level commons area with a wall of vending machines where sodas, chocolate bars, and the occasional snack cake were available for purchase during lunch and after school.

It was not long after Robert and Barbara returned to Halfway that the distance between them grew. Seeking solace, Barbara returned to gardening. Firing up a slender cigarette, she would clip away browning petals and turn the soil for the seeds she brought home from a local nursery.

—

Days after his sixth birthday, Cory shared with his father that he wanted to play sports. The small school offered baseball, basketball, and with miles of country roads available for training, the sport of cross-country. Bored on the three-man team, he quit cross-country at the end of the first week's practice. Finding the courage, he tried out for the school's basketball team. With only nine boys in the lower school's combined classes, he was seen as a star, and immediately placed on the team when he was able to sink four free throws in fifteen minutes.

When a change in schedule forced Robert to leave work to pick him up after practice, it did not take long for him to realize the family needed hired help.

One evening, when Robert was unable to pick him up from a make-up game, forcing the recently hired housekeeper to do so, a family meeting was called. Placing fisted hands on aproned hips, the exasperated housekeeper demanded their undivided attention. "If I have to grab Cory after basketball practice and those two-bit circus games that coach of his calls a triumph, then you're in charge of the laundry and dishes," she barked at Gina, who had days earlier moved back home. "And if you're going to ride that pony, you best be gettin' up early to feed her."

"Pepper is not a pony. She's a Fox Trotter," Gina sassed.

Hoping to calm the situation, Robert jumped in. "She knows she's a Fox Trotter, Gina. That's what we ride in Missouri. I believe she told me she once rode…"

"It doesn't matter what I rode or when I rode it." Hot arrows shot from her bulging eyes. "Cory isn't old enough to play sports. His job is to stay home and help me around the house."

Having witnessed her brother dragging bags of trash out to the barrel, Gina came unhinged. "Help you? You treat him like he's your errand boy."

"Gina, that is enough," Robert shouted. "I think it's best we enjoy this fine lasagna dinner she's prepared."

"Prepared? Dad, she found it in the frozen food aisle at Dullie's."

Pushing his plate aside and ignoring his daughter's sassy remarks, Robert turned to Cory. "As for you, my young man, I will take you to practice and bring you home. It'll be our time together. Just the two of us; father and son."

Hearing the enthusiasm in his father's voice, his face lit up. Grabbing the glass of chocolate milk Barbara poured him, he sipped the straw to the drink's last drop.

From a young age, he enjoyed his chocolate milk in a chilled glass along with his breakfast, but later in the day, closer to bedtime, he preferred to sip the cold milky treat while rocking in the wooden chair his father had made years earlier, several months before Kirby was born. Often in envy, as they watched their baby brother rocking back and forth in a steady rhythm, his brother and sisters lovingly nicknamed him Thumper. It was about this same time he settled into a pattern of lying on the bed with the blankets a tussled mess under him. Placing one hand over the other, he would slowly lower his head and repeat a single word, "Thumper," over and over until sleep calmed him.

Sometime later, long after Kirby, Gina, and Jill were living on their own, he and his father returned from basketball practice only to discover that, in their absence, the house had been emptied. Standing in the small alcove that until now held the refrigerator, Robert stood paralyzed. The house was robbed of all the furniture, including the coffee maker and blender he brought with him from St. Croix. Gone were the refrigerator and its contents, a window air-conditioning unit he bought when a house he was building had a surplus, and the washer and dryer he purchased with credit and for which he still owed money. Also empty were all the closets. The only things left behind—a foam cooler and an unopened hair coloring kit.

Turning to Cory, whose eyes were wide open and hungry for answers, Robert fell into a belly laugh. "Son, I do believe we've been taken to the cleaners."

A week later, Robert was served with divorce papers. Until he could refurnish the empty house he had been left with, they slept on a foam mattress and cooked their meals on a two-burner camping stove he purchased at Sears with coins he counted from a jar the thieves overlooked.

Forced to leave Halfway, his dad took a job in Memphis. Still a minor, he had no choice but to move with him. While Robert welcomed the change, his heart grew heavy. For him, it was like starting over once again.

CHAPTER 10

Before allowing his young team to enjoy the fruits of their labor, Cory treated the pool with bromine, a water sanitizer a clerk at a pool store recommended, and with an algaecide added to kill and remove impurities. He hosed down faded lane ropes he found behind the changing rooms and attached the blue and white lane dividers to the rusted clips at both ends of the pool. Making a run to the pool supply store, he picked up a chemical kit. He did not know how to use it, but he would learn. The budget did not allow for pace clocks, display boards, or scoreboards—equipment usually found on the pool deck where elite teams practiced and competed—but his pool would be crystal clear and clean. Thunder's pool would not be a place where there would be pool records to beat or meet records to set, but until he found a home for his team, it would serve its purpose.

The team's first practice in the new pool had them in good spirits. Standing along the pool's edge, his small team admired their new training facility and looked forward to returning to a routine of practice drills, timed sets, and the social interaction training with kickboards allowed.

Feeling like a kid himself, he invited the team to enjoy a brief game of Sharks and Minnows, a game where one swimmer, the shark, swims after the other swimmers, the minnows, hoping to tag them before they reach the opposite end of the pool. The last swimmer to remain in the pool became the unfortunate minnow. As expected, it turned from a playful game to one of competition. When the shark grew tired, the faster and more skillful minnows had no choice but to sacrifice one of their own. Holding a teammate at bay, they waited to free the victim until the hungry shark was an arm's length away.

"We've enjoyed a few days off from swimming, and before we focus on our strokes, I want you all to know how proud I am of you." Turning toward the sparkling pool and clean deck, he spread his arms out wide in front of him. "You made this possible." When the cheers and roars died down, he tapped his clipboard against his thigh, a habit he was unaware of. "I have one question." Letting the anticipation build, he paced the deck. When he decided the kids were ready, he asked for their attention. "Who's ready to swim?" This time, his team jumped up and down, clapped their hands, and cheered louder than any he had ever heard. "It's time to return to our training drills. Okay, my little yahoos, grab your goggles and line up behind the blocks."

Days later, luck presented itself when a reporter for the local newspaper showed up during practice. Any other time, he would have asked that an interview be scheduled at a later date, preferably when the team was not practicing, but because luck had passed over him his entire life, he welcomed it with open arms.

Exchanging pleasantries, the reporter, who shared that he had been a so-so swimmer in high school, found this new team newsworthy. He had read recent articles about Silvie and Margo, and now with a new team in town, he wanted to be the first to break the story. "Every time I turn around, someone's talking about you."

"I hope they're saying good things," he chuckled.

Holding a dulled Ticonderoga in his hand and a spiral notebook on his lap, the reporter leaned back in the plastic chair. "What do you want the swimming community to know about Thunder?" His interest was undeniable.

Instructing his team to follow the 200 warm-up with catch-up drills, he took a seat under the awning. The corners of his smile and the life in his eyes relayed to the reporter seated across from him that he would speak from his heart.

"Memphis Thunder may be the new kid in town, but we're not new to swimming. I think of us as an embryonic team. We're developing, we're growing, and we're learning. Great things await us—I feel it in my heart. I'm fortunate to coach a team of dedicated and disciplined swimmers who give their best to the sport. As their coach, I step into the shadows when it comes their time to shine. Each time they compete, they are pushing their trained and natural abilities to the cutting edge. When you get to know them, you come to understand chlorinated water is in their blood. They would rather wear the scent of salt tablets and enzymes than a department store's best-selling fragrance. I sometimes wonder if my little amphibians bleed chlorine.

"They've watched the Olympics, they've cheered their favorite swimmers, and they understand what it takes to succeed. Their success has nothing to do with me. I'm a coach they trust to guide them. When the gun fires, I become their cheerleader. They work well together and support one another in reaching their individual accomplishments. In doing so, they are learning valuable lessons and skills they will take with them on their journey through life. What I'm hoping they will take away from their time with me is character building. *Stand tall, be honest, and always take the road that promises a better outcome.* They are also learning that hard work can be fun. On those days we play games, they are practicing teamwork. Watching their personalities unfold and seeing their friendships develop, I believe these are the attributes that will stay with them for a lifetime. It's easy to imagine the adults they will become."

Twenty minutes had passed when his team interrupted the interview to ask what they should do next. "A 300 pull. Go hard every third length. When you're done, grab your fins and give me a 200 kick."

With the interview coming to an end, the reporter asked to take a picture to run with the article. Pulling his team from the pool, he asked that they form a line on the diving board, a common pose among swim teams. Wearing their team suits and proud smiles, Memphis Thunder let the newspaper's readers know they were prepared and ready to compete.

———

Arriving at the pool the following afternoon, Cory found a stack of phone messages waiting for him.

Cutting coupons from a local advertising rag, Donna sipped the coffee she picked up earlier at her favorite donut hole. "That was an impressive article in the paper this morning." Pointing to the yellow notes he held in his hand, she leaned over a napkin while taking a bite from a glazed donut she dunked in her coffee. "Looks like you're going to need your own telephone number, and a secretary."

He had read the article during breakfast. The reporter called Memphis Thunder an *elite swim team*, words that made his smile mirror those of his team in the paper's black and white photo. Shuffling through the messages, it was evident word of his new team was spreading. "Hold the phone, Donna, Donna, Bobanna Fannah. A secretary isn't in the budget just yet."

"By the way, before I forget, Miss Kitty's been swallowing rocks again. And you know what happens after that." Donna paused to enjoy his uncomfortable frown. "Yep, sounds like a gunshot every time she passes a rock on the hardwood floors. Anyway, you might want to tell your kids to stay out of the gravel. Vet tells me once a rock eater, always a rock eater."

"Thanks for the heads-up. By the way, are those Jordache?" he asked, recognizing the jeans she wore from those his sisters wore during his childhood.

Smiling, Donna fell into a model's pose. "They sure are. I bought these when I was in college."

"Would that have been in the late sixties?" he teased.

Shaking a finger at him, Donna enjoyed the banter. "Late seventies, smarty pants. Did I mention they still fit?"

"May I add, they look great on you?"

"Listen up, swim coach. I haven't said this to very many swim coaches.

Come to think of it, I don't recall having ever said this to anyone. You're a great role model for these kids. I'm no expert, but your love for them, and theirs for you, well, it's obvious. Just keep doing what you're doing. Someday, these kids of yours, these yahoos, snotchkins, or whatever you call them, will look back on these days. If they stay the course, they will appreciate all you've done for them and the way you did it. You're a good man, my friend."

Humbled by her kind words, he gave a wide smile. Worried he might be brought to tears, he stepped out to the deck. Donna's words would never leave him, but in truth, he received from these kids far more than he gave. At the end of each practice, they went home to their families. He, however, counted the minutes until they returned.

Pulling a cell phone from his pocket, he returned a call to Lisa Augger, a woman unknown to him. "All my daughters ever talk about is joining Memphis Thunder. My oldest girl knows Silvie Mercer from their days at Gymboree."

Scratching his head and unfamiliar with "Gymboree," he envisioned a highfalutin musical where dance students kicked up their heels under a gym's backboard, but because Lisa never stopped to take a breath, he soon lost interest. Desperately needing to finance his new team, he suggested she schedule her daughters for a tryout session.

Two days later, when Lisa arrived at the pool with her daughters, he was surprised to find her outfitted in a cropped leather vest, pleather pants that hugged wayward curves and accentuated her dimpled flesh, and tall, leather boots that showed signs of frequent wear and tear. He was tempted to ask where she parked her motorcycle, but fearing she might ride with an international bike gang, he kicked curiosity to the curb. Standing a safe distance behind their mother, Haley and Harley Augger listened with little interest as she bombarded him with questions. "Is that junker car out there waiting to be towed?"

Finding Lisa a petite woman, her bloated voice surprised him. On the telephone, she had sounded sing-songy—her voice rising and falling in a musical sort of way reminding him of the many times his sisters forced him to watch *The Wizard of Oz*.

Tired of the question, he simply nodded. "It's going to be here for a while. It's mine."

Learning he was the car's owner, Lisa turned her attention to the pool. "Will they be using those boogie boards? When I stopped by that swim place on Evergreen, those kids were playing with boogie boards and splashing every which way."

He was not aware a team practiced on Evergreen. "Are you sure about the street?"

"I'm telling you it was Evergreen."

"Mom, that wasn't a swim team."

"Sure it was. They were dressed in the same suits."

"They were wearing *Hello Kitty.*"

"Whatever. I'm not going to pay for my kids to be on a swim team when they can do that for free in our neighbor's pool."

Trying not to laugh, Cory's cheeks turned the color of his Jetta. "No, Ma'am. No boogie boards here. I think you might be talking about kick-boards, which we use to teach the proper kicks for the butterfly and breast strokes." He did not think it was necessary to mention the boards were also used for the freestyle and backstroke kicks.

Arching penciled eyebrows, and sporting a disapproving frown, Lisa bobbed her head. "How about snorkels? The girls use those at home when they're diving for those colorful rings."

"Those are pool toys, Mom," Haley corrected.

This time, he chuckled. "No. No snorkels or boogie boards here, and no diving for pool toys."

"That's good to know. I've watched the Olympics and I've never seen anyone with a boogie board or snorkel."

Ready to move on, Cory suggested the girls take a step up on the starting blocks. "I'm going to have you swim a 200. Fifty each of the four strokes in medley order."

Unsure what he meant by medley order, Haley whispered to her sister, who believing she knew the order, stood tall and confident. "Start with freestyle and then do the backstroke..."

"No, no, no. It's butterfly, back, breast, and then free. Always in that order, unless it's a relay, then it's back, breast, fly, free," he corrected. Chewing on his lower lip, he watched the sisters serpentine the lanes, stopping occasionally to catch their breath or flush water from their drowning goggles. Pumping their legs and thrashing their arms about, they finally resorted to treading water. Watching as they worked to keep their heads above water, he came to understand they were not what he or any coach worth their salary would call competitive swimmers. When the girls finally finished the medley's freestyle stroke, he waved them out of the pool. "You're good swimmers, but I'm thinking you might need a little more time at pool school." In his hurry to end the session, he turned to their mother. "If they continue with lessons and are still interested in six months, bring them back by here and we'll give it another shot."

Many of the tryouts he was forced to endure over the next several weeks were often entertaining and pathetic, but mostly, a waste of time. And, given time was a commodity he learned to value and appreciate, he would have rather spent it scrubbing toilets at Grand Central Station, cage-fighting mutant fire ants, or suffering through the preparation period before a colonoscopy.

One girl, he was asked to call Summer Cat, smelled like a shaggy dog left out in the pouring rain. She slapped the water each time her dive turned into a belly flop. When she asked to be his assistant coach, he suggested she visit the team on Evergreen.

Asked to demonstrate her best platform dive, another swimmer threw her head over her shoulders, arched her back, and once she was airborne, spread her arms out wide. Bringing them together over her head as she prepared to enter the water, she executed a decent swan dive.

When another young girl jumped into the pool with her arms wrapped around her knees, he laughed so hard he doubled over with stomach cramps. Her winning cannonball drenched his hair, soaked his shirt, and had him close to wetting his pants. When she asked about her dive, he nearly split his sides. "It wasn't just great, it was *waterful!*"

Eight-year-old Alexandra arrived wearing a bikini that, bursting at the seams, failed to squeeze eighty pounds into a twenty-pound suit. Her bangs were so thick they covered her forehead like duct tape. When she slipped her arms into water wings, memories of his youth on St. Croix and the floaties his father made him wear danced in his head. "Hey, Walla Walla Bing Bang, do you need those floaties, or can you swim on your own?"

"My mom says I have to wear them all the time so I won't drown."

Hearing whispered voices behind him and a symphony of giggles, he gave his team of curious onlookers a face they understood to mean they were to be quiet. "Those are nice floaties, and your mother is right to have you wear them, but we can't wear them during swim meets."

Dressed in a yellow and white smocked dress, nine-year-old Marta looked like a hard-boiled egg. As she skipped her way over to him, he soon realized she was wearing a full-face dive mask. Pulling up the rear, her mother wore a long skirt and a knitted beanie. When he noticed the Velcro strap on her thick walking shoes, he expected her to feed the birds seeds from her embroidered bag. "She's had that snorkeling mask on since breakfast. Paid a dollar for it yesterday at Ike's."

Tongue-tied and dumbfounded, he searched the air for words. Pushing aside memories of watching *Mary Poppins* with his sisters, he rushed Marta to the pool. "Well then, we'd better get you in the water."

Demonstrating the dog-paddle, a stroke not recognized in competitive swimming, Marta appeared at war with the water. Trotting along the surface left her exhausted and him near tears.

"Have you had swimming lessons?"

"I don't need lessons. My mom told me I'm the best swimmer she's ever seen."

Getting a whiff of the young girl's onion breath, he took a step back. Days earlier, when he spoke with Marta's mother, he noticed she spoke with an accent, and in her effort to communicate, butchered the English language. Believing he heard her say "shawim," he had to ask her to repeat the purpose of her call. "Marta, do you know how to swim the backstroke or butterfly?"

Fighting to catch her breath, and unclear what he was asking, Marta tilted her head until it came to rest on her shoulder.

"Marta, Marta, Marta, I think we've done enough swimming for today. If you're still interested in six months, or maybe ten, or in a year or two, please come back for another tryout."

His eyes lit up when Patricia, a student at a private catholic school, and whose family lived within walking distance of the club, zipped through the water. She timed her flip turns with an accuracy to be admired, and her stroke technique needed little improvement. When he shared with her she was the type of swimmer he wanted on his team, she reached her arms to the sky and gave a happy dance.

When twelve-year-old Carter DeMarco arrived for his scheduled tryout, he tried to hide his surprise. Out of the corner of his eye, he noticed his team had stopped midway through their assigned drill, and eager to watch the young boy display his best effort to join Thunder, they formed a closed circle when he crossed the deck. Asking Carter to step up to an open lane, he then instructed his team to swim another 500. Aware of their curiosity, he wanted their focus on training, not on the young boy who would soon enter the water. "Okay, Carter, show me your best stroke."

Pulling tinted goggles over his eyes, Carter moved to the edge of the pool. Expecting all eyes to be on him, he stood tall, smiled at his father, and with the confidence of a skilled champion, shot off the starting block. When he surfaced, he glided effortlessly through the water. Watching the young boy balance his strokes with strong and steady kicks left everyone in awe. Coming out of a winning flip turn, he pushed on to a strong finish.

Crouching at the wall, Cory spoke in a low voice. "Carter, there are other venues available to you."

"My dad always tells me when it comes to swimming, there isn't anything special about me." Pulling off his swim cap, he gave a winning grin. "People keep saying I have a disability, but other than missing an arm, I'm just like everybody else."

Admiring Carter's determination, he offered a high-five and a knuckle exchange. Looking over the young boy's shoulder, he shared a warm smile with his father. "Carter, I don't know the rules about swimming with one arm, but if it's possible for you to join USA swimming, I want you on my team."

From this moment on, he vowed he would accept only those swimmers who had potential, were eager to better their swim time, and displayed respect for their fellow teammates and coach. Loss of limbs would not play a role in growing his team.

⁓

October's arrival brought new challenges: a drop in temperature and Memphis Thunder's first swim meet. Weeks earlier, Cory spent his evenings perusing the meets scheduled in the Southeastern Conference. Taking advantage of Mississippi's close proximity, he announced to his team they would enter meets in Jackson, the state's capital, and Laurel, a town close to home, and the upcoming Memphis Tigers Invitational. "We have a small team and that's a disadvantage in some respect, but we're a strong competitor."

Silvie raised her hand. "I have a question."

"Hit me with it, Hi-Ho Silver."

Rolling her eyes, Silvie skipped over the nickname. "Coach Cory, will you be driving that pink car to the swim meets?"

He waited for the laughter to settle down before answering. "It's red, Hi-Ho, and of course I will. I can't walk that far, and besides…"

Cutting him off, his team shouted together, "It's paid for!"

CHAPTER 11

For Cory, entering the swim center on Echles Road was bittersweet. Walking the famed Tiger Tunnel, the center's vast hall lined with plaques and posters of swimmers who went on to compete in the Olympics, he recalled the first day he entered the aquatics office. He was so nervous that when he was introduced to the coaching staff, he stumbled through his own name. He enjoyed his position with the Memphis Tigers, but coaching a team was the icing on every assistant coach's career. He was no exception.

Following behind, and stopping occasionally to chat with old teammates and friends from school, walked his proud and ready swimmers. After checking in at the coach's table, he received a warm welcome from Dick Fadgen.

"It's good to see you, Cory."

He was relieved to find his smile sincere, fearing his departure appeared he had abandoned ship. "It's great to be here. This is our first meet, and I have to admit, I'm the only one who's nervous."

Always a kind and giving man, Coach Fadgen patted him on the shoulder. "I'd like to tell you those nerves go away, but I'd be lying. After all these years and hundreds of meets under my belt, my stomach still does somersaults when the announcer starts the meet."

"Well, I'm glad we're here. It feels like I'm coming home." At that moment, his thoughts raced through the many houses he called home during his childhood. Feeling a twinge in his stomach, he hurried to forget the past. Memphis was his home. He had friends he trusted to keep the secrets he shared, and when asked, to calm his fears. Needing to return to his team, he offered his hand. "I have to get moving. I'll meet up with you on the deck."

Carrying the heat sheet at his side, he returned to his flock, a name he thought sounded more professional than snotchkins.

"Coach Cory, what's my first event?" Silvie asked, twirling about.

"Fifty breast," he answered without taking his eyes off the heat sheet.

"What's the time I have to beat?"

This time, he gave Silvie the attention she wanted. "I can't recall your previous time. All you have to do today is go out there and give your best."

Hearing his familiar words, Silvie rolled her eyes. "You always say that, Cory."

"And I always mean it." Addressing his flock, he pointed a marker at Margo. "Your first event is the 50 back." Turning to Katie, he placed a hand on her shoulder. "Free and breast means do your best." As always, he got a laugh from the girls.

When Sunday arrived, the last day of the three-day meet, Memphis Thunder Aquatic Club made its name known. Margo bettered her time in the 50 back, one second faster than the 1997 Meet of Champions where she swam the event in 31.0. She also shaved time off the 100 back, beating her Meet of Champions time of 1:07.78. With a time of 1:20.15, Silvie had a personal best in the 100 breast. Kelli's freestyle finishes were equally impressive. Swimming the twelve and under group, she had personal bests in the 50, 100, and 400 freestyle events. Katie's strong legs helped her take first place in the freestyle and breaststroke events.

When Will McCawley entered the water, all eyes turned to see if he would beat the records he set in the 1997 Gabrielle Rose Classic. He did not disappoint the onlookers when he touched first in the 50 and 200 freestyle events and bettered his time in the 100 breast and 200 individual medley.

As Thunder swimmers navigated the water, the deck, and the Tiger Tunnel, where swim gear was offered for sale and food vendors prepared simple sandwiches, toasted bagels, and tossed a healthy garden salad, they proudly displayed the *marks of excellence* drawn on their cheeks.

The swim meet in Laurel was equally impressive. The sportsplex on Highway 84 offered eight lanes in a heated fifty-meter pool. In addition to the white swim caps his team wore during practice, and at the Tigers meet, he gave his swimmers black swim caps to wear when swimming the meet's finals. He beamed with pride on the last day of the meet when every member on his team donned the winning black cap. Thunder was on fire.

Already thrilled about their momentum, he became even more excited after their next outing at Jackson's Sunkist Challenge. On the morning of the meet, he dressed in his usual attire of belted khaki shorts, a white Thunder shirt, tube socks, and running shoes he recently retired from competition when the soles logged over two hundred miles. His team looked prepared and strong in the warm-up, and each swimmer remembered to wear the white swim cap. After the national anthem had been sung, the announcer called the meet's first event. Already at the starting block, Silvie stood ready.

Walking the deck with the heat sheet at his side and an ink pen clenched in his teeth, he smiled when she executed the perfect dive. Later, when she placed first in the breaststroke, he was again reminded of his reasons for starting his own team. Silvie Mercer wore the face of a champion.

Like Silvie, Margo blasted through the water like an upside down torpedo, winning all of the backstroke events in her age group. He later learned her times were faster than those of the meet's older swimmers.

CHAPTER 12

As the year drew to a close, Cory was thrilled to learn Kelli had been invited to compete in the Meet of Champions. Days before Christmas, and surrounded by her teammates, she was the first Thunder member to post record times for the team. Swimming the 50 free in 25.25, she beat her previous best time. Pumped with adrenaline, she finished the 100 free in 54.36, the 200 in 1:56.11, and the 500 in 5:07.12.

The following month, January 1999, Margo posted a team record at the Pilot January Classic when she swam the 50 back. This same year, she bettered her times at the War Eagle and Supersplash meets. Each time Margo celebrated a victory, she gave credit to him. In return, he praised her determination and work ethic. Always observing, he watched as Margo gained on Silvie during practice and in competition. Thinking back, he now recognized in Margo the competitive spirit he admired in Gabrielle. Watching them now, he aimed for a higher goal. He would take both Silvie and Margo to Olympic level.

Moving away from the breaststroke, Silvie was now noticed in the butterfly and individual medley events. In 2000, while competing in the twelve and under age group, she set team records during the short course season in the 100 individual medley, and at districts in the 400 individual medley.

In February, he took his team to Huntsville, Alabama, to compete in the Groundhog Invitational. A member new to Thunder set a team record in the mile with a time of 18:33.01. Swimming in the fourteen and under age group, Kelli continued to set team records in the freestyle events.

March's calendar kicked off with the Senior Regions Short Course where Kelli competed in the 1000 free. The first to touch the pad, she set another team record. In the following weeks, Thunder was off to Districts and the SES Short Course Championships where Silvie set records in the butterfly and the individual medley.

In October, Thunder traveled to Tuscaloosa. The BAMA Open, hosted on the Crimson Tide campus in the student recreation center, promised fast times, not only for Thunder but all teams. "It's a fast pool," he reminded his team.

That same year, Mary, an eight-year-old new to Thunder's roster, and whom he was quick to nickname Mar, took the swimming community by storm when she powered through the water setting a team record at the BAMA Open. The following month, while competing in the Germantown Thanksgiving Invitational, she set a second team record in the 50 free.

When Margo and Silvie qualified for the SES Long Course Championships, he fist-pumped the air. He was proud of his team. Watching Margo push to the next level, he understood it was her hard work and discipline that defined her. Silvie's times were still impressive, but when she spent more time visiting than training, he grew concerned that perhaps she was resting on her laurels. The following day, he gave his team a motivational speech. When Silvie took notes on her arm, he put his concerns to rest.

C H A P T E R 1 3

Cory got his first taste of conflict when several mothers who thought they were being helpful and generous, arrived at a Saturday morning practice with dozens of powdered, chocolate-covered, and glazed donuts. Once his team spotted the familiar boxes, their interest in swimming began to wane. The younger ones complained, *"We're just too tired to continue,"* while the older kids shouted between strokes that they were starving. When practice was over and Silvie reached for a treat, her mother stepped in. "Silvie isn't allowed to eat donuts or any sugar snack."

Hearing the commotion, he hurried to address the parents. "Donuts are allowed on the first Saturday of the month. I'll tape a sign-up sheet to the door. If you want to participate, commit to a date." By month's end, the sign-up sheet and the donuts had gone missing.

However, a more serious problem soon replaced the donut conflict when several mothers who often gathered under the awning during practice shouted for their daughters to swim faster than their teammates, often calling out names.

This forced him to make phone calls. "I will not tolerate this type of sabotage. I want to hear the parents cheer for the team. I understand you want your daughter to do well, but we are a team. We work together as a team. When you cheer, you cheer for Thunder."

The arrival of cooler temperatures posed another minor setback. Unable to heat the pool, he installed a solar cover. The cost ate up most of his savings, and until the new cover had a chance to warm the pool, the team was out of the water. Not wanting to stall their training, he introduced them to running. "Stay on the sidewalk, away from cars. You'll be surprised how running will strengthen your legs."

Although the girls initially complained, their attitudes were soon reversed. Jogging through the East Memphis neighborhood allowed the older girls to catch up on happenings at school, activities on the calendar for the youth groups they attended at church, and plans for the upcoming weekend. They enjoyed leaving practice with dry hair and their skin free of the strong odor swimming in chlorine left behind.

Days later, when the water was still too cool for swimming, he added calisthenics to their routine. "Today we're doing dry-land training. Partner up and take a place under the awning." When everyone had settled on a partner and quieted down, he asked for their attention. "Raise your hand if you know how to do sit-ups." Having done sit-ups in school, the kids laughed. "Super. I was worried I'd have to ask one of you to give a demonstration. Take turns counting for each other, and when you're done there, do the same with push-ups. Give me fifty of each."

Leaving the kids to stretch and moan, he stepped out of the room. When he returned, he was pushing a crippled and dusty rolling cart. On the top shelf was an old black and white television Donna warned was stubborn. When the team finished their push-ups, they watched a swim video he borrowed from the university's library.

During the movie, Will announced he would be returning to Memphis Tigers. He did not mind swimming with the girls on the days Carter came to practice, but in recent days, Carter had been sidelined with activities that kept him out of the water. "I don't want to be on a girls' team."

"With you here, we're not an all-girls' team. Besides, it could be worse," Silvie spouted.

Will looked at her with curious eyes. "How could it be worse?"

Interrupting Silvie, Cory jumped in. "They could be ugly."

After the laughter died down, he asked him to reconsider, but once a young boy himself, he understood when Will explained he was missing his friends.

Practices at the club were running smoothly until the club's manager, a rotund man with a slow-growing beard and high-waist slacks, showed up minutes before a Saturday practice. "We've had some interest from other teams who want to use the facility, and they're eager to sign a lease."

Disbelief overshadowed his disappointment. "Come on, I thought we had an agreement. I've put a lot of time and money into cleaning the pool and making the changing rooms functional. I need a place to train my team. Is there anything I can do or say to get you to work with me? I mean, look around. These children are your children, your neighbor's children, and kids you see in church. I made a promise to them. If I can't live up to my word, then this is nothing more than a boondoggle."

Nodding his head in agreement, the manager looked to the ground. Extending his hand, he took a deep breath. "Just forget I was here. I'll see what I can do."

Wrapping his arms around him, he surprised the man with a bear hug. "Thank you." Watching him walk away, he realized the problem he now faced. If he wanted to keep the pool, he would have to find a way to bring in more dollars. Turning on his heels, he glanced at his Ironman watch. He had twenty minutes until practice. Taking a seat on the old sofa in the clubhouse, he scoured the heat sheets he saved from recent meets. On a yellow legal pad, he wrote the names of those swimmers whose times showed promise. When his eyes fell on the pages dedicated to male swimmers, he leaned back onto the sofa. *Had it become necessary to recruit male swimmers?* Intending to keep the girls' focus off the boys and on swimming, especially as they entered their teens, he had never considered adding boys, other than Will and Carter, to the roster. Shaking his head, he tossed the heat sheets aside and grabbed his phone.

"What's up, son?" Relaxed on the beach with a pina colada to quench his thirst and a book he could not put down, Robert Horton listened while he explained his predicament.

"I'm just trying to eke out a living. I can't cut costs and I don't see how I can live on less."

"I know, first-hand, you're to be commended for your budgeting skills. Can you start by recruiting those girls who would most likely pose the greatest challenge to your team?"

His father could not see the grin on his face, but he was sure he heard his chuckle. "Those girls are already on my team."

"I think you know what you have to do, Cory."

"I was afraid you would say that. How am I going to do this? I swore I'd never recruit from other teams."

"No one said you are. They'll come to you. Keep in mind, you developed this team to fund Silvie's training. Don't look at this minor set-back as a sacrifice, but rather a compromise you're willing to make to reach your goal. It's a stepping stone, not a stumbling block."

"This is why I look to you for answers. You are a wise man, Kemosabe."

CHAPTER 14

As the meet in Jackson was coming to a close and Cory was gathering his gear, a man approached him with two children in tow. "Hey, I'm sorry to bother you, but I want to ask about your shirt. Are you moving your team to Jackson?"

Confused by the question, he shook his head. "No, we're from Memphis."

"I live in Memphis. I don't recall having heard of Thunder. Where do you practice?"

The two men continued their question and answer session, which included Bob Compton giving his name and asking his.

He spoke of leaving the Memphis Tigers to develop Thunder and the neighborhood pool they called their training facility. "It doesn't have all the perks the other facilities in Memphis offer, but right now it works for us. We're a small team, but we're big when it comes to talent."

Calling his daughters to his side, Bob, who stood an inch taller and was comparable in weight, explained they, too, were swimmers. "Country club right now, but I'd like to see them get involved in a team sport." Giving a smile, he patted his stomach. "I should take my own advice."

Talking sports and exercise, their conversation continued out into the parking lot. Opening the car door, which he no longer bothered to lock, he tossed his duffle bag over the front seat's torn headrest and into the backseat.

"Is this your car?"

He turned to see a look of disgust on Bob's face. "It's paid for."

Eyeing a cycling sticker in the back window, Bob wondered if it had been slapped on to keep a growing crack in the glass from spreading, but looking at the dinged doors, worn tires, and scratched hubcaps, he arrived at a very different conclusion—the car had earned early retirement. "Do you ride?"

Like a kid at Christmas, his eyes lit up. "Road racing and triathlons." Having noticed the pat Bob gave to his stomach, he gave him the once over. "Are you a cyclist?"

"Me? Hardly. I do have a bike, though. Right now it's hanging in my garage collecting dust bunnies and cobwebs."

"I understand. Mine's done that a few times. Listen, I've enjoyed talking with you, but I have to get back to Memphis. I ride with a small group and we're riding early in the morning. Even if you don't have time to wipe down your bike, you're welcome to join us."

"I'll pass on the ride, but I'd like to talk with you sometime. I have a proposition I think you might be interested in."

His interest piqued, he pulled a business card from his wallet. "Let's meet for lunch sometime."

Shaking hands, the two men parted.

CHAPTER 15

Fourteen days later, and after as many lunches with Bob and the team of professionals he trusted to manage his portfolio, Cory was still feeling uneasy about the many compromises and sacrifices he was about to take, including Thunder's monthly billing system. Earlier, when itemized billing had been proposed, he was reluctant to give his approval, but after some convincing, he agreed it was more efficient than his current method, which was usually a shout-out at the first of the month that fees were due.

"If it's a going business, you have to run it like a business," the balding accountant muttered under his breath. "Keeping track of expenses and income will help your accountant when it's time to prepare your taxes."

Before the ink dried on the paperwork, he found himself pacing the floors of his new apartment, worried he would be late for practice. "How we doing there, guys?"

Glancing over his shoulder, a beefy man with a twisted goatee and sleeves of tattoos, put down the kitchen chair and floor lamp he carried in from the delivery truck. "All we got left is the box spring and mattress."

"Great. The place is looking good," he said, stealing a peek at his watch.

The man with the inked illustrations, which he assumed journaled paths his young life had taken, nodded to the cardboard boxes stacked in front of the patio door. "Is that all you got, man?"

"Well, and those few pieces of bachelor furniture behind you." Embarrassed, his face reddened when the man's eyes fell on the folding chair in the corner. "Everything else went into the dumpster. I have a coffee table and a few family pieces I'll bring in later. My brother is coming in from Nashville to help hang pictures and line the kitchen cabinets." There was no way he was going to share with these big guys that he asked Kirby to help pick out things to fill the kitchen cabinets and bathroom linen closet, and later, to help line those same shelves with a spongy material he was told was necessary to preserve the cabinet and its wares.

Weeks earlier, when Bob presented the proposition, the job offer included an apartment in a newly constructed development. He had not expected it would be outfitted with new furniture, art for the walls, and fancy area rugs with well-groomed fringe. He appreciated the framed art, but the pencil drawings the kids gave him were worth far more than any Monet or Picasso.

Standing in the apartment's kitchen, he scanned the new furnishings. Observing the floral patterns and throw pillows he felt were wasteful and far removed from his simple taste and easy lifestyle, along with a gift basket of raspberries and long-stemmed strawberries dipped in a creamy dark chocolate he found neither visually appealing nor tempting, he was left wondering who had done the shopping.

When the movers announced their job was complete, he tipped them with the gift basket.

———

Driving along East Memphis' winding streets, Cory did not think about the Jeep's heated seats, the spare tire he caught sight of each time he glanced in the rearview mirror, or the power steering the high-energy salesman pointed out was an upgrade from the 1980 two-door Jetta he left at the dealership. He focused his thoughts on the license plate on the

Jeep's rear bumper. "*A teacher's car tag,*" the man at the dealership had said when he handed over the plates. He had not entered a college nor had he graduated from one. The closest he had ever been to a higher education was walking across campus. Thinking about Bob's proposal and the pool it included, he did not need a college education to know he had been handed a great opportunity.

Once the aquatic center was completed, his swim team would have a training facility that would allow them to host swim meets. The extra money in his pocket would take a load off his shoulders, and having the new Jeep at his disposal was a welcomed perk. A passing thought had him wondering if his ride was paid for.

CHAPTER 16

About the time construction was getting underway at St. George's Collierville campus, plans for the Compton Aquatic Center were unfolding. Asked for his input, Cory walked the staked property with Bob.

Standing in a field of tall weeds and working ants he worried would carry him back to their colony, he pointed to a small patch of grass. "Is this where the locker rooms will be?"

Glancing at blueprints, Bob shook his head. "That's the sidewalk." Waving a hand to the east, he surveyed the area. "It leads this way out of the pool center."

Looking over Bob's shoulder, he pointed to a second building. "Those are the locker rooms over here? In a separate building?"

"Two small locker rooms. Boys are over here on the left and the girls are on the right. There are plans to put vending machines between them."

"I don't know about this, Bob. It can get pretty cold out here, and in a wet swimsuit, the kids will freeze to death. I'm thinking the locker rooms should be attached to the building."

"They will be attached to a building. A gymnasium is going up over there." Pointing to the north, Bob gave a reassuring smile. "The kids will be okay. It's really not that far."

"It's far when it's cold and dark. Who is going to monitor them when they run out during practice to use the bathroom? You have a lot of trees out here, and from what I can see on the drawings, there is very little lighting."

"You have a dim view, my friend. It's going to be great. They can buddy up, hold it until after practice, or do what most kids do—pee in the pool." Pulling a pen from the pocket of his shirt, Bob placed four small circles on the blueprints. "Good catch, my friend. I agree. We'll add lights over here and near the parking area. Trust me, in the end, it will all work out. No pun intended. Now, let's talk about the inside of the building." Scouring the plans, Bob took several steps back. "I believe I'm standing in the middle of the main pool." Aware of Cory's questioning look, he counted off steps before planting a foot on a fallen tree branch. "This is the smaller pool. Twenty-five meters. If I'm not mistaken, it will have six lanes. The architect referred to it as a lesson pool. I'm not sure about starting blocks or the depth, but it won't be as deep as the 50-meter pool."

Other than the locker rooms' distance from the pool, he was impressed with the plans. Dodging fire ants, and feeling a pinch from prickly cockleburs that clung to his socks, he continued along the area inside the knee-high stakes. "How big is the building?"

"One point seven million dollars will buy twenty-eight-thousand square feet. The ceiling will be vaulted, and east of the pool, we'll have six rows of bleachers. Starting blocks on the west and north sides. It's designed for both long and short course training. I've been told that when it's all said and done, ours will be West Tennessee's largest indoor pool facility."

"My hat's off to you, Bob. It's going to be great."

"As the aquatic director and head coach for St. George's, you'll have your own office, and of course, the pool will be the home of Memphis Thunder. If I were you, I'd be thinking about adding to our coaching staff."

CHAPTER 17

Saturday morning's ride along Forest Hill's Gate, a mountain bike trail outside the city limits, required each rider to come prepared with plenty of water and a snack. Once a respected and prominent cattle ranch, the property went into a trust when the landowner passed away in his sleep. In recent years, frequent bike rides had flattened the soil, creating a haven for mountain bike enthusiasts.

On this day, the temperature was unusually cool and the morning sun took refuge behind a continuous wave of low-lying clouds. The threat of rain and a muddied trail tripled the attendance. Parked on a mountain bike, Cory was the first to enter the trail, allowing him to set the pace.

The first mile of the rugged descent was a cakewalk compared to the rest of the trail. Silt and sludge sprayed the air as the cyclists rode through shallow puddles. The following miles proved more difficult as the group of experienced off-road riders became more challenged as they biked through plowed fields, over root gardens where, if they lost control, threatened a dangerous outcome, and around mud-filled ruts that had been known to turn a champion rider into a desperate one. Making a tight twist over a narrow bridge, he pulled back on his speed, bent his knees, and lifted his rear off the saddle. Waiting ahead was Dead Dave's Curve, the trail's most grueling challenge. To reach Jewel Lake, the property's 300-acre watering hole and the trail's only rest area, he would first have to pass through a narrow opening in an old, wooden fence. He cringed when he recalled the last time he paused at this spot. On a day when Memphis' weather adopted temperatures better known to California's Santa Barbara, he made it to the other side, but not without first scraping his elbow against the fence. It took days to remove the splinters and weeks for the swelling to go down. He was one of the lucky ones. Several riders had been thrown from their bikes and others met up with century-old trees less forgiving than the fence's rotted wood.

Hearing his name, he glanced over his shoulder. Squinting through muddied sunglasses, he could not make out the rider's face.

Biking up alongside him, the young woman removed her helmet. "I'm Terie. I don't believe we've been formally introduced, but I've noticed you around Memphis State, and I believe I've seen you once or twice at the Shrine Building. If I'm not mistaken, I think we've exchanged a glance, maybe two."

His heart aflutter and his tongue tied and twisted, he pulled from memory the number of times he had admired her beauty, and along the way, her shapely legs. Unable to forget her and the first time he laid eyes on her, he gave a blushing grin. "That's right. You're a..."

Holding her helmet in one hand, she used the other to tease her hair. "I'm a wader. I walk the pool after a workout. I get teased about it all the time, but the truth is, it helps me unwind."

"Hearing you call the university by its old name tells me you're a local."

"Born and raised here."

Many times, he had watched as she climbed down the ladder, walked a lap in the pool, and then exited the center. Looking into her eyes, he hoped she never caught his laugh. Meeting her on this ride, he saw she was far more the athlete than he had given her credit. Alone, along a popular trail off the beaten path few athletes dared to explore, he enjoyed talking with her, hearing her unusual southern voice and gazing into her captivating eyes. Hearing a rumble in the near distance, he was forced to return to the present. "It's time to tackle that nasty fence."

"If I survive Dead Dave's Curve, I'll see you on the other side," Terie promised, giving a look she knew he would understand.

Hell's Curve, a rut jumping, log dodging, two-mile stretch over the trail's most treacherous and rugged terrain, had been renamed Dead Dave's Curve after Dave Archila, an off-road daredevil, pierced his beating heart with an iron post after failing to execute a bunny hop over a rolling log. Knowing this, he proceeded with caution. Smitten by Terie's beauty and confidence, he did not want to damage the heart he hoped to give away.

When the ride was over, and both survived the trail's notorious and unforgiving curves, they refueled with a cold beer he pulled from a cooler he kept in the Jeep's cargo space. While quenching their thirst, he helped Terie load her Huffy mountain bike into the back of her truck. "If you're not seeing someone, I'd like to see you again, maybe take you to dinner sometime."

Grabbing a pen from a canvas backpack, Terie placed the cap between her lips. While he watched, she scribbled on his hand. "That's where I work. Come by this week and I'll show you our pool."

His thoughts a scrambled mess, and worried sweat might wash away the digits, he put to memory the inky numbers. Leaning against a tree that had taken root decades earlier, he watched Terie fasten her seat belt and lock the old truck's door. Backing out of the graveled space, she leaned out the window. Calling his name through a cloud of dust, she asked if he needed a ride.

"No, no, I'm…I'm okay. You go on ahead."

Pointing to the white Jeep parked under a mature tulip poplar, Terie shouted again, "Is that yours?"

He gave a simple nod, "Yep."

"Dang. I was looking forward to teasing you about that pink rust puppy I've seen you driving and the faded hula dancer glued to the dash." Throwing the truck in drive, Terie sped away.

CHAPTER 18

It was the third straight day in a row Memphis was paralyzed by freezing temperatures. Snow blanketed the streets as sand trucks crept along Walnut Grove, Poplar Avenue, and Summer, the city's principal streets. Behind them, traffic slowly resumed.

Escaping cabin fever, Cory ventured out into the cold. His destination? The pool. Knowing their coach never canceled practice, the team readied their swim bags and took to the road.

Arriving minutes before him, the kids took advantage of November's ice storm and the fast and slick surfaces it left behind. Falling victim to the long stretch of cold days where the sun went into hiding and freezing rain pelted everything in its path, the club's baby pool was transformed into a solid sheet of ice. Taking turns on the small space, they skated across the baby pool, falling on their bottoms when their shoes clipped jagged pieces of debris and embedded leaves recent windstorms had left behind.

Those same storms ripped the pool's solar cover from the deck and off its reel. Foregoing their time on the rink, the older swimmers helped drag the heavy cover from the fence. Because the pool had been exposed to the snow and ice, swim practice was canceled.

Hustling his team indoors, he hurried to bump up the thermostat.

Wearing his coat until the old system kicked in, he rubbed his hands together until the old heater warmed the small room.

"Who wants to play foosball?" he asked, combing the floor for something they could use for a ball. "First one to find a ball or a piece of popcorn gets to be my partner." Recalling an old Gene Autry film, he placed his hands on his hips. "Now, git along, my little doggies."

"I'm not a doggy," Silvie sassed.

"You're right. I stand corrected. Move along, my annoying little mutants."

"Can we use this?" Patricia asked, offering a wad of gum.

Giving the pink plug a once over, he curled his lip. "You can chew it, but we're not playing with it." Taking a second glance at the wad, he noticed a hair running through it. "Drop that in the garbage and keep searching."

Using a cheese puff he found hidden deep in the sofa cushions, he and his partner easily scored the winning fifteen points over their opponents' single-digit score.

Taking a new partner, he enjoyed a second victory. Scanning the small crowd, he resorted to a round of eeny, meeny, miny, moe to choose his next partner. Pulling at his sleeves, the kids fought for the position. Waving their arms overhead, they shouted, "Pick me! Pick me!" Winning the counting rhyme, Silvie took her place at the table.

When their unworthy competitors whined, he pulled Silvie off to the side. "I'm going to let them win a few points." After whispering the game plan in her ear, they returned to the playing field. Older than most of her teammates, Silvie had more fun playing the game than having to win it. Partnered for the next round, they challenged their eager opponents with fighting words. "You don't mess with the best, 'cause the best never lose at cheese puff foosball!"

Employing poorly timed kicks, missed shots, and finding themselves unable to block their opponents' mighty puff, he begged for a rematch when he and Silvie fell behind. When his request was denied, he shuffled his way to the sofa.

—

Desperate to heat the pool, Cory searched the classifieds and swim magazines until he found a solution. The sale price of a commercial pool dome, which promised to withstand high winds and heavy rainfall, included a blower. When he learned it came with a heater and a revolving door with a zippered entry, he placed a call to the number listed in the ad. As promised in print, the bubble arrived on a flatbed trailer three days later. Needing to watch his pennies, he recruited his friends and swim team parents to help with the installation.

Training in the bubble created a stir when several of the swimmers broke out in a rash. While most were willing to show him their inflamed arms, legs, and backs, a shy one complained about the irritation on her bottom. "It gives me the itchy scratchies." Known for giving nicknames, he quickly dubbed her Bumps on the Rump.

During practice, the bubble filled with a chlorine fog, making it impossible to see an outstretched arm. Those times when the team could not see him or when the noise from the blower made it hard for them to hear, he was forced to shout their drills. "Cave swimming," he called it.

It was not until freezing temperatures and high winds downed the bubble that he understood its bargain price and quick delivery. Each time someone passed through the small, revolving door, the bubble hissed its warning. Within seconds, it began its gradual descent as it slowly collapsed into the water. In his hurry to prevent the heavy door from sinking out of sight, he rushed to bump up the blower. By Thanksgiving, this rescue mission became an everyday occurrence. When a swimmer asked to leave the pool to visit the bathroom, he had to jump into action.

"Listen up. If any of you need to use the restroom, now's the time to go. This is the only bathroom break until the end of practice." Rolling his eyes, he chuckled when every member of his team climbed out of the pool.

In the passing days, the bubble continued to collapse and the tired and overworked blower battled a croupy cough. Fighting the door and the bubble's heavy canvas, swim practice became a challenge. Their noses red and runny, the young swimmers begged to stay indoors. Always up for foosball, he challenged them to a game.

For the kids, it was all about winning, especially when he was on the other side of the table. When things heated up, he distracted them with wet willies. Covering their ears, they ran from his outstretched finger. When the game resumed and his challengers were ahead, he rubbed his face while whining that his jaw hurt. "My dog jaw is acting up again."

Curious about their coach's dog jaw, several of the younger children asked to touch it. When he was certain he held everyone's attention, he growled and then bared his teeth at the outstretched hand when it was inches from his face. Those kids who had already been a victim of his playful prank laughed along with him, while those unaware let out a scream and backed away.

"How do you do that, Cory?" they asked, touching their own jaws.

"I was born this way," he answered with teasing eyes.

———

At month's end, the club's manager arrived again at practice. "Hate to do this to you, but we're closing the club at the end of the month for a total remodel. I'm not even sure if the pool will be staying. All I know is, you'll need to be out by the thirtieth. I'm really sorry, Cory. If I hear of a place where you can train your team, I'll give you a call."

CHAPTER 19

With a skip in his step, Cory strolled through the double doors of the workout facility. Passing by roaring treadmills, aging members reading the morning paper while pedaling stationary bikes, and young mothers clad in tight-fitting yoga pants, he searched the large room. When he caught sight of Terie, his heart skipped a beat. Dressed in spandex and running shoes with her hair pulled back in a side braid, she took his breath away. When she took him in her arms, he was left blushing. A welcoming squeeze to his shoulder rendered him speechless.

"I'm so glad you called. For a while there I thought maybe you lost my number."

Again, he blushed. "Impossible. It's forever in my memory."

Hearing this, a smile played on Terie's painted lips. "Come on, follow me. I know you're dying to see the pool."

His head in a fog and his face still red, he failed to notice she had taken his hand. Pausing their workouts, the center's members looked on, curious about the young man who put a smile on Terie's face. Following behind, he blushed a third time when a reflection in a floor to ceiling mirror caught him checking out her backside.

"I work out every day. It's one of the perks," she said with a flirty smile.

Entering the pool area, he quickly noticed the six twenty-five-meter lanes were occupied. "Is it always like this?"

"We get a lot of swimmers in the morning and late afternoon when area schools let out, and we have water aerobics classes in the afternoon."

"I really appreciate your help in arranging for us to swim here."

"Right now, I can give you three lanes. I'll make sure they're always side-by-side. Two hours each day, from four to six. I'm still working on getting a couple of mornings for you, but right now, we're obligated to keep the pool available to our paying members." Leaning in, she whispered in his ear. "When they feel cheated, they get hostile."

"I'm not a betting man, but if I were, I'd say you could outrun them." Watching her enjoy a laugh, a smile filled his face.

Hers was not an ordinary laugh. Throwing her head back, her eyes danced and deep dimples appled her full cheeks. "This will work. We're just lucky to have a place to train."

"Oh, one last thing. You'll need to tell your team they have to sign in at the front desk each time they enter the building. I know it's a hassle, but it keeps the scrounge-a-muffins and grit monkeys from sneaking into the club."

Having heard those terms before, he nodded his understanding. "One must pay to play."

While he and Terie continued to make small talk, his team slowly trickled in. Speaking over each other in loud voices, their parents rushed the deck. They wore a look of disappointment on their faces, but with Terie at his side, he did not feel the time was right for addressing their concerns or answering questions.

"Hey, kiddos. The locker rooms are just outside the door and down the hall on the right. We'll be swimming in the first three lanes." Leaving Terie on the deck, he ushered the parents out into the hall.

"It's a long way to drive, Cory."

Before he was given an opportunity to respond, another parent piped in. "It's always rush hour on Germantown Parkway, and it's especially worse this time of day."

"I understand, but please keep in mind this is only until I find a better situation." He pleaded, but still the complaints continued.

"Traffic is crazy and parking is impossible. I sat in stop and go traffic so long, I darn near grew a mustache."

"I'm parked behind a car. I left my flashers on. I got tired of circling the lot, but I wasn't about to let the girls walk in without me."

"I have all of you beat. I circled the lot three times, drove over a downed stop sign, *tapped* a car with my bumper, and dodged a wreck when somebody failed to yield. On top of that, a gray-hair honked at me and then flipped me the bird."

Hoping to calm frazzled nerves, he again asked for their patience and understanding. "This is a temporary situation. Until another pool is available, this is our training pool. Once the pool at St. George's is open and ready, this will be a distant memory. I know it hasn't been easy—all these interim pools—but in the end, we'll have a training facility that will be the envy of every team. I want you to know I appreciate your dedication and commitment to the team. In the meantime, I don't want you to worry about parking. When you get here, just drive up to the front of the building. I'll be waiting at the door." While their complaining continued, he spoke over them, explaining he would sign each swimmer in at the front desk. Getting an odd look from most and an evil eye from one, he shrugged his shoulders. "Management requires it."

During the following weeks, backed-up traffic, fender benders, and lack of parking caused practices to be shortened, delayed, or worse, canceled. Later in the month, when he was offered an opportunity to train at a sports plex, he jumped at it.

Located miles away from the schools his team members attended, and off I-240 in an industrial park near horse stables, a federal prison, and a buffalo range, the sports plex's pool had originally been constructed as an outdoor facility. In recent months, a screened breezeway was added, connecting the bubbled eight-lane pool to the main building. When unforgiving winds slapped against the simple structure, the small corridor roared like an industrial vacuum at its highest setting. Inside the bubble, overhead lights flickered, the raised floor shook, and those members caught in the storm ran for cover.

Just as it had been at Colonial Acres and the workout facility, Thunder was still not in a position to host swim meets. With this in mind, the search for the perfect training facility continued. In the interim, the sports plex would have to do.

In addition to searching for a pool, he added several swimmers to the roster, including those he would later coach during the summer months at Ridgeway Country Club, a job Bob encouraged him to take.

Turning his focus to his team, he took Thunder to the Germantown Thanksgiving Invitational, a well-attended meet close to home. Because Germantown shared a border with East Memphis, overnight stays in costly hotels were not necessary.

Situated in the heart of Germantown, the center provided plenty of parking, access to affordable restaurants, and a water park with tennis courts just a lob away. Thunder was among twelve teams to attend the three-day meet. Their competition included the host team, the Memphis Tigers, and Wimbleton's Makos, another local team. During closing ceremonies, he learned seven members on his team broke just as many pool records, a feat to be admired.

December's calendar included several out-of-town meets. First on the schedule was Nashville Aquatic Club's NIKE Music City Invitational. An unforeseen problem presented itself when one of the parents, an aggressive woman with a face made of stone, reserved an entire block of rooms at the only hotel within walking distance of the Tracy Caulkins Swim Center, forcing the other families to search for hotels throughout the city. When he learned of the situation, he had the block of rooms released, but because many of Thunder's parents had been forced to secure rooms demanding non-refundable charges, those rooms near the swim center went to visiting teams.

After returning to Memphis, he sent an email to the parents suggesting that in the future, each family should only make their *own* hotel reservations.

CHAPTER 20

U pon spring's arrival, a time when area country clubs prepared for the coming months, Cory opened his mail to find a packet of information from Ridgeway Country Club, a private club near Collierville. Inside the large envelope was a parking pass and a leather-bound copy of the club's employee manual. Clipped to the parking pass was a handwritten note letting him know he needed to stop by the human resources office for the keys to the pool deck and adjoining locker rooms.

From May through August and until after the city swim meet, he coached the Tidal Waves, Ridgeway's team. The Tidal Waves participated in the Memphis Summer Swim League, a swim organization that gave recreational and seasonal swimmers the opportunity to compete for ribbons, trophies, and a chance to have their winning results posted in the newspapers.

His employment agreement with Ridgeway allowed him to use the club's outdoor pool for coaching his own team. Arriving at eight o'clock, Thunder practiced until the club's team arrived hours later. Because many Thunder swimmers also swam on their own country club teams, which allowed them to compete in the city meet with school friends, he did not schedule afternoon practice.

The pool's dive well offered one board and was separated from the swim lanes by a fiberglass rope. On a morning after a hard practice filled with long sets, drills, and a closing mile swim, he directed the team to the dive well. "Who wants to play corkscrew?"

Eager to play, the kids grabbed their swim goggles and hurried to circle around him. Handing each swimmer a pack of sour punch straws, a chewy straw-shaped candy, he divided them into relay teams. Lining the teams alongside the pool's edge, he reminded his team of the game's rules.

"You must have the entire pack of candy in your mouth before the first swimmer enters the pool. We're going to mix up the medley a little bit, so listen up. You can start with any stroke you want, but after the first stroke, you must immediately change to a different stroke. One stroke breast, one free, one back, one fly. You can pick the order, but you must flip from stroke to stroke after each single stroke. Up and back. Diving is not allowed. If the straws are not in your mouth when I start the race, your team will be disqualified. Who wants to tell me what happens then?"

"We have to wash your Jeep."

"Winner, winner, chicken dinner." Holding their attention, he held up a paper bag. "Oh, and there's a prize for the winning team."

Cheering on their teammates, the kids laughed each time one messed up. Dizzy from flipping from stroke to stroke, many had to stop to get their bearings and regain equilibrium. Waiting for stomach cramps to subside, others grabbed onto the rope. Those who pressed on to the finish, raced to the locker room once they were relieved of their duties. Eager to participate, the swimmers waiting to enter the water offered encouragement to their teammates. By the time the last swimmer exited the pool looking a little green and unsteady, wet and gooey straws hung from open mouths.

When he announced the winning team, they pumped their fists in the air. "What did we win?" they asked in unison.

Wearing a smirk on his face, he reached into the paper bag. Waiting and teasing until their eyes grew wide, he presented each winner with a pack of sour punch straws.

CHAPTER 21

September was a busy month for Cory and his team. Their first practice at World Overcomers, an outreach ministry on the corner of Winchester Road and Kirby Parkway, in Memphis' Hickory Hill Community, took place on Labor Day.

As he drove up to the entrance, he was greeted by two rows of brightly colored flags representing the world nations. Security guards in golf carts, whose job it was to monitor the premises, occupied the main entrance to Word Dome, as the campus was known. He observed the parking area's many posted traffic signs and water features. Unable to forget the parking nightmares at the fitness center, he did not expect to hear any complaints. Noticing his was the only vehicle in the back parking lot, he was confident his team would find him.

The church's eight-lane pool was heated, and the locker rooms were just steps away from the deck. Parked in a swivel chair under rows of fluorescent lights, a wall of windows provided Cory an uninterrupted view of the pool. Always overwhelmed with heat sheets and upcoming meet brochures, he was thrilled the narrow office had built-in filing cabinets.

Having taken on competent swimmers from the country club and coaching children who attended World Overcomers' after-school programs, Thunder's roster tripled in number. Recalling his conversation with Bob Compton when he referred to Thunder as "ours," he decided the time had come to hire an assistant coach.

His first choice was Keith Anderson, an old friend and former landlord when he lived at The Hobo. A real estate developer, Keith swam in high school and college. An accomplished swimmer, he set pool records in both the butterfly and freestyle.

"The job doesn't pay much, but what you'll gain working with these kids will enrich your life in ways you can't imagine." After an abbreviated pause, he spoke with an enthusiasm Keith appreciated and admired, and feeling a comforting warmth in his heart, he listened in envy. "It's like I've found this great fishing hole others have overlooked. I threw out my line and you know what took the bait? The fastest fish in the pond. I've seen kids turn to sports to escape problems at home. With a little hard work and discipline, they later walked through doors that would have otherwise remained closed to them. I believe a coach, a really good coach, can help save a lost child." With love and emotion in his voice, he continued. "I'm blessed to coach them. Every time I step on the deck, I feel like I've won the lottery."

Sharing a basket of buffalo wings, he tore at a fried appendage before dipping the fleshy meat in a red sauce the waiter described in two words: blistering hot. Trusting the waiter's description of a beer the restaurant's bar offered on tap, they sipped a local ale he found hoppy and bitter. Licking sauce from his fingers, he reached for another wing. "These kids get the concept. Every time they shoot off the starting block, they represent the team. And you want to know something else? Some of the best coaching happens after the meet. These kids look out for each other. They'll praise a solid effort and offer words of encouragement when it's needed. This is their family. Sometimes, this little team feels like an extension of my own."

Wiping sweat from his forehead, Keith hurried to accept the assistant coaching position. "A hundred times over, I wish I could be like you. You are like rust—you never quit. Don't kid yourself thinking you're the one who won the lottery. These kids are lucky to have you, my friend. Now, before I reach for the check, let's discuss the duties that warrant my meager salary and when I can expect a raise."

The next afternoon before the team was scheduled to arrive for practice, they met at the pool. "Now that the older girls are aging up, we need to focus on the younger kids." Pulling a copy of the roster from a deep drawer in his desk, Cory handed it to Keith. "You'll be working with the Silver group. I call them my trifecta team. They always win, place, and show. They're always consistent in their outcome. I think there will come a day when the order rotates, not because they're driven, but because they're so competitive. The kids in the Black group are strong swimmers with a lot of potential, but I'm limiting them to afternoon practices. I don't want them to burn out." Reading Sophie's name on the roster and recalling a recent meet, he fell into a contagious laugh.

"When Sophie came up from her dive, her goggles were hanging around her neck. When I asked her later why she didn't open her eyes, she complained about the chlorine. Everybody watched as she swam all over the place. She pulled through the water and her arms stayed with the stroke. She bumped into the ropes, slapped at the water, but somehow managed to remain in sync with her arms and legs. Everyone cheered her on. People came up to me later asking if she was blind. What was amazing was she won not only her heat, but also the event." Throwing his head back and slapping the desk, he spoke through the laughter. "There was this one time she chased me around the pool singing Blondie's song, *One Way or Another.*" This time he laughed so hard, he had tears in his eyes. "She ran behind me singing, 'I'm gonna getcha, getcha, getcha one way.' I couldn't get that song out of my head for days."

When the team arrived for practice, he introduced Keith. "We're fortunate to have this guy on our team. Keith and I go way back. He set a few records here and there, and I can't help but imagine what a great swimmer he would have been if I had coached him."

Laughing along with his friend, Keith gently shoved him aside. "I have a lot of respect for Coach Cory. Having seen him struggling to keep his head above ankle deep water, I can honestly say I was surprised to hear he chose the life of a swim coach as his career. I guess he finally learned he couldn't make a living eating popcorn." Enjoying the attention, he held up a bucket of sour punch straws. "Cory tells me you respond well to bribes. That's a good thing to know."

Hanging on each word their coaches spoke, and enjoying the banter between them, the kids joined in the laughter. In the days to come, they eagerly accepted Keith, the Harley he rode, his five o'clock shadow, the baggy jeans he constantly pulled up to his narrow waist, and the frosted tips in his dark hair.

Together, they recognized the team's potential and worked to strengthen its weaknesses. At the end of every practice, they went through the roster, discussing the performance of each swimmer, the goals he or she hoped to achieve, and how they fit into Thunder's swim program. Working side by side, they outlined a training program to benefit each team member. Together, they agreed on one goal. Keep the swimmer interested in the sport.

On a day like any other, Cory noticed that Caiti, a seasoned swimmer, was falling behind in the practice drills. "Karate Chop," he called out. "Swim over here."

Hearing the name he pinned on her, Caiti took a deep breath before diving deep. Staying below the swimmers in the lanes above her, she dodged fierce breaststroke kicks as she navigated toward the wall. When she surfaced, he was waiting for her.

"What's up, Karate Chop? Why are you letting everyone pass you?"

Treading water in the pool's deep end, Caiti pushed her goggles up to her forehead. "I'm sorry, Cory. I have an audition tomorrow and I'm so nervous."

Leaving Keith to coach the team, he crouched low. "What are you auditioning for?"

"A musical at school. I have never been so stressed."

"Do you know the song? All the words?"

"Yes, but I feel I need to sing it several more times before tomorrow's audition."

"Go ahead and climb out of the pool. Grab your towel, dry off, and meet me in my office in five minutes."

Worried she might be in trouble, Caiti did as she was asked. Minutes later, when she walked toward his office, she saw through the window that several of her teammates were circled around him. Looking up from his swivel chair, he waved her in. Taking a deep breath and preparing for the worst, she pushed through the door.

"Karate Chop, take whatever time you need to warm up your pipes. When you're ready, sing like this is your audition."

CHAPTER 22

"How much should I spend on a ring?" Cory asked.

Holding a hand to her face, Jill gasped. "What? Are you thinking about getting married?"

"If she'll have me."

After a noticeable pause, Jill did her best to hide her disappointment. He had not dated much, and she worried he was rushing to the altar. Admiring her own wedding band, she remembered the sapphire ring he received after their mother passed away. Afraid he might lose it, she held on to it for him. Feeling a little guilty, she did not bring it up now. "Well, if you're sure about this, you can buy a simple band. Later, when you've had time to save money, you can think about buying a diamond."

Cory's proposal of marriage did not take place at the end of a treacherous bike ride, or at the popular Nora Champagne, a restaurant adorned with crystal lighting and a tuxedoed wait staff whose presence was known to encourage romance. He did not surprise Terie by bending down on one knee or asking her father for his daughter's hand in marriage. Instead, he chose to propose in the privacy of his apartment with a ring made from hemp that she admired weeks earlier in a boutique shop on Highland Avenue.

Pulling at a stubborn ringlet, he hurried to place her hand in his. "You are the tater to my tot, the sun to my flower, and the nutter to my butter. The way you look at me tells me I'm the luckiest man in the world."

Nuzzling close, he inhaled the sweet fragrance she sprayed on her neck, along her delicate wrists, and in the shadows of her chest. Brushing her hair aside, he placed a gentle kiss on her forehead. He did not have to tell her he loved her—his actions told her what she wanted to hear. Exchanging a kiss, he pulled a box from one of his khaki shorts' many pockets. "Forever and always I want you at my side. Terie, will you do the honor of being my wife, my partner, and my best friend?"

With a tender kiss, Terie accepted his proposal. Taking the ring he offered, she wrapped his hand in hers. "I accept the love of a fiery redhead, a loving man I trust to guard and protect my heart."

Pulling her from the sofa, he lifted her into his arms. Holding his face in her hands, she whispered, "I can't wait to be your wife and the mother of your children."

Celebrating with sparkling wine, the engaged couple made phone calls to family members and close friends. "We're getting married!"

CHAPTER 23

Many changes took place over the next two years. Margo and Silvie learned to drive, and swimmers from as far away as Arkansas and Mississippi took an interest in the team. Overnight, Thunder doubled in number, billing statements were prepared and mailed by a staff unknown to Cory, and monthly swim fees nearly tripled. This was not a bad thing, considering the team would soon have its own facility. Unfortunately, problems started when an aggressive accounting volunteer with a business background and a no-nonsense attitude, who paid monthly fees for her own children to swim on the team, raised questions about Silvie. Because she had no knowledge of his commitment to the Mercers, she wanted only to get the team's books in order. "Cory, I can't find any information for Silvie. I don't even have an address."

Standing on the deck while his team raced through a sprint drill, he was not in a position to discuss his arrangement with the Mercers. In fact, he was not sure he would ever disclose the agreement with anyone. "If you wouldn't mind leaving her statement on my desk, I'll take care of it."

"I don't mind calling Silvie's mom. I just can't find their telephone number."

Forced to continue the awkward conversation, he turned his back to his team. Ready for the next drill, they remained quiet, waiting and listening. In past months, he overheard a number of parents, many who followed him when he left Tigers, pretend to have knowledge of his commitment to Silvie. By no fault of her own, she had become the topic of conversation. These same parents shunned Silvie and her family when they heard, through gossip, he formed Thunder for the sole purpose of financing her training. "I'm sorry, but I have to coach my team now. Please leave Silvie's statement on my desk."

The following afternoon when his team arrived for practice, a sign taped to the center's door greeted them. *Effective Immediately. Parents are requested to refrain from interrupting practice. All conversations with Coach Cory and Coach Keith will take place after practice.*

A man of his word, he kept his promise to Silvie's parents. On the first of each month, he wrote a personal check to cover her fees and expenses. A man of honor and pride, he ignored the negative comments and odd looks a small circle of naysayers wanted him to endure. Taking the high road and turning a blind eye, his silence put the matter to rest.

CHAPTER 24

When Cory learned of the Tour d'Esprit, he wanted his team to participate in the 24-hour run. Held in East Memphis on the grounds of the Church of the Holy Spirit, the proceeds of the race benefited the Holy Spirit Medical Clinic in the town of Croix-des-Bouquets in Haiti.

On a day before practice was underway, he talked about the race with his team. "The actual race starts at three o'clock. The course is a one-mile loop around the church." Envisioning the neighborhood, he tried to picture in his mind the race's location. "If I'm not mistaken, I think it runs along those tall power lines you see on Poplar Avenue when you enter Germantown. It must be south of Kirby Parkway." Pausing to read the trifold brochure, he scanned the detailed map on the entry form's back cover. "Oh, wait. We'll start in the parking lot, and we'll run on gravel, grass, and through a wooded area. This shouldn't be a problem for us. We will be given one ankle chip and that one chip must remain on the course at all times. That means if a wild squirrel chases you, you must stay the course. We'll take turns trading off so we can eat and sleep. The race ends at three o'clock the following day. It's for a good cause. I think it'll be fun. Any questions?"

"Where will we sleep?" the kids asked, talking over each other.

"I'm working on that. We can bring a camper and some pup tents. I'm fresh out of campers at the moment, so if anyone knows where we can get one for the night, let me know."

Questions continued while he explained the silent auction and spaghetti dinner. Scanning the brochure, he answered questions about breakfast. "They'll have omelets, fresh fruit, and French toast. I think it's safe to say we won't be running on empty stomachs. There's a wrap-up party after the race. There will be live music, hamburgers, and hot dogs." Squinting, he muttered to himself. "I can't read the fine print, but I think they're trying to get The Beatles and Elvis Presley to perform. They're opening with Josie and the Pussycats." When his team did not laugh with him, he laughed alone. "You do know The Beatles are no longer together, Elvis has left the building, and Josie and the Pussycats is a comic book band?" Their blank stares let him know they were not up on their music history. Again, his was the only laugh they heard.

One week later, on the day the race kicked off, he and his team decorated a rented trailer with strings of Christmas lights and strands of red and gold Chinese lanterns. A large sign with Thunder's logo stood front and center. Steps away, an artificial turf rug led to the front door. Inside the spacious Northwood Skyline, a small refrigerator was stocked with energy drinks and a supply of fresh fruits. Several bags of popcorn were on the counter. In the grassy area next door, Thunder parents pitched four two-man tents.

Standing alongside the marked course, the team cheered as he stood ready to run the opening mile. At the pop of the start gun, he shot off. Staying in the back of the pack, he waited for an opening. When he saw a chance to take the lead, he took off with a vengeance. Taking the lead, he felt strong and confident. Years of running and biking had strengthened his legs. Rounding a tree-lined curve, he looked to find his team running alongside him. Keeping his pace, he waved them away. "What are you doing out here? You need to go back. Save your legs for your turn."

Twenty-four hours later, at the end of the race, Thunder had logged over 200 miles. "The first place trophy was not ours to claim, but second place is *nothing to sneeze at*. What's important is we had fun."

———

In early November, they competed in the popular Fall Frenzy meet. Neighboring teams and envious coaches took notice when a Thunder member placed in the 100 free with a time of 56.56, and her teammate touched the time pad at 59.92. Cory beamed with pride when Margo, Silvie, and several other members of his team walked away with personal bests in their individual events.

This same year brought significant changes to the team. Several new members joined the roster, and the meets they attended brought recognition far greater than he expected. The newspaper's sports section often mentioned their successes, along with pictures of the team's rising stars.

The following year was also a busy one. Training alongside him, and often biking upward of one hundred miles in blistering heat and through sheets of rain so thick he learned to keep his focus on the rear tire inches in front of him, Bob Compton was physically and mentally prepared for upcoming triathlons.

With their future home base still under construction, Thunder continued their training at World Overcomers. At year's end, they were a strong presence at the NAC Winter Invitational held at the Tracy Caulkins Swim Center in Nashville.

———

The opening of the Compton Aquatic Center brought much relief to Cory and his Thunder family. Bouncing from pool to pool had taken its toll, and now, having a place to call home, he was able to put aside real estate searches and give his attention to what he loved most—coaching his team.

Days after Thunder settled into the Collierville campus, when overhead lights had been adjusted and new starting blocks were secured to the concrete deck, Walt Rider stopped by. Greeted by Cory, he asked for a tour.

The two friends, who were also fellow triathletes, soon found themselves in a conversation regarding a possible venture. "Come by the house. I'll introduce you to my sons. The older boys are already competing in triathlons, but it's the youngest one who shares my love of the sport."

His curiosity piqued, he made a visit to Walt's Germantown home the following day.

When a knock on the front door went unanswered, he made his way around to the side of the Rider's two-story brick house. Entering the carport, he observed the canopy of bikes hanging overhead. Recognizing the yellow Cervelo time trial bike Walt rode the last time he sailed by him on the course, he recalled a recent triathlon where Walt, an older athlete, successfully demonstrated the benefit experience had over youth's ambition. Before knocking on the windowed door to the house, he stopped to admire a vintage car parked in the carport's far bay. Just as he peeked through the open window, he heard a cough.

"It's a '76 Jensen Healey. It runs when it wants to, which in my opinion, isn't often enough."

"I saw one like this at a car show in Vegas a long, long time ago. That's interesting fabric on the seats. Is that what they call argyle?"

"Paisley. Back in the day, it was all the rage. I can appreciate it, but it doesn't suit my fancy. When I get some free time, I'm going to recover them with a buttery leather I saw at a trade show a few months ago." Moving to the door, Walt kicked aside a running shoe. "Let's go inside. Excuse the mess." Stepping around crates and boxes, he brushed a hand over a disabled bike. "These are the tools of the trade. The clutter drives Mary crazy. I just closed my Germantown shop last week, so I had to move everything here. I liked having a place where my customers could stop in and I could tinker with new parts. Anyway, I got tired of the traffic. I had to cut through three lanes of traffic to turn left into the parking lot, and to exit, I had to turn right, go through the intersection, and then circle back to get home."

Entering the house, he found himself amidst baskets of washed laundry, nylon backpacks, and a myriad of bicycle parts—new and advanced products expected to live up to their promise of shaving time and increasing speed, and recycled parts hoping to hitch one last ride. Stepping over, on, and around bike tubes, tire pumps, chains, and cranks, he worried he would land on his nose if he failed to navigate the entry hall's obstacle course.

The dining room offered more of the same. Race wheels hovered in the corners, and race jerseys blanketed the oval table. Each of the table's eight chairs held bike helmets, bicycle shorts, and damp socks waiting for their turn in the dryer.

Following Walt through the foyer to the den, he searched for a place to sit.

Clearing a chair, Walt tossed a stack of old race brochures and crinkled magazines aside. "Have a seat."

Keeping with the home's athletic theme, T-shirts, race numbers, and plastic bags filled with race goodies littered the hardwood floor. Falling into a chair he cleared of newspapers, Walt took off his running shoes, and after stretching his long, narrow feet, slipped into a pair of gray and black toe-loop jacquard sandals. "Are you familiar with Iron Kids?"

"*The triathlon series where every finisher is a winner?*" he said, drawing a chuckle from Walt. Searching his memory, he recalled hearing that as a young boy Lance Armstrong participated in the Sara Lee Corporation's triathlon series.

Leaning back against a throw pillow, Walt's face lit up. "Good. You've heard of it. I'm in the business. For over twenty years, I've made a living in the sport of triathlon, and aside from this mess, I'm good with bikes. I'd like to talk about working with your Thunder kids."

"What do you have in mind?"

Eager to show him his home's recent addition, Walt jumped to his feet. "Come with me." With him following behind, Walt headed out to the garage.

"Nice boat, Walt." He slid a hand over the fiberglass wings.

"It has a 450-horsepower engine and moves through the water like, well, like your team."

"Nice paraphrase. Where do you ski around here?"

"We usually go over to Greer's Ferry. Clear water is great for seeing what's below, especially when we're tubing. And the boys like the cliffs. Speaking of the boys, you just missed them."

The garage's second floor had little lighting, and exposed two-by-fours gave a glimpse of the conduits that traveled away from the room's four corners. Similar to the area below and to the home's living space, bike parts were laid out on the unfinished floor.

"I want to reach a young age group. I'm talking as young as six. Competing in Iron Kids is a great way to introduce them to the sport. Last year's races were in St. Louis, Tulsa, and right here in Memphis. A few years back, the national championship was out in Sacramento. We stayed a few extra days for a family vacation. I think we can draw some interest from the kids at St. George's. We'll have the pool, and right out the door we'll have easy access to running and biking trails. What do you think about an after-school program that focuses on the three sports? We can tap into their interests and strengths and guide them through the process of appreciating the value of putting those sports together. Think about it. The possibilities are endless."

He thought Walt might be on to something. "We have the perfect setup with the pool school. Tell you what, I'll run it by Bob the next time I see him." Making his way outside, he stopped to read the framed engagement announcement on the wall near the garage door. "The Dunn Rider wedding?" Stepping aside, he failed to stifle a laugh.

"It could have been worse. Before I met Mary, I dated a girl whose last name was Rump."

Together, they shared a laugh and a smile. Still chuckling, he promised to talk with him in the coming days.

Later in the day, when practice was underway, Cory noticed the circle of mothers watching on from the bleachers. The answering machine in his office blinked with telephone messages from these same parents, each wanting him to know they expected their daughter to swim in the upcoming meet's relay events. He had heard the messages but waited to respond. Overhearing their comments, he jumped into action.

"I need the twelve and under girls on the deck. The rest of you move over to the far lanes and finish your drill sets. If you finish before I'm done here, kick a 400. No fins this time." Speaking louder than he needed, the eyes in the back of his head let him know the parents were watching with bated breath. He then turned to the girls standing closest to him. "I want each of you to take a starting block." Addressing the remaining swimmers, he explained the drill. "Grab a board and line up behind them."

Moving along the deck, his eyes locked with those of one of the women. A smile crossed his face while a sneer came over hers. Understanding her message, he moved along. Knowing tension was rising with several other mothers believing their child was better than most of the swimmers and deserved special and added attention, he hoped she would not cause a schism.

"You will be swimming the free relay in the next meet," he addressed the girls on the starting blocks. Pointing to the girls as he spoke, he ignored the commotion from the bleachers. "First one to touch the wall will swim anchor." When the swimmers hit the water, he turned his attention to the flock of swimmers who waited to hear his instructions. "You will swim the medley relay. We'll start with backstroke. Go ahead and get in the water. First one to touch the wall swims the back. When we're done there, we'll do the same with the fly, breast, and free. Get ready, and go on the whistle."

Minutes later, while the parents watched on, he responded to their telephone messages when he announced the relay teams. The woman, who earlier offered a sneer, now had her lip in a snarl. Instructing his team to grab kickboards, he turned to the parents. "It's important to *play nice* in the sandbox."

CHAPTER 25

When news of the grand opening of the Compton Aquatic Center made the front page of the newspaper, Cory's excitement exploded. In bold print, the cover story announced the names of the medaled champions who would participate in an exhibition event with Memphis Thunder when the team hosted its first meet.

As the celebration unfolded, hungry visitors waited in line at the concession stands and crowds gathered on the pool deck hoping to rub elbows with the celebrities they followed on television. Cameras focused on Pan Pacific gold medalist Michael Phelps, world record holder Misty Hyman, Memphis' own Gabrielle Rose, and Kristy Kowal, the first American female to win a world championship title in the 100-meter breaststroke. The athletes mingled among the swimmers, often pausing to pose for pictures and sign their autographs to swim caps, heat sheets, and the meet's commemorative shirt.

Moving through the aquatic center, he burst with pride. On the wall behind the starting blocks, the results clock flashed a welcome to the famous athletes, and in the pool's four corners, pace clocks sat ready. Minutes earlier, he watched as race officials gave the touch pads a last-minute test run. Volunteers with lanyards around their necks, stood at their assigned posts, and meet officials took their positions. On the far wall was an enormous thunderbolt, the team's logo. Hustling about on the deck, his swimmers wore winning smiles. Years earlier, when he made the decision to go after his dream, he never imagined it would place him here, or that his team would grow in five years from four members to sixty.

When Cory heard a voice call out his name, he turned to find Donna heading in his direction. Dressed in denim gauchos and a western-fringed blouse, he noticed she had not changed a bit since the day they met at the pool on Helene, except perhaps, being a little slow in her giddy-up.

"Oh, Cory, you've come a long way since Colonial Acres. I imagine this was how Dorothy must have felt when she arrived in Emerald City." Pulling a Polaroid camera from a pink tote bag, she insisted on a picture. Keeping him at her side, she posed for a second photo. When the chemicals were dry, she compared the images before tucking the better picture in her bag. "Here, you can keep this one," she said handing him the other one.

Making his way along the wide deck, he mingled with coaches from as near as Germantown and as far away as Irvine, California. Curious neighbors, who followed the construction of the state-of-the-art facility, toured the center. Taking their place near him, his team was suited up, energized, and eager to get the meet underway.

When he reached for a marker, Sophie tugged at his sleeve. "Cory! My tooth is loose!" She pointed to a baby tooth hanging by a twisted thread.

Crouching to her level, he searched her mouth. "I can pull that for you." When she opened her mouth a second time, he gloved his hand with the corner of the swim towel draped over her shoulders. "This won't hurt," he promised with a quick grab.

Taking the tooth her coach offered, Sophie ran her tongue over the bleeding divot. "You pulled the wrong tooth!"

"Well, I'll have to pull the right one later." He laughed while looking into his young swimmer's mouth a third time.

When the meet announcer asked for their attention, the center grew silent. On the platform with a microphone in her hand, Caiti stood tall and proud. As the flag of the United States raised, she proceeded to open the meet. Singing the national anthem, she brought a smile to many faces and a tear to others. "You have the voice of an angel," he whispered when she stepped to his side.

Taking the microphone, he welcomed visiting coaches and their teams. When he introduced Michael Phelps, the crowd cheered, called his name, and rising from the bleachers, gave him a standing ovation. When he called attention to Gabrielle, the locals in attendance went wild as they cheered their hometown athlete. Turning to his own staff, he introduced Keith.

Impressed with Silvie's warm-up, Michael Phelps took the microphone and announced he was confident he would someday see her compete in the Olympics. A proud smile covered Cory's face as he and those around him nodded in agreement.

Gabrielle's friends from high school and former teammates cheered when she challenged Michael Phelps, Kristy Kowal, and Misty Hyman to a freestyle race. Wanting to involve the crowd, Michael extended the challenge to include Cory, who tried to wave them away. After continued insistence and cheers from his own team, he soon found himself stepping up to the starting block.

Adjusting the goggles he was offered from the gold medalist, he took a deep breath. Hoping to shake off nerves, he rotated his arms in the same circular motion he encouraged his team to do each time they prepared to enter the pool. He was certain he looked ridiculous as he lowered to a squatting position to stretch his weakening legs. When the announcer called his name, he did his best to stand tall and give a winning smile. The wave he gave was followed by a shrug of his shoulders. "Let's get this over with," he shouted with a laugh.

When Phelps reached for his hand, the crowd shouted his name, cameras flashed, and embarrassed by the undeserving attention, he grew weak in the knees. A photographer from the newspaper captured their high-five and his broad grin and red face.

Taking their marks, the five swimmers leaned over and grabbed the edges of the starting blocks. Then, halting the race, the medalists stood tall. One by one, they removed their swim caps to reveal Thunder's black cap. Again, the natatorium roared with loud cheers. Asking for silence, the swimmers took their stance.

Waiting for the pop of the gun, his knees buckled, his heart raced, and his face turned cherry red. He lowered his head and prayed he would not land face first, or worse, hit hard with a belly flop. Feeling nervous, he considered a cannonball entry but knew his team would never let him live it down.

Hearing the gun, he shot off the block. Executing a worthy dive, he made a small circle on the water's surface. Pulling through the water and kicking through a cramp, he turned over his stroke as fast as his arms would let him. Turning for a breath, he failed to catch a glimpse of his worthy opponents. It was not until he reached the far end of the pool that he understood the kindness his guests had given him. Instead of diving off the blocks, they jumped in feet first, and foregoing the freestyle stroke, dog paddled across the pool. The huge smile on his face let those close to him know he was living his dream. In his journey to create and coach his own team, a vision he nurtured for years, he allowed himself to dream it, believe in his own abilities, make sacrifices and compromises, and in the process, work hard to succeed. This moment would stay with him forever.

By the end of the meet, his team celebrated many successes. A member in the ten and under age group set a team record in the 50 fly and in the 200 individual medley. Competing in the twelve and under group, another member claimed records in the 500 free and the 100 individual medley. Surrounded by his team, he gave a deserving applause. Catching Sophie's smile, he called her to his side. "The only loss Thunder suffered was Sophie's tooth."

Left to right:
Ryan Weaver, Sophie Kramer, Mary Jensen
Nease, Michael Phelps, Sarah Kramer

CHAPTER 26

"Look at me, Cory! I'm bouncing!"

Glancing up from the pace clock, Cory did a wide-eyed double take. Edging closer to the pool, he watched as several members of the team bounced from one end of the pool to the other. Bobbing heads went out of sight, and breaking the surface, shot up only to disappear again. At first glance, he wondered if they had springs in their pants.

"Watch me, Cory. I'm on a trampoline."

Tossing his wallet aside, he stepped out of his shoes and pulled off his white tube socks. Foregoing goggles, he dove into the deep end. Swimming to the wall, the team watched as he moved along the bottom of the pool, stopping every few feet to brush a hand over the gunite's deep and widening cracks. Pressing on air-filled bubbles, he grew concerned for his team's safety. Out of breath and gasping for air, he shot to the surface. "Everybody out of the pool. Now."

Climbing from the pool, he shook his head in worry, and making his way to the small pool, he cupped his mouth with his hands and shouted to Keith. "Get everybody out of the pool. We have a problem." Scratching his head, he worried he was facing another roadblock. *Would he have to ask his team to go on tour again? He was running out of pools.* Although he would never allow the words to escape his lips, his greatest fear was failing his team.

Long after the kids had gone home and Bob Compton and the engineers he brought with him had time to examine and access the damage, he was relieved to learn that, although the fifty-meter pool required major repairs, the small pool had not suffered any damage. He would have a place for his team to swim. His team had grown since their days at Colonial Acres when playing foosball was as important as swim practice, and unlike those days when the cold pool caused him to cancel practice, he was thankful he would not be forced to hunt for a temporary training facility. His only job now was to change up the training schedule.

The following afternoon, when the team arrived for practice, they were handed a copy of the revised training schedule. Accommodating those families whose children practiced at different times had been a challenge, but in the end, once again, he asked for understanding and patience.

When he arrived at the pool the next morning, he was surprised to find the parking area blocked off. Parking his Jeep in the narrow lane behind the school's chapel, he walked over the footbridge. When he noticed the above-ground pool on the far side of the tennis courts, he picked up his pace. Spotting Bob Compton in a conversation with a circle of men wearing hard hats, he slowed his steps. It was not until Bob waved him over that he sprinted past the pool center and through the parking lot.

"They're going to build a deck around the pool," Bob said, pointing to a stack of two-by-fours. "And a safety rail and some stairs."

"Can we use the school pool?"

Answering for the group, a man with blueprints tucked in his armpit turned to face him. "It appears to be okay. I'm going to have another look at it. There's been some shifting under the big pool. It has suffered some significant structural damage. It looks like it might be awhile before any repair work can start. At this point, we don't know if it's an engineering issue or poor construction that's responsible for the collapse. There's a lot of moisture in the ground out here. You have the Wolf River in your backyard. It's possible this is a wetland area. I don't know, but I'm guessing there's a whole lot of sand under us."

Stuck without a pool, quick thinking had him planning a different workout for his team. When the older kids arrived minutes later for morning practice, he was ready to present it. "Instead of swimming this morning, we're going out for pancakes. My treat."

While his happy team poured maple syrup over stacks topped with creamy melted butter, he explained the problem. "Once the above-ground pool is filled, we'll still have to wait for it to heat up. So, I'm thinking we should go canoeing."

Speaking with her mouth stuffed with muffin crumbs, Silvie's eyes grew wide. "Are you saying a day trip, or are we camping somewhere?"

"Definitely a day trip. I thought we'd go up the road, past the street that turns into the school. There's a really neat place back there. I think it's part of the Wolf River." Not hearing any complaints, he took their silence as approval. "We're going to need bug spray." While they finished their short stacks, he started the phone chain.

Later that afternoon, when the younger kids arrived, he asked them to grab a partner. Leaving the school's campus, they walked along the unfinished dirt road, stopping occasionally to pick up rocks or scratch at an insect bite. When they ran out of road, they trekked through tall grasses, jumped over fallen branches, and stepped around sunbaked cow patties.

"Be on the lookout for meadow muffins," he warned.

Swatting at flies, ducking under hornet's nests, and searching for water moccasins, they cheered when they came upon the Wolf River. Clearing tall weeds, they kicked off their shoes and ran over the sand. Once they eyed the canoes, they sprinted over the sandbar's shallow shoals, calling a race to the water.

The hours flew by as they enjoyed their afternoon on the water. On the walk back to the aquatic center, the kids talked over each other, each telling what they had enjoyed most and asking when they could do it again. He was about to break down the workout they had just pushed through, paddling their canoes and walking to and from the cool river, when instead he decided to let them enjoy their break from practice.

—

When his team arrived the following day, Cory had a surprise waiting for them. "We're going on a field trip." Reading from the list he prepared after speaking with their parents, he assigned carpools. "First stop is Bogey's Deli." After a breakfast of bagels smeared with cream cheese, he made an announcement. "Next stop is Whitehaven."

Crossing over Elvis Presley Boulevard, the short bus ride from the parking area to Elvis Presley's home had many of the kids hearing for the first time the King of Rock and Roll's many achievements. Born long after the King's passing three decades earlier, his name was familiar, but his music was not. Keeping a safe distance behind, they kept their guide busy with questions at each stop along the tour from the moment they stepped into Graceland's grand entry hall, through the colorful jungle-themed room, until the tour came to an end after a visit to the Meditation Garden.

During the ride back to the parking area, he called for their attention. "Raise your hand if you want barbecue."

Later, when they exited the Rendezvous, a popular rib joint, he ushered the kids down the long alley and over Union Avenue and into The Peabody hotel. Had they arrived five minutes earlier, they would have witnessed the hotel's famous ducks making their daily pilgrimage along the red carpet from the lobby's large fountain to the elevator they took to return to their rooftop suite.

Stepping onto Beale Street, the team posed for pictures next to a bronze statue of musician W.C. Handy and his trumpet. They continued along Beale's bricked streets and took a self-guided tour of The New Daisy, a music venue popular among Memphis' music lovers. When the kids begged to stop at A. Schwab, he raced them to the door. When he exited the small shop, he was the proud owner of a B. B. King coffee mug and a paperback about Edward H. Crump, a determined man who, like Henry Loeb, twice held the office of mayor.

Before returning to East Memphis, they visited Mud Island. Riding the tram, he looked down the forty-foot drop to the island's amphitheater. His thoughts quickly turned to the concerts his previous salary had forced him to miss. Once, when he had the extra cash, he bought tickets to a James Taylor concert. Singing along to *Carolina in My Mind, Fire and Rain,* and *Copperline* justified the tickets' steep price. Years earlier, he had been given tickets to see Bruce Springsteen. Up front and personal with "The Boss" only added to the crowd's enthusiasm as they belted out *Born in the USA.*

He reflected on the many music festivals he attended. When he grew tired of the crowds, loud music, and the rain's poor timing, he took to the blues clubs. It did not surprise him that he knew every word to Marc Cohn's hit song *Walking in Memphis*. Humming the words, Jeff Buckley came to mind. The first time he heard him perform *Hallelujah,* he was brought to tears. Later, he shared with his friends that not only had the song moved him, but he wanted it played at his own funeral. It was only recently he learned the famed music artist had drowned in the waters below.

Looking to the north, he admired the new bridge that had been funded in part by a popular fundraiser. A hefty donation allowed the donor to claim one of the two hundred vapor lights draping the bridge from Memphis to Arkansas, its neighbor on the other side of the Mississippi River. The thought of his own wallet reminded him he would never have the kind of money it takes to buy a bulb for any fixture other than the lamps in his own apartment. Walking with his team along the Mighty Mississippi, he came to realize he did not require a lighted bridge to be connected to what he needed. The only bridge necessary was the one he built with the young kids who always hurried to gather around him.

C H  A P T E R 2 7

Months passed, and still little progress was made in the pool's repair. A drop in temperature forced Cory to take his team out of the above-ground pool. A phone call to an old friend he worked with at Tigers gave his team a place to practice. The Collierville YMCA offered a pool the coach was happy to share. Don Waters founded Collierville Swimming, a US competitive swimming program. Prior to developing his own team, Don worked alongside him as an assistant coach under Coach Fadgen, the Memphis Tigers coach.

———

Four months later, the Compton Aquatic Center was back in business. Swim practice ran smoothly, meets were scheduled, and Walt Rider set up training on the deck.

He arrived on the campus with his car filled with bike tires, indoor bike trainers, and running gear he would need after riding. The kids who signed up to train with him hurried to help him unpack. Throwing their swim bags on their backs, they loaded their arms with the gear he handed them. Exchanging a wave with Cory, he made his way to a cleared area just beyond his office. He placed the bike trainers in a semicircle and anchored the racing bikes the young triathletes brought to practice.

Their program faced challenges right from the start. There were times when, just as Cory had lined up the team for practice in the pool, he would call them to the deck. Other times, Cory was forced to shout over the pool equipment and the drills he gave his team.

On a day when chaos halted swim practice, Cory gathered his team on the bleachers. "You are here to swim. When my practice is over, you are free to bike and run."

This routine worked until area triathlons pulled many of his swimmers away from daily swim practice and out of upcoming meets.

In a private conversation, Cory and Walt decided to part ways.

CHAPTER 28

The night before his wedding, nearly eight months after Thunder's first home meet, Cory sat with Kirby and Gina on the white sands of Orange Beach, an Alabama coastal town. An October moon lit up the sky and an unexpected autumn wind coming in over the gulf ruffled his hair. Mesmerized by the rhythm of the lapping waves as they tapped the sleeping shore, he settled into an easy sway. Each time he closed his tired eyes, he silently wished his mother could be here to celebrate his wedding. His face warmed when he spoke of Terie and their future life together. "Every time she enters a room, she takes my breath away. When she calls my name, a sense of calm comes over me."

Earlier in the day, the family gathered at the marina for a dolphin cruise. Setting out on the water, he sat next to his father. While the others held cameras ready to capture gray dolphins at play, he turned his focus to his family. Conversations were plentiful, laughter was easy, and watching the exchange of smiles, he felt love's presence. Before the boat returned to shore, any qualms he may have felt were cast out to sea. For as far back as he could remember, he was forced to wage life's battles, but through all the disappointments, he continued to dream. Perhaps dreaming helped him to survive. He had been blessed with family and friends who not only believed in him but also encouraged him. Standing beside his father, he rested an arm over the old man's shoulders. Reaching across his chest, his father placed a hand on his. "I'm happy for you," he whispered.

"She's the only woman I've ever loved. I knew when I met her I wanted her to be the mother of my children. Can't you just imagine all those little red-headed children swimming through the water?" He laughed at the thought.

The following afternoon, a small circle of friends and family joined them on a terrace overlooking the gulf. Steps away, the waves rested. Admiring the scenic backdrop, Cory recalled his childhood. He had always taken an interest in boats under sail, fishing boats, and observing and learning from his place on the pier. Everything about the moment felt right.

On a terrace leading from the hotel's banquet room, a table draped with white linen held woven baskets overflowing with long-stemmed lilies rising above feathery ferns and a two-tiered red velvet cake his bride had always dreamed of having on her wedding day. At its side, a champagne fountain flowed bubbly to be enjoyed later, after wedding vows were exchanged. Anchoring a nearby table were tall candles he refused to call tapers. Placed between them were trays of green and black olives, a variety of aged cheeses, and seared chicken and soy nuggets pierced with plastic cocktail forks. A tower of gulf shrimp and crab claws over shaved ice invited guests to graze before the seated dinner.

Taking his place next to Kirby and Bill, his best men, he gave thanks for the warm sun overhead and the gentle breeze that promised the perfect beach wedding his bride desired. A knowing nod from his father told him he was proud of the man he had become.

Standing under a canopy of Monte Casino Aster, dark red wax flowers, and Queen Anne's Lace, he waited for Terie to make her grand entrance, which was delayed while Christopher, Jill and Bill's son, meandered the narrow path, dragging the ring pillow at his side along the way. When the toddler was finally at his father's side, all eyes turned to the bride. Locking eyes with Terie, he was spellbound.

Wearing an off-the-shoulder vintage gown made of white silk and sequined tulle, and her hair pulled up in a loose twist, she floated along the stone path. Not once did she take her eyes off him. In her hands, she carried a single calla lily. On her face, she wore a gentle smile. As he reached for her hand, they looked upward toward the heavens. When they turned to each other, dark clouds rolled in. Following a flash of lightning, they were left standing under a driving rain and darkened skies. A second bolt sent their guests running for cover. Fearing the unpredicted storm was an omen, she began to cry.

Pulling her close, he brushed away her tears. "It's a sign of good luck when it rains on a wedding. It means this will be the only storm our marriage will suffer."

While the catering staff hurried to rescue the cake, they insisted the wedding go on. Taking refuge under the awning, the wedding party and guests sipped champagne while toasting the newlyweds.

When the rain did not let up, the reception was moved indoors. Feeling a chill, and their clothes damp, they hurried the photographer to the hotel's lobby, where, huddled together, they smiled for the camera.

Hearing the band start up, the newlyweds took to the dance floor. Their friends and family looked on as they danced to Pat Green's *Wave on Wave*, his favorite song and music entertainer. Dancing cheek to cheek, he whispered the song's words that always brought him back to her, "All I'm looking for is you."

Country music played while everyone dined on fresh seafood and rosemary chicken, and servers circled the small room offering flutes of champagne, along with chocolate-covered strawberries he brought with him from Memphis.

As the night moved on, the newlyweds and their guests slowly made their way outdoors to the beach. Holding Terie in his arms, with wet sand between their toes, he looked into her eyes. "I love you, Mrs. Horton." His heart was filled with joy as they sipped from personalized champagne glasses, a wedding gift from Jill and her family.

Although they enjoyed a long weekend in Orange Beach, work

schedules and swim practices delayed a honeymoon. The following month, weeks after they exchanged vows, they traveled to Dallas where a busy weekend awaited their arrival. Their first night in the "Big D" had them at the Texas Stampede and Pat Green concert. When the singer opened with *Wave on Wave*, they hit the dance floor telling those nearby that the country hit had been their wedding song.

Two days later, they were off to Cowboys Stadium. A huge Cowboys fan, he looked forward to watching his favorite team play New York's Buffalo Bills. Mapping out the day, their plan was to grab an early lunch, catch the DART, Dallas' rapid transit service, and tailgate until the large television outside the stadium announced the game's kickoff.

Arriving hours before the mid-afternoon game, they danced along to the music of local bands. An earthy woman, known as Heaveny, traveled the stage wearing a fedora hat, fringed boots, and a red, white, and blue bandana. When she noticed him singing along, she invited him to join her on the stage. Taking the microphone, he continued to sing and kick up his heels. The game was in its fourth quarter when he realized they missed not only the kickoff, but also watching his team celebrate a victory.

He later told his friends the weekend in Dallas was one of the best moments in his life.

CHAPTER 29

Hosted by Memphis Tiger Swimming and held at the University of Memphis Student Recreation and Fitness Center, the Gabrielle Rose Invitational took place in late January. Limited to 600 registered swimmers, the short-course meet was well attended.

After acknowledging the host team, Gabrielle spoke of the many hours she spent training in the center's pool. Always a gracious host, she introduced the coaches, including Cory, who she claimed insisted she *train hard while still having fun*. Writing her autograph on heat sheets and posing with swimmers whose parents stood by with cameras, she stepped up to the podium to announce the meet was underway.

When the three-day meet closed, Memphis Thunder set team records in the 50 back, 100 fly, and the individual medleys. Swimming for Thunder, Gabrielle set a team record when she swam the 200 individual medley in 1:59.58.

Months later, in April, Thunder returned to the University of Memphis. This time, they competed in the Dash n' Splash Biathlon, an event sponsored by the university's Department of Health and Sport Sciences. A fundraiser for the department, the biathlon included a two-mile run and a fifty-meter swim.

When Cory realized this might be the only time he could team up with Silvie or Margo, he offered his running legs for the dash. Winning a thumb war with Silvie, Margo agreed to swim the splash portion. "I'm glad we're doing this, Margo. You'll be going off to college soon and this might be our last chance to compete as a team. Speaking of college, I'm glad you're going to Auburn. Back in the day, I thought about going to Auburn or Alabama." Although the thought was brief, it still existed in his memory. "Did you know Rowdy Gaines swam for Auburn? Richard Quick was his coach."

"I've heard that. What about Alabama?"

"What about it?"

"What was it about Alabama that had you considering riding the Crimson Tide?"

"Two words. *Deacon Blues*." When the Steely Dan song sailed over her head, he did a quick turn-about. "Another man. Different words. Bear Bryant. One of the greatest football coaches that ever lived."

The thought of leaving Thunder and the only coach she had ever known left Margo with a heavy heart. She wanted to shout that she would make certain to see him every time he visited Auburn, but instead she patted him on the shoulder. "Cory, I'm going to miss you."

"And I'll be missing you." Breaking a smile, he shared with her that Silvie was torn between Ole Miss, a college in Mississippi many of her classmates were planning to attend, and the University of Nebraska, a college that always reminded him of the scars on Spitty's chest.

"Silvie will do well at either school, but if she wants to continue swimming, I don't think Ole Miss has a program."

"I think you're right. I'll talk to her about it. I can't imagine she wouldn't want to continue swimming."

On the evening of the race, Cory jogged a short warm-up with his friend, Lesley Brainard. Arriving at the starting line, they found themselves surrounded by fellow swimmers and triathletes, and new recruits from Millington's Naval Base who were outfitted in full camo gear, heavy boots, and rifles slung over their shoulders. He hoped they were not loaded.

The announcer thanked the participants and the race sponsors, and aware a railroad track separated the campus from the pool, reminded everyone to be on the lookout for trains. Believing he heard a gunshot, Cory fell to the ground, rolled into a ball, and threw his hands over his head. Hearing laughter and the familiar sound of running shoes slapping the pavement, he realized in his fear he had mistaken the starting gun's pop for what he believed was a misfire from a nearby rifle.

Later, when awards were presented, he was named the first recipient of the event's "Duck and Cover" award.

CHAPTER 30

The early morning hours on the Fifth of July had Cory looking forward to the days ahead. In recent months, he stayed up into the late-night hours studying tapes he recorded of previous summer Olympics, hoping to take away a relaxation technique or catch a glimpse of the slightest detail that improved a swimmer's dive or strengthened their kick. If there was an advantage he could apply to his coaching, he wanted to study it and the success stories behind it.

He wished Terie would be joining him in Long Beach for Olympic Trials, but she was committed to her own work schedule. Once the Olympic Trials were over, he and Terie would finally be able to make time to be alone together. He had already packed his bag with the usual suspects—white tube socks, khaki shorts, and Thunder shirts—when he spotted Terie's house keys on the table. He glanced at his watch. If he hurried, he could run by the fitness center on the way to Memphis International, the city's airport. Throwing his bag in the Jeep, he headed out the door.

Traffic moved smoothly along Germantown Parkway and signals flashed green in his favor. Worried he would be stuck in slow-moving traffic or come to a standstill due to unexpected road repair, he took this as a good sign. Never one to speed, he laughed when he recalled the many times he had been accused of holding up traffic. "*What's the hurry?*" he always responded. Years earlier, he had been ticketed for driving twenty-five in a forty. Arriving at the fitness center, he rushed to the door.

"Hey, Cory. Aren't you supposed to be out of town?"

"I'm on my way to the airport." Holding a brass ring, he dangled a set of keys in the air. "Terie's going to need these. Do you know if she's training someone?"

The receptionist, a young woman with braces on her upper teeth, gave a full-on metal grin. "I think she's in the break room." Glancing at the daily schedule taped to the wall, the young woman looked back over her shoulder. "She has someone scheduled in about ten minutes."

Returning a smile, he rounded the corner and quickened his step. He walked the narrow hall to the back of the building and passed the small office he once shared with the center's personal trainers and class instructors. Overhead, speakers delivered Willie Nelson's award-winning hit, *Always on My Mind,* at a deafening volume. As he entered the break room, his eyes fell upon Terie. He wanted to call her name, but something held him back. Remaining in the shadows, he begged his heart to be mistaken. Through different eyes, he watched the woman he vowed to love for a lifetime slip away from him. Her back was turned to him, and standing close was a man who held her attention. When the young man whispered in her ear, she responded with a laugh. Their faces inches apart, her whispered words brought a smile to the man he knew only as a stranger. Standing feet away, her words were unclear. When the young man pulled at her ponytail, he steeled his spine. Backing out of the room, he made his exit.

Passing by the receptionist, he placed the keys on the counter. "Please make sure Terie gets these."

CHAPTER 31

Standing an arm's length from the Stanford University and USA Olympic Team swim coach, Richard Quick, Cory cheered for his former swimmer and good friend, Gabrielle Rose, as she prepared to compete in the final of the 100 free. She had come a long way since her training with the Memphis Tigers. Thinking back on the many years he coached her brought a smile to his face—an upturned muscle pull his face had not exercised since leaving his wife's keys at the sign-in counter at the fitness center.

"Margo, time to hit the warm-up pool." Trying desperately to keep his focus on the meet, he browsed the heat sheet. Hearing the announcer call the 400 free, two events away from Margo's backstroke event, he circled his arms at his side. "And do some windmills."

"Please, let me stay to watch Gabrielle," Margo pleaded. "She's in the final, Cory."

Knowing Margo was a fierce competitor and always brought her A-game to the pool, and recalling Gabrielle and Margo had attended the same private school, he relented. "The second she touches, I had better see you hustling your way to the warm-up pool."

Swimmers readying themselves for their events rushed the crowded pool deck. In addition to team suits, all wore swim caps identifying their team. Nervous coaches were heard giving last-minute instructions to their swimmers, but not him. He trusted Silvie and Margo to know the drill.

Taking her place in the far lane, Gabrielle stepped up to the starting block. Dropping the heat sheet to his side, he watched as she went through the routine he helped her develop a decade earlier. She pressed a hand against her shoulder and crossed an outstretched arm in front of her. Satisfied with the stretch, she did the same with her other arm. Shaking her arms at her side, she then pressed her goggles to her face. She gave a ready nod as she arched her back.

At the sound of the referee's "take your mark," the swimmers rocked back. With the pop of the starting pistol, they started the race. Although he witnessed it daily with his own team, he continued to be awed by the synchronization as the row of swimmers shot off the blocks. Watching Gabrielle execute the perfect dive, a grin owned his face. The young women raced against not only each other but also the ticking of the clock as the natatorium rang out with cheers from the pool's deck all the way up to the bleachers' highest row.

From the sidelines, he watched as his former Tiger swimmer, and at times, unattached Thunder member, pushed through the water. In the prelims, she gained an advantage on her flip turns. Finishing with a time of 55.42, she improved her time in the semis. Now, as the clock ticked away and race officials monitored each stroke and kick, she touched the pad with a time of 56.07, placing her eighth in the final. Climbing from the pool, the look on Gabrielle's face told onlookers—him included—she had given her best.

Joining Coach Quick and Cory, Gabrielle made introductions. Giving an admiring nod, Coach Quick glanced at his shirt. "Thunder. You've produced some real talent. I want to tell you, I'm honored you passed the baton off to me. Gabrielle is a strong swimmer and a fierce athlete. Also, I want you to know I appreciate the young kids you've sent out to my camp at Stanford. I know it's not easy letting them go, exposing their hungry minds to a different coach with different methods, but I'll tell you this, it speaks highly of you. I found it interesting when I learned they all went to the same private school in Memphis."

Humbled by the compliment, he thanked the US Olympic coach. "Gabi's hard work and dedication have always paid off, and the girls have found a way to manage their commitment to education and the sport of swimming. It's a delicate balance." Hearing the announcer call the backstroke events, he extended his hand. "It's been an honor meeting you."

Instead of letting go, Coach Quick tightened his grip. "I have a feeling we'll be hearing about you for a good long time. I have no doubt you'll be standing here someday, walking the same path I have followed. There were great coaches before me, and there will be great coaches who will follow you. You have what it takes, Cory." Leaning closer, he placed a pointed finger on his chest. "Keep the passion close to your heart. You just keep doing what you're doing and I promise you will make a difference."

Moving with a new confidence, he carried himself like a winner. He locked Coach Quick's words in his memory and turned his attention to the pool as Margo took her place. Pacing on the pool deck, he hoped that in a field of fifty-four swimmers, she would make the cut. Although he had rarely heard her speak of it, he believed her hard work, commitment, dedication, and perseverance, along with the countless sacrifices she made, told of her desire to represent the United States in the sport she loved.

Nearing the starting block, Margo stood tall and proud in her black Thunder suit and matching cap. Looking confident, she gave a wave when the announcer called her name. Like Gabrielle had done before her race, Margo stretched her muscles and secured her goggles. Unlike her former teammate, she eyed the swimmers at her side. Cracking knuckles, rocking on their blocks, and repeatedly adjusting their goggles, she thought they appeared nervous, too. Again, unlike Gabrielle, Margo was about to swim in the preliminaries. It was her performance the previous month at the Janet Evans Invitational that qualified her for these Olympic Trials. Entering with a time of 1:03.67, she hoped to shave some off. She did not have to look at him to know he was both nervous and proud.

Instructed to enter the water, she held a firm grip on the starting block. Tucking her head and waiting for the familiar pop of the starting gun, she thought the passing of time was moving at a snail's pace. Once she was given the signal, she threw back her head, arched her back, and pushed off the wall. She had trained for this moment. Gliding through the seventy-eight degree water, she kept her breathing steady, the stroke count precise and accurate, and her eyes on the ceiling. Her stroke looked strong and her technique admirable. Passing under the signal flags, she turned to her stomach, and taking a single stroke to the wall, executed a flawless flip turn. Pushing off the wall, she pressed on to the finish. With a single hand to the touch pad, she hurried to remove her goggles. Looking to the results board, she searched for her name. Disappointment took over when she learned her prelim time of 1:04.36 was not fast enough to qualify for the semis.

After checking in with Cory and the meet officials, Silvie lined up to swim the 100 breast, her only qualifying event. Focusing on the event, she was not aware Margo had not moved on. Having learned the qualifying times of the girls she would soon swim against, she held little hope of making it to the finals, but that did not matter. She was here to do what she loved most. *Swimming.* In the back of her mind, though, she could not forget the troubling look she saw on Cory's face at the airport. Before they boarded the plane in Memphis, she could see he was upset. Because theirs was a relationship where they shared triumphs and victories, she was not comfortable discussing personal problems.

Waiting for her event to be announced, Silvie's thoughts turned to the Janet Evans Invitational. She had qualified for Olympic Trials with a time of 1:15.31, her personal best. Waving the heat sheet overhead, Cory had been so excited when the scoreboard flashed her winning time. Watching him pump his fist in the air, she laughed when he fell to his knees. When she went to him, he whipped out the black marker he always carried. Instead of a single "mark of excellence," he decorated her cheek with two. When the invitational came to a close, he allowed his team to parade on the deck.

Now, here in Long Beach, she understood her work was cut out for her.

Standing on the block, she turned to him. This time, she thought he looked disconnected and tired. Taking her stance, she wanted nothing more than to swim her best. Making him proud of her was all that mattered.

Anticipating the pop of the start gun, she rocked back. When she felt her foot slip, she hoped it would not cost her time. Coming up from her dive, she worried she had gone too deep. She focused hard on her stroke and kick, and continued on, but after throwing a hand at the touch pad, she looked away from the scoreboard. She knew her chance of making the finals had slipped away when she slipped on the block. Exiting the pool, she ran to him.

"I'm so sorry, Cory. I was awful."

Placing a hand on her shoulder, he pulled a permanent marker from the pocket of his khakis. Unaware nearby coaches were watching, he drew on her cheek. "You earned the mark of excellence. You gave your best, which is all I ever ask of you and all you should ever ask of yourself. Every time you swim in a pressure-packed meet, which this is, you exceed my expectations. I'm proud of you and your fighting spirit."

Hearing this, she forced a smile. "You are the best coach, Cory."

With the day's events coming to a close, he and the team met up at a restaurant near the hotel for a quick dinner. The mood was somber, with Margo anxious about her upcoming event.

"I want you to go back to the hotel, crawl into bed, and focus on resting your mind and your body. Swimming a bad race is not the end of the world and there will always be a next time. All you should ask of yourself is to do the best you can, believe in yourself, and have fun while you're doing what you enjoy. All the greatest athletes have suffered a setback and informed judges have ruled in error." He was taken by surprise when, out of nowhere, images of his mother raced through his tired mind. "And reputable surgeons have botched a surgery. Every time you give your best, you are a winner."

Later, after he showered and settled in for the evening, his thoughts were not on swimming, but on his marriage. He used the time alone to question the events of the past several weeks and what might lie ahead in the coming months. Several times, he checked his phone, only to be disappointed he had not missed a call from Terie. The time on the bedside clock reminded him it was too late to call home. Staring at the ceiling, he worried his time in Long Beach would only serve to place more distance between them and open the door to irreparable damage. Until he returned home, he would have to keep his focus on his team.

CHAPTER 32

"**I** have to untie the knot."

While Gina listened, Cory shared with her the sleepless nights he suffered, the images he could not shake from his memory, and his uncertain future. "I can't stay married." He shared with her the words he recently overheard in a conversation between a reticent father and his troubled daughter: "*When you trust your heart to guide you, allow your ears to listen and your eyes to see. If they've misled you in the past, be wise to your actions. When an answer arrives, accept it with all your might. You're going to have to be truthful and trusting not only in your heart but also in your future.*"

Miles away, Gina held the phone to her ear. It pained her to hear him so lost and broken. "Cory, I'm so sorry you have to go through this. Clearly, you have some thinking to do. This is your future we're talking about. Look to find some clarity. If you're asking for my advice, I think you and Terie need to talk when you get home. Whatever it is you decide, just know I'm here for you."

"This is killing me, Gina. What am I supposed to do? I'm not sleeping, I can't focus, and I'm drinking so much coffee I'm darn near percolating. I recall every second after I rounded that ugly corner, and now, when all I want to do is run from it, I'm left feeling it's holding me hostage. I don't want to be a fool's defender, you know, pushing a rock up a hill to nowhere."

"I want you to promise you won't let the fear of what lies ahead keep you from moving forward. Sometimes, all we need is a different rudder. Don't be afraid to lean on others for support. For your own sanity, forget what's in the rearview mirror. You want my advice? Dust off your broken heart and step on the gas."

—

Days later, when Cory arrived home, he opened the door to find the apartment dark and empty. Still in the thick of it, and feeling beat up, he worried what the coming hours would bring. In his rush to see his wife, he did not notice the walls were now blank and the shelves had been emptied, and it would be days later when he would learn the good china and candlesticks, *along with the tapers*, had gone missing. Moving through the apartment, he was surprised to find Terie seated at the kitchen table. She wore a high neck sweater with a three-inch zipper that threatened a chokehold should she make a sudden move. A thin leather belt circled her miniscule waist. Earrings made of a stone similar to lapis fell from her lobes. A suitcase was at her side, and on the table in front of her a drinking glass held small cubes of melting ice. A ring of water circling the glass let him know she had been waiting for a while. The look on her face and smeared mascara under her eyes told him all he needed to know. When she did not welcome him home, he slowed his step. The tightening in his chest begged him to pace himself and prepare for the worst. Although there was silence between them, her body language was loud and clear. Foregoing a smile, she remained in the chair. The message she sent was understood. Their marriage was over.

Leaning against the counter, he shoved his hands into empty pockets. "We can't fix this with rose petals and scented candles." Lowering his head, he cleared his throat and continued. "Truth is, you deserve a chance at love, and I don't want to ruin that for you." He hated that he was still in love with her, and what was more painful was, he probably always would be. Stuck in a narrow path, he could never forget what his eyes allowed him to see.

Leaving the comfort the chair offered, Terie moved aimlessly about the room. When she came to him with outstretched hands, he backed away. Glancing over her shoulder, he saw a stack of unpaid bills. Remaining a gentleman, he did not ask her to pitch in.

As the minutes ticked away, they talked about what their futures held, and spoke openly as they shared their feelings and thoughts about the life they would no longer share.

"In that moment, when I asked you to be my wife, you smiled at me, and then we smiled at each other. You looked more beautiful than any woman has ever looked. Angelic, almost." Needing to regain his composure, he paused for a moment. Lowering his eyes, he waited for the lump in his throat to smooth. "At our wedding, when you walked toward me to become my wife, my heart was so filled with love I thought it might explode. It was a moment that physically took my breath away. With you at my side, my life was all I ever wished it to be. I had never known such magic. When we exchanged vows, your love for me made me forget about everything in my life before you entered it. In your eyes, I saw how much we loved each other and how happy we would always be. I believed ours would be an ever-lasting and solid union. And when we were caught standing in the rain, I was convinced we had survived our worst storm. I never imagined we would be here today."

Closing the space between them, he moved to her side. "I'm sorry it has all faded away. Our marriage is too young, and it's too soon for us to be here in this uncertain place. My only wish for you is that you will find whatever it is you need to be happy. When we pledged our everlasting love, I believed you had found all of those things in me." Swallowing hard, his voice cracked and his lips began to quiver. Wiping away a tear, he worried he could not continue. "I love you so much, I'm willing to let you go." Hanging his head, he searched for words that would not only make sense to her, but also to him. "This is my final act of love."

Standing at the door's threshold, Terie reached for his face. Breaking her silence, her lips trembled and her shoulders fell. Stroking his cheek, she whispered her apologies.

Before he allowed her to walk away from their home and out of his life, he pulled her into his arms. "We have been left with little to offer each other." Brushing her hair aside, and cleansing his eyes with tears he wanted to hide, he placed a kiss on her forehead.

CHAPTER 33

Although Cory continued to grieve his failed marriage and struggle with the "what ifs," he decided to embrace Gina's advice and put the pedal to the metal. Looking to his future, he sought solace on the open road.

⁓

"Dust off your bike. We're going for a ride." Seated across the table from Bob, Cory referred to the lightweight carbon fiber racing bike his friend kept on an extension rack in his garage. "We've done the Tour De Wolf and now, drum roll please, we're training for Memphis in May."

Resting his elbow on the table, Bob gave him a quizzical look. "When is the race?"

"In May, of course. It's a triathlon. Come on. We have to do it. It's in our backyard and it's what Memphians do."

Early in their training, with him pushing their average speed upward of twenty miles per hour, he had little doubt his friend would do well in the upcoming event. Riding three days a week and swimming every morning, sometimes alongside Thunder's swimmers, finding time to run became their biggest challenge. Most days, they scheduled their own eight to ten mile runs.

On the morning of the triathlon, they made the drive to Edmund Orgill Park in Millington, Tennessee. After checking in with race officials and racking their bikes in the designated area, the good friends and training partners wished each other a safe and successful race. Because they were scheduled to swim in different waves, they arranged to meet up later near the finish line.

Bob placed thirty-fourth in his age group, finishing the 1500-meter swim, the 24.9-mile ride, and the 6.2-mile run in under three hours. Fourteen miles into the ride and seconds after crouching over his bike's aero bars, Cory was forced to withdraw when a brake cable split in half.

Later, they cheered with the crowd that gathered near the water as the awards were presented. The winners took center stage and celebrations got underway. Thunder member Katie Siegal placed second in her age division, and David Carl Jones, Kurt Arthur, and Thunder's Taylor Flynn placed first in the mixed relay. Posing with their trophies, Katie and Taylor gave a shout out to him.

On their late morning drive back to Memphis, Bob rode high on his finish. "The whole time I was out there on the ride, I kept thinking we should go to France."

"Well, although I like the cold water, dirt roads, and the flatter-than-a-flit grassy fields out here, I'm sure the views in France are more amazing. We could tour all the great sites and dine on my two favorite French foods—croissants and French fries." Amused by his own silliness, he gave a tickled laugh. Jokingly he added, "And, hey, while we're there, maybe we should stop by the Tour de France. Better yet, let's sign up and show them what cycling's all about. They'll forget about Lance—what's his name—and the daily mail."

Bob's face lit up. "Let's do it, Cory. Let's do Tour de France."

"Hold your handlebars, Lance Armstrong. I think you have to qualify to compete." For a passing moment, he wondered if Bob had lost his mind out on the course. "And it would cost a bundle. Have you heard of the Tour de Corn? We can do that. It's a ride through cattle farms and miles of dirt roads, cornfields, and pastures. On a windy day, you can see dirt devils vacuuming the fields."

"Heard of it? No. Want to do it? No. We're going to France, Cory. We're doing the Tour de France. It will be my way of paying you back for all the training."

Slowing the Jeep and taking his eyes off the road, he turned to Bob. "Are you serious?"

"Dead serious," Bob answered, placing his hand over his heart. "We'll sign up for the first five stages."

"You know it's in July? What is that, two months from now?"

"Yes, and that gives you plenty of time to get that brake cable replaced, or better still, upgrade your ride."

He always defended his faithful and aging Schwinn, but in recent months, had come to admire the newer, lightweight frames cycling enthusiasts always brought to races and into conversations.

The following afternoon, when thoughts of the Tour de France continued to linger in his mind, he reached a milestone. Counting out a stack of twenties for a red and black Specialized bike, it was the first time in his life he purchased something brand spanking new. It set him back a few bucks, but in his eyes, it was worth it. Seated in the butterfly saddle, he felt he could conquer the world and outride the competition. Rubbing his hand over the sleek frame, he imagined pedaling alongside Lance Armstrong and the Postal Service team.

The fifteen-hour flight from Memphis to Luxembourg gave him an opportunity to read up on his new bike. Seated next to him, Bob had plenty of time to study the race material and map out the adventures their free time would allow. Arriving three days early, they taxied the streets of Luxembourg, stopping for lunch, posing for photos, and touring Notre-Dame Cathedral. Struggling to understand their guide, he asked what language he was speaking. Expecting to learn it was French or German, he snorted a laugh when the man answered, "Luxembourger."

The eighty-ninth edition of the Tour de France, which totaled 3277.5

kilometers when the racers crossed over the finish line in Paris, started in the early morning hours on July 7. Because they were only biking the first five stages, they set out on the course long after the race's professional participants were underway.

The first stage, a distance of 192.50 kilometers, circled the city. The race's second stage took them 181 kilometers to Saarbrucken, Germany. Riding by St. John's Basilica, he promised to return someday. Arriving in Metz, they visited the Covered Market, one of the oldest markets in France, where they sampled traditional local foods. After dinner, they noshed on dark chocolates and drank Moselle, a white wine produced along the Moselle River. Taking in the night air and breathtaking views, they strolled along cobbled streets where young artists begged to paint their portraits and freshly baked treats and Mirabelle plums were sold from a one-man kiosk. When a sculpture, waterway, or cathedral caught their eye, they posed for pictures they were eager to share with friends back in Memphis.

Later, when they arrived in Soissons, the fifth and final stage taking them 195 kilometers to Rouen, they were exhausted. Including the Tour's prologue, they had biked 817.54 kilometers, the equivalent of 508 miles.

—

Returning home to Memphis and his team, Cory continued to wear the Live Strong wristband included in his race packet. His love of the sport led him to return to the states with a box filled with the popular signature bracelets he later awarded to his team during practice.

Addressing his team, he put into words what he took away from the experience of a lifetime. "First and foremost, if you're going to ride five hundred miles, make sure both your bottom and your bike seat are well cushioned. If I ever decide to ride this ridiculous distance again, you can trust I'll be packing Preparation H." Pausing to laugh at himself, he continued when the only reactions he received from his team were curious looks and awkward frowns. "The tour taught me more about teamwork than I've learned my whole life. For our team to be successful, we must rely on each other to be honest, loyal, and dedicated to the sport we love and enjoy. With hard work, perseverance, and determination, anything is possible. It's a success only when we work together. In addition to physical preparedness, we must focus on mental toughness and positive thinking. From this day forward, these fundamental rules will apply to Thunder. Now, if you'll excuse me, I need to soak."

CHAPTER 34

By summer's end, when the city meet was over, the kids were all aflutter about the upcoming school year. Understanding their excitement, Cory encouraged them to visit during the kickboard and resistance drills. A kid himself, he listened as the girls talked nervously about homeroom teachers, class schedules, and clothes they would need in addition to the school uniforms they were required to wear. As he walked along the deck in his black flip-flops and white ankle socks, he ignored his cell phone's repeated vibration. When practice was over and he was able to glance at it, he was surprised to find text messages from Jill, Gina, and Kirby, each asking that he call immediately.

The following morning, he was on a flight to St. Croix. Arriving on the island after a two-hour delay out of Memphis and a longer one out of Miami, he arrived at the hospital only to learn his father had not survived a heart attack. While Kirby filled out the required paperwork necessary to return their father's body to Missouri, Gina made funeral arrangements. With Jill's help, he packed up their father's belongings and arranged for shipping. In the evening, after dinner, they shared stories about their father as they took turns summarizing his life for the required and expected obituary.

On the afternoon before their evening flight home, Cory and his siblings drove through the island's sub-districts and along the coast, stopping to take pictures at Fort Christiansvaern and Salt River Bay, a place where members of Christopher Columbus' expedition were known to have visited. Although they did not snorkel, they joined a boat ride to Green Cay, a small outer island popular with snorkelers and scuba divers. Before returning to their father's rental, they made their way to Christiansted, a place they once called home.

Walking along the cobblestones and under windswept trees, the siblings admired colorful stone buildings, visited scuba shops, and perused the menus of the town's many restaurants. Hailed by local artists hoping to sell their wares, he stopped to admire a painting awash in colors he found warm and soothing. Recalling the naked wall in his apartment, he arranged to have the painting shipped the following week. Approaching a row of cabana rentals, they stopped at a marina to watch an approaching cruise ship make its way through calm waters to the island's port of call. While the island's mariners moved at a slow and leisurely pace, the ship's tourists rushed the boat's deck in their eagerness to explore the island's long stretches of postcard-perfect beaches.

Gina and Kirby could recall having visited the wharf, but he was exploring it for the first time. When they arrived at Schooner Bay, they hurried to find the old rental.

"I think it has a red roof," he offered. When Gina pointed to the many red-roofed homes, he joined in their laughter.

It was Gina who recognized the white stone rental. Winding along the beach path, he grew excited when he, too, spotted the single-story house. He glanced out at the water and grew quiet when he saw the old dock. Stepping around water-filled puddles, he thought of the many times he had searched the Caribbean for the otters his father pretended to catch a glimpse of before they dove out of sight. Wanting to preserve his memories, he reached for his camera, removed the lens cap, and checking the film roll, held the camera to his face. Recalling a conversation he had with his father years earlier, he looked out at the pier. *"You can always return for a visit, but you can never go back."* Understanding his father's words, he placed the cap over the lens and returned the camera to his backpack. The pictures he held in his memory would never fade.

Searching the shore, his face lit up when he spotted Spitty and *On the Fly*, his old fishing boat. Picking up his pace, he hurried to greet his old friend and neighbor. It had been decades since they last spoke, and although he wanted to say age had been kind to him, the old man appeared to be on his last leg. His skin had leathered, cataracts clouded his eyes, and many of his teeth had parted ways. When Spitty removed his hat to wipe a damp brow, he was surprised to see he had gone shiny on top. Back in the day, he sported more hair than his dog.

"It's good to see you, Cory. I heard about your dad. I sure am sorry. He was a good man. I wish we were reuniting on a happier note."

Wrapping his arms around the old man, he kept his face at a safe distance. Time would never allow him to forget the reason for the old man's nickname. A glimpse of Spitty's chest told him he had been kind when years earlier he shielded the young Cory from his desire not to be resuscitated. "I'm just glad he didn't suffer. When it's time to go, it's best to go quickly. You're looking good, my friend. Where's that pooch of yours?"

"What's that? You'll have to speak up. I've lost my high-frequency hearing and sometimes I hear an awful echo. These good-for-nothing hearing aids are worthless."

"I was asking about your dog."

"No need to shout. Hurts my ears, if you know what I mean. Did I tell you Fenndus died a few years back? Best worthless dog I ever had the pleasure of serving. I was fishing on the flats, you know, near the barrier reef, when all of a sudden my fishing rod arched like a rainbow. Fenndus went crazy. He ran back and forth from one end of the boat to the other and then collapsed at my feet. Sort of like the time my sister and her half-breed pooches came to stay with me. Back then, I thought he was showing off for the females, but maybe he was always a little crazy in the head. Anywho, I think Fenndus reacted to my panic. He flew the coop 'bout the same time I landed the big one. Jumped overboard and out of sight. Vet told me dogs know when their time is up. I've always said if we had been on daylight savings time, I think I could have rescued him. In any crisis, an hour can make a difference between life and death. Anywho, I always said that when I die I want to come back as my dog. Eat, sleep, and walk the beach a bit. The next day, repeat steps one through three, but not necessarily in that order. When I need a change, I'll play with a squeaky toy or chase my tail."

At a loss for words, he hoped Spitty interpreted the awkward silence as his condolences. "Well, you're looking good, Spitty. What number are you putting up these days?"

"You're going to have to speak up. I got a tin ear. Did I mention I don't hear well?"

"I was asking your age," he shouted through cupped hands.

Pondering a response, Spitty pulled at his thinning beard. "Before my heart attack I kept track. Now I count the years since the day I was given a second chance at life. Doctors told me to expect another ten years. You know what's interesting? I've outlived all of them."

"I remember a long time ago when you told me you spent your days relaxing. You're living right, Spitty." Patting him on the back, he promised to call the next time he was on the island.

Early the next morning, after a sleepless night in Memphis, he threw a duffle bag in the backseat and racked his bike on the Jeep. Driving through the night to Springfield, he thought back to his wedding. The weekend in Orange Beach was the last time he had seen his father. Although his dad had recently been diagnosed with a heart condition, he could not recall him looking ill. His father had been concerned about his health, but at his age, aches and pains appeared normal and par for the course.

———

On August 7, 2004, seven days after their father's passing, Cory and his siblings sat quietly as their Lincoln Town car serpentined miles of unkempt, dusty roads outside Rogersville's city limits. The narrow back roads framed with deep ditches and overgrown sprays of wild daylilies ran alongside grazing cattle too busy to notice. The dirt road turned to gravel at the entrance to a single story church abandoned seasons ago by its aging parishioners.

Passing old grain silos adorned with untamed wisteria, and exchanging waves with farmers who sucked on straw while mending fences, he and his siblings entered the gates of Spring Hill Cemetery, a place they gathered decades earlier when their mother was laid to rest.

Standing under a cloudless sky and feet away from a mound of newly turned soil, he listened as the minister read from a leather-bound Bible the passages his sisters requested. After reciting The Lord's Prayer, he stepped forward. Wiping away tears, he placed a single white rose on the pearl-gray casket. Lifting his face to the heavens above, he promised his father he would see him again.

CHAPTER 35

It was Thursday, May 5, 2005, three days before a triathlon, when Cory and his friends entered Panama City just as night began to fall. The air was damp, and ominous black clouds threatened a shower moving in from the south.

As they arrived at the Crow's Nest, a light sprinkle began to fall against the windshield, and the conversation changed from discussing heavy traffic to giving thanks for dodging bad weather. Stepping from the backseat, he was quick to appreciate the scent of pine and sea salt a gust of wind carried inland from the shore. Kicking off his shoes and tossing his socks aside, he allowed a carpet of wet sand to cool his feet.

The two-story, beachfront rental was raised a safe distance above the stretch of pristine sand and rising tides known to flood the area when seasonal hurricanes blasted the coast. A widow's walk offered an expansive view of the horizon as well as a safe haven for roosting white-winged royal terns who fished the low tide's shallow water for unsuspecting shrimp.

Parking in the covered space under the main floor, they hurried to unpack the Suburban. Recovering from a broken ankle, Lesley was not able to help with the heavy lifting, leaving it to the others to unload the many duffle bags, race tires, and water gear they needed for the long weekend and upcoming race. While everyone scattered in different directions, Lesley's husband, John, took to the task of assigning rooms in the rental. Eager to compete in the Panama City Beach Half Ironman, they agreed that stocking the refrigerator was their first priority.

While their friends settled in, Cory and Doug Ruddle, a friend and fellow athlete, made a beeline to the grocery store. To save time, each grabbed a cart. Parting ways, Doug took off toward the seafood section while he hurried in the opposite direction. Later, when they met up in the middle, their baskets were overflowing, and he wore a look of accomplishment.

Shaking his head, Doug looked curiously at his friend's shopping cart. "You're buying a grill?"

He returned a silly smile. "We'll need it to grill steaks."

Turning to his own basket, Doug pointed to a slim package wrapped in butcher paper. "I picked up salmon."

"I thought we were fishing for cobia and tarpon?"

Again, Doug shook his head. "This is big-time fishing in these waters. You have to have a license, my friend."

With a devious grin on his face, he reached back and tapped his pocket. "I just so happen to have one."

"Very funny. A driver's license won't cut it with the game warden. You need a fishing license to fish these waters. What else do you have in there?" he asked, looking over at his basket.

"Charcoal, two boxes of cereal, and a gallon of milk. Under the grill, there's a case of Bud Lite. I also picked up stuff to make pasta. Oh, and a bottle of red wine."

Back at the Crow's Nest, he commandeered the spacious kitchen. Tossing thick noodles with the ingredients he purchased at the market, he served up a nasty pasta dish. The sauce tasted like the tin can it came in, the noodles were undercooked, and the watery cheese was far from aged. His friends teased that he should stick with foods he knew how to reheat in the microwave or order off a menu. "Popcorn, pizza, and hot wings."

The following morning, soon after a breakfast of hot coffee and cereal loaded with fiber, he and his friends trekked out to the shore. Holding a camera, Lesley promised to take pictures.

Expecting to be welcomed by warm water, foxtail palms, annoying sandpipers, and aggressive sea ducks, they were roughed up by crashing waves, a barrage of tangled seaweed, and water so cold and raw it turned their skin blue. Shivering in knee-deep water, he rushed back to the house to change into a wetsuit he hoped would keep him warm in the unseasonably cold water.

Leaning against his friend, he slipped into the black and yellow swim fins he brought along for one reason—bodysurfing.

Caught in a war with unforgiving winds, he kicked hard against the rough water hoping the strong currents he fought would die down before Saturday's race. Yards away from the shore, he eyed a triple wave coming at him from the east. Drifting along and hoping a riptide would not get him, he waited until the perfect wave was on his tail. Patiently riding along on his chest and pulling through the water, he finally caught it. He fought the water's quick current and the strong wind pushing at his back as he tried to turn onto his side. Unable to catch his balance and his breath, he was thrown into a barrel roll. Tossed about, he fumbled forward, slapping the water with his face and hands. When the toss was over, he learned he lost a fin along the way. As the violent waves eased their anger, he crawled along the sandy floor until he reached the shore. Shaking it off, he returned to the water in search of the next great wave. It was not until he grew hungry that he surrendered for the day.

—

Saturday morning's triathlon drew thousands of triathletes ranging in ages from 15 to 74, and hailing from as close as the Panhandle's Emerald Coast to as far away as Europe's Czechoslovakia.

When Cory arrived at the Edgewater Beach Resort, the beginning and ending site, he did one last check of his race wheels. Spreading out the towel he would need after the swim portion, he racked his bike in the marked area. A quick observation let him know he was good to go.

Wearing the neon green swim cap that identified his age group, he stood at the water's edge. Shaking off nerves, he vowed this triathlon would be his best performance ever. In recent months, in preparation for this day, he logged double digits in the pool, covered hundreds of miles on his bike, and worn the soles off his running shoes. He was fit and ready.

Once he was given the signal, he entered the cool water. Surprised by the brisk seventy-four degrees, he turned to the other athletes in his wave. Watching their calm reactions, he hoped the playing field was even. He paced his stroke for the mile-plus out and back swim, and worked to stay in the forefront. When an opportunity to pass opened up, he swam through it. Pushing through teal blue waters, memories of his first triathlon popped into his head. The thought created an untimely chuckle, and he grew embarrassed at the thought of drowning from a nose full of saltwater.

Entering the bike chute, he pulled off his swim cap, threw it to the ground, and hurried to replace it with his racing helmet. The 56-mile bike portion took him inland, away from cheering spectators and curious passers-by. Ten miles into the ride, the sweat on his brow had him aware of the climbing temperatures. While pedaling through Conservation Park, he was reminded of Memphis' Shelby Farms. Bodies of water invited resident coyotes and wild turkeys to quench their thirst, and to avoid the commotion, snakes and other ground-hugging crawlies hid in hollowed tree stumps. Fathers and sons leaned over pedestrian bridges, their fingers pointing to the ground below. In the distance, a family of white tail deer grazed in tall grasses.

Running alongside beachfront properties, he was relieved the thirteen-mile run held to a flat course. By the time he reached the ten-mile marker, his legs were fatigued and his body needed refueling, but once the finish line was in his grasp, adrenaline carried him through the final chute and over the finish line.

On their last night at the beach house, he and his friends relaxed around the kitchen's picnic-style table. Dining on grilled fish and drinking a pinot noir they agreed smelled like a medicated Band-Aid, they gave a toast to the triathlon and their individual performances.

Raising his glass into the air and tapping it with a spoon, he made an announcement. "I'm just glad I got through the swim without needing a lifeboat." Having heard stories of his earlier attempts, his friends roared. Poking around his plate with a fork, he turned to Doug. "What are these purple things?"

"Those, my friend, are olives." Again, the room filled with laughter. "And those of us with advanced palates call it tapenade."

Sporting a serious face, he smeared the olive mix on a piece of French bread he tore from the loaf Doug remembered to grab at the market. "Is it a fruit or a vegetable?"

"A little bit of both." Watching his friend enjoy the dinner he prepared, Doug promised to make it for him. "Anytime, my friend."

Soon after the table was cleared and the dishes washed, the friends headed to the beach. Huddled around a glowing fire pit, they were entertained with the pictures Lesley had taken throughout the weekend. Asking for copies they would later frame and forever treasure, they passed the camera while laughing at the candid moments she captured.

Hoisting his glass to a starry sky, Cory made a second toast. "Here's to a perfect day, an uneventful triathlon, and an amazing dinner. I love you guys and I'm blessed to call you my friends."

The smiles he received in return let him know the sentiment was mutual.

CHAPTER 36

Three days later, in the late morning hours on Tuesday, May 10, 2005, unseasonably mild temperatures begged Cory to strap his treasured Specialized frame onto the Jeep's double bike rack. He was disappointed when the kids who often rode with him could not join in the ride as end of the year finals required their attention. He was comforted in knowing that once school let out for the summer, they would enjoy many bike rides together.

Before heading out the door, he called Doug. "You know that olive spread you put on the fish? Tampa something or other? I'm thinking of making it for dinner tomorrow. Do you have time to give me the recipe?" While Doug reeled off the short list of ingredients, he scribbled away on the back of a receipt he pulled from the kitchen's trashcan. Taping the recipe to the wall, the friends promised to get together the following weekend. "Don't forget the olives," Doug teased before hanging up the phone.

Driving away from his apartment, he navigated the property's many loops, tiger tails, and hairpin turns. The weather not only persuaded him to enjoy the day, it had also encouraged runners, mothers with strollers, and amateur cyclists to take to the asphalt trails that kept them a safe distance from the heavily traveled Houston Levee Road. On the days he was tight on time, he rode these same trails. In recent days, he grew frustrated when social riders ignored or disobeyed the trail's posted rules. He could not understand why it was so difficult to stay to the right, give a shout out when passing on the left, or when riding in a group, maintain single file.

With the onset of the three calendar months area schools recognized as summer rounding the corner, he knew that in the coming days, traffic on Houston Levee and Wolf River Boulevard, an intersecting parkway to the east, would triple. Teenagers with newly acquired driver's licenses and college students returning home for the semester's break would travel these roads, leaving in their path empty bottles and food wrappers from fast-food restaurants they tossed out the windows into the streets. He gave up biking these streets when a passing motorist came so close to him he was forced onto the sidewalk.

Committed to a routine he adopted in recent weeks, he parked the Jeep, leaving the keys in the ignition, in the driveway of the home of Kathleen and Craig Clark, parents of Thunder members Caiti and Chris.

On this day, Kathleen greeted him as he pulled his bike from the Jeep. Eager to begin his ride, he was quick to exchange pleasantries. Securing his helmet, he mounted his bike.

"Be careful, Cory!" Kathleen reminded.

Biking away from the house, he acknowledged Kathleen's shout with an easy wave. Cursing a cramp in his calf, he pedaled on, knowing that with each passing mile, the cramped muscle would warm up. Pushing through it, he followed the advice he often gave his team: "Warm it up and stretch it out."

A quick inhale of the roses Kathleen nurtured near her home's driveway entrance confirmed spring was finally in the air. Turning east, he welcomed the wind on his face as he took to the open road. Looking upward, the sky's blended colors had him recalling a watercolor he admired when he attended a garden concert at The Dixon, a museum near the university. That evening was one he would always remember. Laid out on a blanket, he and his friends ate from a picnic basket and sipped wine from Waterford crystal stems. The name meant nothing to him, but the oohs and aahs he heard told him he indulged in a stem far better than those he purchased in bulk when he stocked his kitchen cabinets.

Riding under canopies of branches laden with thick leaves and the occasional low-lying strays, he welcomed the timely sliver of shade the treetops offered. Dodging shards of glass, soiled newspapers, and fallen branches littered along the two-lane county road's narrow shoulder, he kept his eyes on the road and his hands steady and secure on the handlebars. The few occasions when he encountered oncoming traffic, he offered a wave to acknowledge the driver's presence. Traffic needing to pass around him usually veered into the open lane to the left, but only after making certain he had adequate space to continue riding.

To his left, an abundance of impressive homes rested high in the bluffs above. Their seemingly endless driveways adorned with custom gates and security cameras provided a pleasant backdrop and an occasional umbrella of shade from the rising sun. Blooming dogwoods and ornate tulip poplars cast their colors upon manicured lawns. Mature larch trees offered refuge to resting birds and curious squirrels, which by the grace of God, dodged Raleigh Lagrange's traffic and the area's hungry coyotes and sly foxes.

Carried by a breeze out of the south, the sweet scent of honeysuckle reminded him of the afternoon he stumbled upon the pool on Helene. A twinge in his heart took him by surprise. *Was it possible he missed the old place?* Worried dehydration was playing games with his head, he reached for his water.

Glancing at the homes to his left, he thought the grand estates were lovely but not the kind of home he saw in his future. He imagined a simple home, one with mature elms along the driveway, a concrete birdbath outside a kitchen window, and a tree swing on the front lawn. If money allowed, he wanted a yard large enough to play flag football, and if life and love permitted him the gift of children, he could see a tricycle or two in the driveway. Smiling at the thought, he realized he had come a long way since his days along Hominy Creek. Grateful to live in a home with running water and a door to the bathroom, he pedaled on.

Milkweed butterflies fluttered nearby, while bumblebees hovered over ditch flowers he recognized from his childhood. When a wayward grasshopper jumped from his gloved hand to his handlebars, he flicked it into a patch of tall grasses and overgrown weeds. It was then he remembered the tule patch back in Springfield that caused him such consternation. He laughed when he thought of all the times the dark water and cattails had sent him running into the house.

Riding along, he was aware of the calm his body carried. His breathing was in sync, his muscles were warm, and the tightening in his calf was long forgotten. It was at this moment he enjoyed nature's unspoiled beauty. Adding a splash of color to a grassy knoll, spikes of tubular red flowers attracted hummingbirds, and wild oak leaf hydrangea ebbed from the shallow ditches coming to rest on the concrete now cooled by the shade of mature bur oaks and sweet bay magnolias. Alongside the road, a shallow creek reflected a road sign and the sun's golden rays, reminding him of the shallow waters near Muscle Shoals. Someday, he wanted to boat the rapid waters of the Tennessee River. Glancing off in the distance, he wondered if the shallow creek flowed from the Wolf River. He would ask his friends about it later.

Basking in nature's sweet fragrances and admiring rocks blanketed with a velvety moss, he looked at the world through new eyes. The smile on his face mirrored the one he wore the day early in his childhood when he stepped into the waters of the Atlantic Ocean. Fearful he would be sucked into an unforgiving undertow he heard his father warn him about time-and-time again, he was surprised to find the water's gentle waves comforting.

Enjoying the open road in front of him, he reflected on the new lease life had given him. He had the unconditional love of his brother and sisters and adored his nieces and nephews. He was proud of his team and grateful to his coaching staff. It was not a corporate veil they worked under, but instead, the easy rules a loving family encouraged.

Appreciating the fresh air, he thought of the many blessings life had given him. He was in good health and had reached his dream with his team. Recalling his days at The Hobo, he was surprised how quickly he had adapted to the constant rumble of the passing freight trains that traveled the double tracks a stone's throw from his window. He took some comfort in knowing it was unlikely the wrestling movie he took part in some time ago would ever surface. Thinking back on the days he and his father shared a mattress and lived without appliances, and on the fact he grew up without his mother, moved from town to town, and bathed in a feeding trough, he struggled to accept that perhaps he had always been an adapter. *Is this a word one uses to define their existence?* Pushing the question aside, he returned his focus to the curve up ahead.

Unable to forget the rust he drove before receiving the keys to his Jeep, made him scrunch his nose. Not only had the car been a mess, it also collected it. The only time he missed the car was in those awkward moments when the kids he coached shared with him they wished they still trained at the club in Colonial Acres. Still in school, he thought they were too young to understand the gift he had been given. *As they grew older, his team would understand the conditions he accepted were meant not only to better him but also to benefit them.* Each time he walked in the door, his new apartment felt like home. Furnished with pieces he would never be able to afford, it was more than he ever expected. He was blessed to call Bob his friend.

Unlike in recent months, when he struggled to keep his mind focused on those things in life that truly mattered, thoughts of Terie entered his mind. Planning the wedding, the disagreements they settled, and the storm that changed the course of their marriage was now nothing more than a blur. His marriage had failed, and now, almost a year later, he finally had all his marbles in a jar. The experience, along with the sweet essence of time, taught him he could be vulnerable to pain but still be strong and remain positive. Taking Gina's advice, he put the past in the rearview mirror, and now that his heart was stronger, it would be foolish to look back. He was itching to begin his new adventure.

Hearing a muffler's roar, he moved to the right. When he caught sight of the car's hood, he looked to the driver. He nodded and the car's driver offered a smile. As the El Camino passed on his left, he wondered about the boat engine hanging off the rear bumper. Giving in to a chuckle, he knew this was a picturesque story he would later share.

Thinking, once again, of his team warmed his heart. They reminded him to appreciate the little things in life, those things that sometimes can only be seen through a young child's eyes. Watching them grow, especially Silvie and Margo, he learned it was okay to make mistakes as long as you learned from them, and that many good days would wash away one bad one. Margo and Silvie. Silvie and Margo. Two amazing swimmers with endless promise. He could not wait to see what the future had in store for them. He had not made them what they had become, he had only carved out a path for them to follow. The blessing was not that they had been given him to coach them, but that he had been allowed the opportunity.

Recalling a recent road trip with the parent of one of his swimmers, he hummed Tim McGraw's song, *The Next Thirty Years*. Ready to embrace life, he sung along in the car often louder than he was aware and in a voice that should never be heard outside the shower. Recalling the song's words, he was grateful for all of his good fortunes and thankful for his many friends. Accepting God's plan, he was excited to learn what the future held for him. *His future.* Thinking the words made him smile. Still young at thirty-five, he had a lot of living ahead of him. In the distance, a church bell rang out. *Its timing could not be more fitting.*

Rolling along at posted speeds, he planned the practice his team would have later that afternoon. Perhaps he would change it up today. A softening in his heart told him they deserved a break after the hard practices he asked of them in recent days. As he pressed the pedal, he questioned if they preferred a game of Marco Polo or a game that ended with a prize-winning bag of sour punch straws. A knowing smile assured him they would enjoy both. Glancing at his wrist, he was surprised to see he had forgotten his watch. Still, he knew the time was nearing for him to turn back. Eyeing a stop sign up ahead, he pulled back on his speed. Clicking out of the pedals, he prepared to stop. Looking in both directions, he continued on.

Pedaling along the familiar route, he mapped out in his head the ride he would bike the following day at Shelby Forest, an area located north of

Memphis. He had not biked the forest in months, and with nice weather in the forecast, he looked forward to the challenges the hills presented. Looking ahead, he made a quick decision to take advantage of the long stretch the flat road promised. Switching gears and picking up speed, he leaned into the handlebars. Breaking a sweat, the constant breeze brushing over his face was a welcomed relief. A glance at the speedometer confirmed what he already knew. He had reached record speed. A rush of adrenaline pushed him to pedal harder. He had just eyed the curve in the road up ahead, a place he designated on earlier rides as a turnaround point, when he heard the sound of an engine. Easing up on his speed, he moved toward the road's narrow shoulder, a place riders who biked along this route often called "a slim alley out of harm's way." Struggling over fallen branches, bits of gravel, and broken rocks, he positioned his hands on the curve of the handlebars.

The truck's driver had driven Raleigh Lagrange Road many times. The tight curves and frequent turns where visibility was limited kept him aware of oncoming traffic, disabled vehicles, and the cyclists he occasionally encountered. A seasoned and experienced driver, he pulled into the left lane, allowing a safe distance between the heavy trailer he pulled and Cory.

Hearing the truck's engine downshift, he looked to his left. Making eye contact, he and the driver exchanged a smile and a wave. In that moment, driver and cyclist agreed to share the road.

As the truck rolled around him, he glanced over his shoulder. The truck's trailer was weighed down with a land leveler, and a red flag waved from the rear of a Bobcat front loader. Just as he caught sight of a stack of concrete cinder blocks, he veered off the road into loose gravel. In his panic, he rushed to regain control of the bike.

Looking through the truck's side mirror, the driver caught a glimpse of the red and black bike just as it slid out from under its rider. When he fell out of view, the driver grew worried he suffered an injury and may need help getting home. Shifting gears, he pulled the heavy truck to the side of the road.

Traveling behind them, a second motorist hurried to slam on his brakes. Forcing his car to a sudden stop, he watched in horror as Cory was thrown from his bike, flown through the air, and while his arms searched the space around him for solid ground, bounced like a rag doll over the concrete before disappearing under the trailer's rear wheels. Running from his car, the motorist cried out for God's help.

As the truck's driver stepped around the end of the trailer, a sick feeling blanketed him. Bloodied pieces of the bike helmet he wore were scattered in the road, many of them crushed into dime-size pieces. Making his way to his lifeless body, he begged for God and his angels to watch over the young man's soul. Kneeling at his side, he could not bring himself to lift his bloodied head. Whispering a prayer, the driver watched as a steady pool of dark red blood trickled from his mouth, and although it no longer pumped from his body, a thin stream of blood oozed from his ears and nose. Distraught, the driver did not notice a jagged piece of the helmet protruding from his skull. Wiping away tears, he prayed for the young man he did not know. A family man with a wife and children, he wailed when he noticed the wedding band on his finger. Taking his limp and bloodied hand in his, he continued to pray for a miracle. Choking on words, he feared his prayers would go unheard. Turning his face to the heavens, he let go a cry. When he felt his hand twitch, he let faith take over.

Within minutes, a rescue helicopter landed in a nearby field. Although the first response team found him with a heartbeat, they quickly learned he was not breathing. Trained in trauma, the team held little hope as they placed his torn body on a stretcher. As the helicopter lifted off the ground for its return trip to The Med, one thing was certain—his future was in danger.

CHAPTER 37

At her home in Texas, Jill was clearing a flowerbed when she heard the telephone. Pulling a garden glove from her hand, she placed the trowel in the other as she made her way through the house to the kitchen. Recognizing Terie's number on the phone's clear screen, she hesitated to answer. Grabbing a pen, she scribbled a reminder to call her when she was finished in the garden. She had already returned to the yard and slipped on the dirtied glove when the phone rang a second time. Making her way indoors, she prepared a list of excuses to cut the call short. After all, Mother's Day was coming up and she had roses to plant.

Unable to understand the words Terie mumbled, she asked that she slow down and start again. "Why are you crying? And what is it you're trying to say?" she repeated. Time stood still as she listened to Terie tell of Cory's accident. Hearing talk of The Med, the trowel slipped from her fingers to the floor. When Terie mentioned a possible brain injury, she dropped the phone.

Shaken and barely able to think or speak, she stood frozen until she remembered she had been asked to call Gina. Fumbling with the telephone, she tried to will her fingertips to dial the phone number she knew by heart. Finding Gina's number had escaped her memory, she pressed a sequence of random and meaningless numbers. Each time she was told she had misdialed, she slammed the phone into its cradle. Taking a deep breath, she prayed the numbers would come to her. Finally, she raced down the hall, pushed open the bedroom door, and ripped her cell phone from the charger. Scrolling through her phone, she pressed the icon identifying Gina's home number. While waiting for her sister to answer, she gave in to the urge to vomit.

Taking advantage of the handful of spring days Floridians enjoyed before summer's sultry days had them wishing December's cooler temperatures would return, Gina planned to spend her day outdoors. She quickly put on running shorts stained with paint and an old T-shirt she retired from her closet. After joining Mike, her husband, for an early lunch, she made her way to the backyard. Connecting the garden hose to the power washer, she attacked the patio's fieldstone deck and the pool's limestone coping.

Hearing Gina's phone, Mike grabbed it on the third ring. Recognizing Jill's voice, he repeatedly asked her to slow down. "What are you saying about Cory?"

"He was in an accident. They airlifted him to a hospital in Memphis... The Med. He's at The Med."

"What happened?"

"Terie told me he was out on his bike...she asked us to hurry."

Before Mike could hand the phone off to Gina, Jill hung up. Returned calls went unanswered.

Gina half listened as her husband repeated his conversation with Jill. "Did she call the hospital to find out if this is true?"

"I didn't ask, Gina. She was beside herself."

"Please keep trying her phone. I'm calling The Med."

Minutes later, after speaking with a desk nurse in the hospital's trauma unit, Gina threw her hands over her head. Trembling in fear, she rocked back and forth. "Oh, dear God. We have to go to Memphis. And I need to call Kirby."

—

Kirby's mind raced with worry, fear, and questions he hoped would soon be answered as he drove amidst heavy traffic along Tennessee's I-240. Gina's words had left him filled with concern, and when he asked about Cory's injuries, she hesitated before calling them life-threatening. She only asked that he hurry. *"They've taken him to the Elvis Presley Trauma Center."*

The first to arrive at The Med, Kirby was quick to notice that nurses and doctors wearing lab coats and sympathetic smiles did not rush to greet him. Checking in at the front desk, he waited only a short time before a nurse escorted him to the trauma unit. After a brief interview with a woman who documented his full name and his relationship to Cory, he was then allowed to see his brother.

Stepping through the open door, he cried out. He understood his brother had been injured, but he had not been prepared to see him like this. Taking a seat at his side, he prayed for a miracle. In the passing minutes, time that in his heart felt like hours, he was shaken that tubes were not checked, blood was not taken, and trays of small paper cups labeled with prescription pills meant to save his brother's life were not placed before him. The health care professionals who entered the room moved in silence as they read monitors and scribbled notes in a white folder that held the secrets regarding his brother's uncertain future. Exiting the room, a woman in scrubs placed her hand on his shoulder, but moving along, did not offer any encouraging words or her condolences. When he looked into her wet eyes, he understood that she, too, was at a loss for words.

His private time with Cory was brief, and once he came to understand his brother's injuries, also painful and heart wrenching. Watching his chest rise and fall with the rhythm of the ventilator, and hearing the constant intermittent beeps on a monitor overhead, had him doubting his brother would make a speedy recovery. When a member of the medical team assigned to his care entered the room, Kirby raised his hand to wave him away. He was not ready to hear updates regarding his brother's condition.

—

In her rush to get to Memphis, Jill hurried to pack an overnight bag. While her prayers were already with Cory, she stuffed the bag with essentials—a toothbrush, a change of clothes, and old pajamas she had been meaning to discard and replace. Before slamming the closet door, she grabbed a simple black dress and shoes to match.

Securing air transportation, she arrived at The Med with her husband, Bill, at her side. Leaving him to park the car, she rushed to the entrance. Her heart raced with worry for what awaited her inside the multi-story building she found intimidating. Passing families who waited outside the Jefferson Avenue entrance to hear word of their loved one's future, she searched their faces for a hint of hope and signs of encouragement. Catching her reflection in a window, she saw that their tired and worried expressions mirrored her own.

Inside, she approached the front desk to get directions to the trauma unit, and in her wait, she noticed a bottle of hand sanitizer, a collection of pamphlets meant to educate readers on current and necessary vaccines and common viruses, and parenting magazines filled with advice and direction. The brochure that held her eye was the only one that offered grief counseling. When the front desk nurse tapped her shoulder a second time, she apologized for drifting away as she forced the brochure deep into her handbag.

"Will you please direct me to the trauma unit?"

Seated behind a wrap-around mahogany desk she shared with a receptionist and a security guard, an elderly woman with skin the color of caramel and a smile warmer than any she had seen in hours, adjusted her reading glasses. "What is the patient's name?"

"Cory. Cory Horton. Cory Scott Horton. He's been in an accident and I was told to get here right away."

"Yes, ma'am," the woman responded kindly while tapping at a keyboard. "Someone will be down in a moment. You're welcome to have a seat in the lounge. There's coffee and chocolate chip cookies on the long table near the window. If you want to read The Commercial Appeal, our daily newspaper, I can get a copy for you."

Following the woman's hand, she surveyed the waiting area. Near the window, a wire cage guarded a flat-screen television. In the far corner, an elderly man lay sleeping across three chairs, while another man, who looked disheveled and worried, cradled a young child in his arms. Take-out boxes from the hospital's cafeteria and a canvas bag filled with books and toys told her the man knew before his arrival that his family's stay would be lengthy. On the floor in front of them was an overnight bag. A white tag hanging from the bag's strap had her believing they traveled by plane.

Seated across from them, a middle-aged woman kept worry at bay with knitting needles and a bundle of yarn. Chewing gum and humming to music she did not hear, the woman never looked up from her lap.

At the children's table, a toddler entertained himself with crayons. When no one ran to help the boy when he fell backward onto the rug, she wondered whom the young child belonged to.

Seated in the far corner, three men huddled close together. Had the temperature in the room been cooler, she would have thought they were trying to stay warm. Appearing anxious, the men shifted about in their seats. Speaking in whispered voices, they lowered their heads and raised their eyes. Peeking over dark sunglasses, their faces wore a look of concern. She was quick to notice when an officer of the law entered the room, the man with a yin-yang tattoo made his exit.

Moving to the windowed area, she began to worry there had been a miscommunication at the front desk. She meant to ask which floor the trauma unit was on and where the elevators were located. Perhaps the receptionist misunderstood that Cory was a patient, not an employee of the hospital. Turning back toward the reception area, she was relieved when she caught sight of Gina. Waving an arm overhead, she hurried into her sister's outstretched arms.

"I got here as fast as I could." Taking her sister in her arms, Gina cried into her shoulder. "Have you seen Cory?"

"We just got here." Speaking in a hushed voice, she shared with Gina the conversation she had with the receptionist. Just as she was about to return to the front desk, Bill was at her side. "Someone will be coming to get us," she offered in a low voice.

Minutes later, when Kirby arrived, a nurse was at his side. Allowing the family their privacy, the middle-aged woman remained steps away until a beep from the pager attached to her hip brought her to their side. Apologizing for the interruption, she let them know that when they were ready, she would escort them upstairs.

Walking in silence, Cory's siblings circled the lobby's atrium before climbing the wide and winding ramp to the Elvis Presley Trauma Center. The nurse, who was trained to handle such gut-wrenching conditions, spoke softly and compassionately as she walked one step ahead along the unit's many halls and nurses' stations they found unusually quiet. Approaching the "Wall of Honor," the nurse stopped to explain the inscribed plaques were given in Elvis Presley's honor. Farther down the corridor, armed police stood guard outside a closed door while others paced the floor. Voices were loud and demanding and the interruption by police radios and walkie-talkies provided constant background noise. Ignoring the comfort offered by loved ones, a thin woman dressed in a shirt several sizes too large for her small frame continued to wail, "Somebody shot my son."

Continuing on to Cory's room, their steps were slow and labored. Noticing the absence of flowers, balloons, and well-wishers, a sick feeling came over Jill. Unable to support herself, she fell against the wall. Sliding to the cold floor, she beat her hands against her chest. "I can't go in there. I don't want to see him. Not here. Not in a trauma unit."

Taking a seat on the floor beside her, Kirby pressed his back against the wall. Wishing he could shield her from what waited ahead, he cupped her chin in his hands. Lifting her face to his, he forced her to lock eyes with him. In his eyes, she saw panic. Looking into hers, he saw a pain so deep it frightened him. Her wet eyes begged him to make all of this a dream and to make it go away. Leaning into her, he held her close. In her ear, he whispered that he wished he could turn back the clock. When she rested her head on his shoulder, he stroked her hair. Listening to her cries nearly killed him. He wanted nothing more than to tell her everything would be all right and that Cory would fight his way back from this, but he loved her too much to give her false hope. Placing a hand on her shoulder and rubbing her back, he allowed her to curse at a world that threatened to cheat their brother of a long and rewarding life. When he felt she was ready to move on, he took hold of her arm. Helping her from the floor, he took her hand in his. At this moment, he would have given anything to protect her from the coming minutes.

As they approached Room 214, she caught a glimpse of Cory through the wall of windows. Unable to move, she fell limp into Kirby's arms. Throwing her hands to her face, Gina let out a whimper. Hearing her gasp, the nurse quickened her pace until she stood at the open door of the room at the end of the hall. *Cory's room.* Although she wanted to lessen the family's pain, the thick air surrounding them warned they should hold little hope.

Recognizing fear and uncertainty in their eyes, the nurse tried to prepare them. "What you'll see may look disturbing, but please know Cory is not in any pain." Along with Cory's family, she silently prayed for a miracle to reverse the inevitable outcome of this tragic and horrific accident. She wished this pain on no one.

Fluorescent lights overhead were set on low, and the room's sterile walls were void of art or any sign of hope. Floral arrangements sent to lift heavy spirits had been placed in the small chapel down the hall. A large clock ticked away the seconds others often mistook for hope, but not today. The room and the absence of a hurried team told Cory's family what they did not want to hear. Holding in secret the magnitude of the trauma Cory's body had suffered, his medical chart remained at the nurse's station. Its only purpose was to document hemodynamic stability and the satisfactory oxygenation of vital organs his family would later be asked to donate.

Suggesting he might be resting, Cory's eyes were closed. A visitor had placed a single red rose at his side. His head and shoulders were elevated, and a starched bed sheet blanketed his resting body. Moving in rhythm with a ventilator meant to maintain his body for its still uncertain future, his chest continued to rise and fall in a familiar pattern. A clear tube taped to his wrist fell from the bed and disappeared under the mattress. His left foot, free of injury, peeked out from under the pressed sheet. Someone, a nurse perhaps, had taken great care to cover the abrasions on his face with wide bandages, and because the trauma to his neck and right shoulder were horrifically grave and severe, only the left side of his body was visible. An intracranial pressure monitoring device covered his skull, its bolts shockingly obvious. Protruding from the surgical helmet were two subdural rods experienced surgeons placed deep below his scalp.

The ventilator's constant hum could not drown out the cries that came from deep within Jill. Moving her eyes over his broken body, she vomited into her hands. As she rushed to his side, she cursed God for allowing this to happen. Giving in to shattered faith and a tightening in her heart, she let out a cry so painfully visceral, it echoed throughout the ICU. Overwhelmed with anguish, and threatening to jump to her death, she threw herself against the window. Never before had she known such suffering and raw emotion.

Witnessing the commotion, a nurse rushed into the room. Concerned for Jill's safety, she offered to arrange for a sedative. Stepping to her side, Gina asked for understanding and compassion. "They are very close."

Tormented and numb, Gina placed her arms around her shoulders. Allowing emotions to take over, the sisters grieved the loss they knew they would never forget, or when time allowed them to heal, begin to understand.

Taking a seat at Cory's side, Jill begged him to wake up. "Talk to me, Cory. Just one word. That's all I need. Open your eyes, my sweet angel. Please look at me." Unaware her siblings were watching, she gently pulled at his ringlets, each time tucking the few strands that gave way into the pockets of her jeans. When Gina stroked her hair, Kirby pulled at her arm. The look he gave told her Jill needed to do this.

"Remember the words we learned long ago? Often, when we are broken, we become desperate," Kirby whispered.

Turning away from Cory, Jill turned to Kirby. "Give me your socks."

Drowning in his own thoughts, Kirby gave his sister a confused look. "What? My socks? You want my socks?"

Disappointment hardened her face. "You know Cory likes to wear socks."

Rubbing his brow, Kirby took a deep breath. Of course he knew Cory loved socks. It was difficult to think of a time he had not seen his brother with his feet covered in thick socks that, allowed to unroll, would have reached his knees. "Jill, I don't think Cory wants…"

Looking at her brother through no-nonsense eyes, she repeated her demand in a guttural voice he found disturbing and uncomfortable. "Give me your damn socks!"

Relenting, he stepped out of his shoes. Holding her with his eyes, he pulled the sock from his left foot. Tucking it under his arm, he removed the other. Placing both socks in her outstretched hand, he worried she would spin so far out of control, he would never be able to bring her back. With his heart aching far more than he could bear, he took his place beside her.

With a tenderness one would expect and admire between a mother and her child, she caressed the arch of Cory's foot before moving to his toes. Rubbing a fingertip over his ankle, she began to tremble. Through wet eyes, she pushed a sleeve up her arm. With gentle hands, she slowly inched the sock over his toes. Careful not to cause him further pain, she pulled the sock over his ankle and up his shin. Gasping, she massaged a bruise near his knee. Leaning over him, she folded back the sheet. When her eyes fell on the thick gauze, she dry-heaved to the floor. Until this moment, she had not known his right foot had been severed in the accident.

"I can't do this. Cory needs to wear socks, but I can't do this for him."

Wiping at her own tears, Gina brushed her hand through her hair. "I'll take care of it." Although Gina could not recall where she heard the words, they rolled through her head at a speed she could not ignore. Placing her hands on her shoulder once again, she whispered in her ear. "One of the toughest experiences to go through is to be someone's strength while you are at your weakest. Lean on me for strength. I will carry you through the valley. And when you're ready, I'll be at your side when you're ready to climb uphill."

Standing at her side, Kirby cried not only for Cory and the pain he must have suffered, but also for Jill. Having moved on with his own life and often living as an outsider looking in, he came to understand their relationship was built on a simple foundation made of trust and love, especially in those times when their father had gone in search of things greater or traveled paths that took him away from his family, leaving her to care for her baby brother. Filled with worry she would never be the same without Cory, he let out a whimper. Looking at her, the tears in her eyes confirmed his greatest fear. She would never be the same.

Cocking her head and twisting her jaw, she begged Kirby to do something, anything, to make things right. She rocked back and forth and screamed angry words, that until this moment, she frowned upon and never allowed to escape her lips.

"No, Kirby. No. No. No. Do not look at me like that. I'm not giving up on him. He's a fighter. He wouldn't want us to give up on him." Looking at Kirby with fire in her eyes, she forced his attention. "If something like this happened to you, would you expect us to give up without a fight?"

Kirby did not know how to begin to answer her question, only that he prayed she would never be placed in this position again. He wanted to tell her there was not anything left to fight for and that all the fighting in the world would not bring Cory back to them. Instead, he tried to calm the rage her troubled heart battled. Pressing his cheek to hers, he held her close. Rocking with her, he tried the voice of reason. "Jill, Cory can't win this fight, and as hard as I pray, I can't fix this. We can't undo what has been done."

"Instead of throwing our hands up, I think we should plan for his care when he leaves here. I'll work out a schedule. If we run into a pinch, maybe Terie can help."

Kirby wiped at a tear. "Jill, Cory's going home—to heaven."

Shocked by his words, Jill threw her hands over her ears. "I can't live knowing I won't see him again." Pulling away and lowering her head, she folded her hands together. "Dear God, I have honored you, obeyed you, but please forgive me, I can't be in this valley without him. I want to laugh with him again, even if it's only for one last time. I'm hoping, praying, begging for a miracle. If it's possible, I hope it will be given to Cory." Placing a hand on his face, she continued. "You are a fighter. I keep thinking this as I sit here watching over you. I will never give up on God's healing hands."

As though on autopilot, she pulled open the slim drawer next to the bed. Grabbing the Gideon Bible, she turned to James 1:6. Reading aloud and stopping only to wipe away tears she could not stop, she pushed on. "Prayer must be offered with confident trust in a sovereign God." Searching her neck for the cross necklace she always wore, she begged for guidance. "Show me the words I need to pray, the words I must say for you to hear me." Her voice cracked and the single tear she cried turned to hundreds. Falling to the floor, she again folded her hands together. "I'm on my knees begging you to let me keep him."

A loud boom and a low and constant beep interrupted her challenging plea. Until the hospital's generators took over, lights flickered, monitors beeped, and alarms sounded. Desperate to understand God's reasons for taking her brother, she believed the flashing lights were a signal of hope. When minutes passed with no one coming to check on Cory, her hopes and prayers faded away. Alone in her silence, she refused to accept what her heart was telling her to be true. Holding her head high, she vowed to prove her heart wrong.

Standing outside the door, a neurosurgeon assigned to Cory's care rubbed his brow and breathed a heavy sigh. He had seen this type of injury far too many times, and having to inform the family of the severity of their loved one's injuries never got easier. In Cory's case, it was even more difficult because he knew he had followed the rules of the road. He wore a bike helmet, signaled passing drivers, and staying to the far right, had done his best to avoid an accident. When he entered Cory's room, Kirby reached to shake his hand, Gina acknowledged his presence with a nod, and Jill, who refused to accept more bad news, turned away.

"There's a chapel at the far end of the hall, but I might suggest taking a moment to visit the chapel off the lobby on the main floor. I find it offers the quiet solitude one who's seeking it might prefer."

Leaving Jill in the room, they stepped out to the hall. In the passing minutes, Kirby and Gina were told of Cory's injuries. When she could no longer bear to hear of shattered bones, abrasions, and torn appendages, Gina returned to Jill's side.

———

Shuffling down the corridor, Kirby rode the elevator to the lobby. His thoughts were a scrambled mess, and like Jill, he hoped to find answers to the many questions racing through his head. Seeking solace in the hospital's chapel, he fell heavily into a pew, took his place on the kneeling rail, and recalled the day Cory was born. Closing his eyes, he took a deep breath.

His mother had called the day *"glorious."* Weighing a hair under seven pounds, Cory arrived just in time to have his birth announced during the evening news. His smile was warm and contagious from his first breath. As his mind raced from one vignette to the next, he recalled the day thirty-five years earlier when his mother was injured in a trash fire. It was an awful time for his family, but especially for Cory, who as a newborn, needed the love and comfort of his mother.

Wringing his hands, he gave thanks that Gina and Jill had been there to take over the responsibilities their mother was too ill to manage. Now, kneeling on the prayer bench, he asked for guidance. He wanted to ask that his life be taken instead, but knew his words were too late. Feeling a hand on his shoulder, he turned to find Gina at his side. Her eyes were wet and her nose was bright red. In her hands, she carried a box of tissues.

Kneeling side-by-side, they exchanged in silence the words neither was able to speak.

—

Several floors away, Jill continued to hold Cory's hand in hers. Massaging his arm, she was suddenly aware his watch was missing. Desperate to have it returned to his wrist, she pressed the call button. "Nurse! I need a nurse in here!"

The door pushed open and the nurse who earlier led her to Cory's room walked to her side. "How may I help you?"

"You can start by finding his watch. It's gray and has lots of dials and buttons. An Ironman something, I think," she shouted accusingly.

Unaware of the watch, the nurse reviewed Cory's chart. "He didn't arrive here with a watch."

"That's impossible. He always wears that watch…when he's coaching, when he's training, and I know I've seen him sleeping with it. Now, get someone in here who can help him. *He wants his watch.*"

Angry and belligerent, she was oblivious to the look of sympathy the nurse offered as she exited the room. Minutes later, when the doctor arrived, he found her running her fingers through Cory's hair. Clearing his throat, he made his presence known. "It's important that he remain still."

Waving him away, she responded in a flat voice. "It's important your staff find his watch."

On staff at The Med for several years, the doctor understood her sudden hostility. "I'll see what I can find out about the watch." Hers was not the first outburst he had heard. Lashing out was normal and expected, especially when the dying patient was young and able-bodied.

Worried what the next several hours would bring—or worse, take from her—she stayed at Cory's side. Growing up together and so near in age, they had always been close. Now, when he needed her most, she would not let him down.

Sliding a cold chair to the side of the bed, she placed her hand on his and laid her head on his arm. Looking up at his face, she understood the wide bandages were not meant to protect his injuries, but to shield her from them. Tormented and burdened with pain, she placed a hand on his cheek.

"I love you, Cory. I know I'm supposed to let you go, but all I ask is to have one more day with you. Without you, my tomorrows will no longer exist. Every day will be just like this day. Please, don't ask me to lose hope." Stopping to catch her breath, she brushed a fingertip along his jaw. "I'm going to miss your sweet smile. Tell me what it is I'm going to do without you? How will I go on? How will I breathe?" Taking his hand, she rubbed her fingers over his. "I'll never forget your laugh and the way you make everything okay when it seems impossible." Closing her eyes, she tightened her grip on his hand. "Oh, Cory, how I need you now." Leaning on her elbows, she folded her hands together. "I have to believe you can hear me. If you are already at heaven's door, I know you can see me. I pray God will help me get through a life without you in it."

Listening to the machines as they continued to whisper, sound, and flash numbers that meant nothing to her, she struggled to understand what she did not want to accept. The machines were not working to save his life. *Cory was already gone.* Crying softly, a pained smile came over her. "You are a gift from heaven, Cory Scott Horton, and I'm not ready to give you back."

Taking his hand, she prayed for time to stand still, but in her heart, the minutes passed faster than they ever had before. The nurses who entered the room did not fluff his pillow, take his vitals, or attempt to ease his pain and discomfort. Instead, they noted the time on the clock overhead, observed and recorded the flashing numbers on the monitor attached to the helmet he wore, and offered a look of sympathy when she locked eyes with theirs. Seated next to him, she felt very alone.

Rushed with anger, she rose from the chair, opened the bedside table, and grabbed the Bible. Looking back at Cory, she threw it to the floor and kicked it into the corner. She had no use for it. Recalling the brochure she earlier tucked into her bag, she ripped it from her purse and tossed it to the floor.

Recognizing a voice she heard coming from the hall, she glanced toward the door. Dressed in a pink vest and tattered denim jeans, Terie talked with a nurse assigned to Cory's care. Catching her eye, she ran to her with open arms.

"His condition has not changed."

Terie shifted her weight, stretched her tired neck, and when she was able to ask, turned to her for understanding. "If it's okay, I'd like to have a moment with him."

Choosing to forget the divorce papers awaiting her brother's signature, she rose from the chair. "I'll wait in the hall." As she passed by, Terie gave her hand a gentle squeeze. "Wait. Please don't leave. Cory would want you to stay."

Wiping away tears, Terie stepped to the bed, bowed her head, and whispered a prayer. Placing a kiss on her fingertip, she traced Cory's lips. "Forever and always, I will love you." Giving a nod, she hurried to catch the waiting elevator.

C H A P T E R   3 8

When word of Cory's accident spread, Thunder parents organized to call the members assigned to them. The moment the young swimmers were dismissed from school, they, along with their parents, rushed to The Med. Questions they asked went unanswered as they were ushered through the building. Soon, the trauma center's waiting area filled with triathletes who often trained with Cory and others who competed against him. They were joined by area swim coaches, close friends, members of his swim team, and other local teams, along with a representation from St. George's High School, including faculty members and students, who in recent months, looked to him for coaching.

Although the extent of his injuries were unknown, parents and friends knew his condition was life-threatening. The Med was not a place known for treating lingering coughs, a bloodied nose, or broken bones, but for providing emergency care to the critically wounded. The Med's staff witnessed patients suffering horrific, life-threatening injuries and managed to save many, who, when admitted by helicopter or ambulance or accompanied by a friend or family member, held little chance of survival. When Cory came into their care, the staff did not rush to treat him. Their job was to comfort his family and prepare his organs for transplant.

Behind the scenes, his friends made calls to their friends, co-workers, church members, and family, asking them to stand ready if a blood drive became necessary. Cell phones that had not been silenced rang out and were quickly answered. Tissues were offered and loud voices were lowered to a whisper. Strangers, acquaintances, and loved ones exchanged embraces.

In the confusion, there was talk he suffered a back injury. Fearing he might be paralyzed and confined to a wheelchair for the rest of his life, others whispered they thought his legs were crushed. Someone described his condition as grim and bleak while another shared that his bike shoes had remained in the clips. Several of the team's younger swimmers huddled together in prayer while promising to meet at The Med each day after school until he returned home.

Carrying a photo album she brought from home, Gina entered the waiting area. Knowing the severity of her brother's injuries, she thought those who gathered to pray and offer support—and should the time come, their condolences—would perhaps find comfort within the album's many pictures of Cory, some taken long ago, and others in recent times. Accepting the comforting hugs and warm embraces his friends extended, she dodged the question on everyone's mind. *Will he walk again?*

Hearing he had been airlifted to The Med, a Level 1 trauma center known for treating gunshot victims and those with little hope of surviving the injuries the hospital's faculty could not undo or make right, friends worried about the seriousness of his wounds. Not wanting to talk about his condition, and having noticed the young kids who gathered together, Gina made her way through the crowded room.

In a circle on the carpeted floor, members of his team sat quietly. While their questions remained unanswered, their tears were understood. Their outpouring of love and the pain of their loss were obvious and heart-wrenching. They had never known such sorrow. Unsure of what to do, they merely observed those who appeared knowledgeable about his condition. Placing herself in the circle, Gina slowly turned the pages of the leather album. The kids took turns sharing with her their favorite moments with Cory. Recalling the many times he had shared these same stories with her, she allowed a smile.

When Kirby entered the room, Bob Compton was at his side. Seeing the pain in her brother's eyes, she asked everyone in the room to gather. Holding hands, Cory's family and friends, along with the swimmers he coached, formed a prayer circle. Clutching hands with Gina and Kirby, Bob did not pray for his best friend to recover, but for the strength to survive a life without him.

Sometime later, when the passing of time no longer offered comfort, a floor nurse interrupted their quiet. She announced visiting hours were ending, but Bob's eyes begged to be allowed to stay a while longer. Offering understanding and giving a sympathetic nod, she quietly made her exit from the room.

CHAPTER 39

Supported by a walking cane, a neurosurgeon assigned to Cory's care entered Room 214. Following behind him was a younger man, who months earlier, transferred from a medical facility in New Orleans. Like his superior, he was well trained in the necessary functions a trauma unit demanded and required. Both wore white lab coats, their names written in calligraphy above breast pockets. The older doctor, a middle-aged man unknown to the Horton family, removed his eyeglasses, placed them in his pocket, and took a seat on a rolling chair a rotating nurse had brought in minutes before his arrival. "I'm sorry about your brother. I've been told by several members of our staff that he was an amazing young man."

Clearing his throat and swallowing hard, the younger doctor offered his condolences. "I didn't know Cory personally, but my nieces swim, and in recent months, I've heard them mention his name." Pressing his back to the wall, he softened his voice. "With all due respect, there are decisions to be made, and unfortunately, time is of the essence." The audible sigh he made went unnoticed. "At this time, Cory is able to donate several organs, his corneas, and tissue."

For Jill, the mention of organ donation made the pain real. Her cries echoed throughout the intensive care unit. Desperate to protect her brother, she hurried to his side. "Stop talking like he's dead. And please, just go away." When angst coupled her pain, she turned to her family. "Kirby, Gina, make them leave us alone."

This time, when the older neurosurgeon spoke, he rose from the chair. "I'm sorry to be standing here today, but please understand that we can't help Cory. He lost the battle long before he arrived here. We understand saying goodbye isn't easy. It never is. Cory can't continue on support. The monitor shows there is no brain activity and..."

Interrupting him, Kirby raised his hand. "We're asking for a little more time to come to terms with this."

"I'm sorry, Mr. Horton." Lowering his voice, the doctor folded his hands. "It's time to think about making arrangements for your brother. For Cory. When you're ready, a donor coordinator would like to talk with you."

Hearing these words, Jill ripped the cross from her neck, and while those around watched with empathy, threw the necklace to the floor. "This isn't right. He's too young to be taken from us."

Drowning in their anguish, Gina, Kirby, and Jill wept as they accepted the truth. Cory would not recover from his injuries. He would not require rehabilitative therapy, and they would never again see his smile or hear his laugh.

When a knock on the open door interrupted their somber moment, they turned to find a woman unknown to them. Distraught, and wanting only for Cory to recover and return to the life he had come to enjoy and appreciate, they failed to notice the young woman's genuine smile. Turning away from her, they were not able to see the compassion in her dark eyes. Allowing time for them to accept her presence, she offered her name. While their hearts filled with sorrow and despair, she knew they would later ask that she repeat it.

"Please allow me to offer my deepest condolences. I was just in the waiting area talking with Cory's friends. Young and old, they were eager to share their stories. I laughed along when they spoke of the silly pranks and games he played, and when they voiced their fears and concerns about his future, I admired the love they have for him and the places he has taken in their lives. It's easy to see how much they love him and feel blessed to know him."

Looking to the tiled floor, Kirby wiped away a tear. "We are all better for having known him, loving him, and being loved by him. He was a good man."

"I understand this is a very difficult time for all of you, and while you will each grieve the loss of your brother in different ways, this is also a critical time for life-changing decisions. This is never easy, especially when a loved one is taken from us without warning. Talking with his friends, I've learned so much about him. The stories they shared have a common thread. He was a giving man. I'm hoping you will consider honoring Cory by allowing him to continue to give by sharing the gift of life."

Lifting her head from Gina's shoulder, Jill's eyes shot to the stranger who stood before her. "Why are you saying this? Why now? Cory's not dead."

Years of training prepared the young woman, a member of a team who valued not only life, but also when it was cut short, in relaying the importance of the gift of giving. She understood that at this moment, his family kept a tight hold onto hope as they continued to pray for a miracle. Meeting them here today and seeing the looks of shock on their worn faces, she wanted to tell them they would embrace acceptance with the passing of time. When the time came to discuss organ donation, it would be her place to help guide them through the gut-wrenching process. "I'll leave you to discuss this, but I want you to know that for Cory to give the gift of life, we will need to begin making arrangements. I'm going to step out, but if you need me to answer questions, I'll be at the nurse's station."

"We'd like to talk this over. Please give us tonight to reach a decision," Kirby begged.

"Of course. I'll be here in the morning. If you've reached a decision, we can talk then. Again, I'm here when you need me."

Offering comfort to her sister, Gina took a seat at her side. Holding Jill's face in her hands, she looked into her eyes. "Please listen, my sweet angel. Cory's not coming back to us. All we can do now is accept this and help each other get through the coming hours." When Jill lowered her face, Gina lifted her chin. "Cory would want us to let him go. It's time, Jill."

Meeting her sister's eyes, Jill squeezed her hand. "We don't need to do this now." Pulling her hand away, she looked to Cory. "He's breathing, Hurricane."

Hearing Jill call her the name Cory had given her so long ago, Gina closed her eyes. In the suffocating silence, she prayed for strength. "Cory is in God's hands now. We have been asked to donate his organs. He would want..."

"Gina, we are not doing this now. He needs more time. He's healthy and he's strong. Last weekend he competed in a triathlon. He's going to pull through this."

"Cory doesn't need more time. We're the ones who need more time with him, but not like this, Jill. He has already left us."

A confused look came over Jill's face. "No, he's still here. He's not a quitter. He's going to get better. I know it, Gina, I just know it."

Holding her sister in her arms, Gina was careful to use words she hoped Jill would accept and understand. "He's been kept on the ventilator so we'd have time to get here and say goodbye." Knowing Jill was fragile and distraught and unable to think clearly, she did not mention the ventilator also allowed the hospital to harvest Cory's organs for donation, should they choose to do so. "I think Cory would want us to donate his organs." She paused to allow Jill a minute to accept her position. "Cory would want to help others."

The look on Jill's face was not only of surprise but also distrust. "You're asking me to let Cory die so others can live? Do you hear yourself, Gina?"

At a loss for words and feeling hopeless, Gina turned to Kirby for support. "I don't mean to put you on the spot, but I need to hear your thoughts."

"Cory is gone. We can't bring him back and we can't allow this to continue." Unable to go on, Kirby lowered his head. "He wouldn't want to be here, like this. In my heart, I'm certain if he could talk to us, he'd ask us to let him go. If he could save the life of someone, or give him or her a chance at a healthier life, he would do it. This is the right thing to do."

~

Needing to clear her mind, Jill separated from her family and the hopelessness and worry she felt in the ICU's sterile environment. Making her way to a bank of elevators, she caught a glimpse of the donor coordinator. Struggling with pain and confusion, she was relieved the woman did not speak to her or attempt to approach her. Seconds later, when she stepped off the elevator, her tired eyes were drawn to a young couple who lingered near the nurse's station. A woman with hair the color of honey held a young child close to her hip. She found it odd that the child wore sunglasses inside the building. As quickly as the thought had entered her mind, it faded.

When she was ready, she returned to Cory's room. As she approached the bed, a chill came over her. Taking a seat at his side, she placed her hand on his. Finding his skin cool sent a shiver through her. *Had he felt like this earlier? How had I not noticed?*

Struggling with a racing heart and shallow breathing, she searched for the right words. She did not want to remember him this way, and she believed in her heart he would not want this for her, either. Afraid she would forget him, she took in every detail. With the tip of her finger, she traced his freckles, and just as she had earlier, ran her fingers through his hair. She had once told him it was as soft as corn silk. She never shared with him she had always been envious of the curly locks he sometimes cursed and often hated. His narrow nose was perfect, and recalling his sweet smile, she worried she would never smile again. Although she could not see them, she knew behind his lids were the kindest eyes she had ever known. She once told him his eyes danced to music he helped others hear. She would have given anything to look into his eyes one last time. Thinking back on the many times he looked into hers, her mind raced with the thought of giving those eyes to someone else. *Will his eyes bring sight to someone who has never before seen the beauty of a sunrise or been in awe of the colors of the sunset? Will I ever see them again? Will they bring a smile to a troubled heart? If I were to cross paths with the person given his eyes, would I recognize them? Will they remember me?*

Fighting a stomach twisted in knots, she rested her head on his shoulder. "I love you, Cory. You will always be in my heart. Without you, the world is a much darker and sadder place. I'm going to miss you more than words can say." Moving closer, she placed a kiss on his forehead. "I'm afraid I'll be looking for you around every corner, and when I don't find you, I hate knowing that the pain I'm feeling now will return." Placing her hand on his, she lowered her voice to a whisper. "I pray that in God's heaven you never again feel pain. I pray you are given perfect peace and that the angels watching over you will love and protect you."

Standing outside his room, Kirby and Gina waited. From the day he joined their family, they watched the bond grow between them. "*Tight as ticks,*" were words Gina once used to describe their relationship. In whispered voices, they questioned if Jill would ever be the carefree woman she was before this accident. Glancing at his watch, Kirby tapped on the door. When Jill moved from the bed, he asked her to stay as he reached for her hand.

"Cory, it's time for us to let you go. I have a feeling you're going to stay busy in heaven. I bet by month's end, you will have put together a team of champion swimmers." Pausing when his voice cracked, he prayed for strength to carry him through. "There will not be a day that I will not think of you. I am so proud of you." Fighting to hold it together, he placed a kiss on his forehead. "I love you, Cory."

Wiping at her face with the palm of her hand, Gina reminded Jill and Kirby the time had come to reach a decision. "Let's take a walk."

CHAPTER 40

Resting at his home in rural Mississippi, Merchant, the name his grandfather had dubbed him long before he had taken his first step, worried not only for his future, which appeared bleak, but also for his family. Ischemic cardiomyopathy forced him into retirement some time ago. Instead of feeling like the man of the house, he felt like a burden to his wife and children. Until recently, he enjoyed fishing the small pond on his property with his grandchildren, but humidity and exhaustion now kept him indoors. While his recliner had given him comfort in the past, it no longer provided relief.

When his condition worsened, he underwent emergency surgery at a hospital in nearby Memphis. Hoping to help his weakened heart, surgeons implanted a left ventricular assist device, or LVAD, under his skin. The surgery was a success, but later, after suffering a third heart attack, he found himself back in the emergency room.

His skin was the color of shucked oysters and each breath threatened to be his last. Each day, as he gasped for air, he was reminded his heart might stop at any moment. Once weighing upward of two hundred pounds, he lost so much body weight, his tired flesh hung on his fragile and frail frame.

Only 57-years-old, he found himself on the waiting list for a heart transplant. He had been notified three times, in as many years, that a heart was available, but each time, he had been passed over. The reasons were different and valid.

One month after his name was added to the long list, he received the call he prayed for each day. A donor's heart was available in Houston, Texas. After meeting with his doctor, it was determined he was still too weak for surgery.

Extreme fatigue, edema, and an infection made him ineligible the second time a donor's heart was available. The third opportunity was the one that continued to haunt him. A lingering power outage had forced him to stay with his grown son in nearby Indianola. It was days later when he learned there had been several calls to his home to let him know that once again he had been considered for a donor's heart.

When he allowed thoughts of a successful transplant to enter his mind, his longings were few and simple. He wanted to enjoy a leisurely stroll with his wife, take a brisk walk with his grandchildren, and again, fish the small pond on his property. He prayed to be free of fatigue, discomfort, and health and financial worries.

He was napping on the screened porch when the ringing of the telephone took his wife away from the laundry room, where she was folding clothes. Hearing the caller say it was possible a heart would be available in Memphis made her own heart race. Dropping the towel she held, she hurried to tell Merchant. Kneeling at her husband's side, she was overcome with emotion. "They might have a heart for you." Brushing his hair aside, she pressed her face to his. Easing his fears, she placed a kiss on his forehead.

Having waited for so long to get this phone call, he wanted to grow excited, but given his failing health, he worried he might not live out the day, much less survive the surgery. Looking into his wife's tearing eyes, he searched for words. "What did they say? Where would we go?"

"We're going to Memphis. It's a strong heart. The young man lived a healthy and active life." Stroking the creases age placed on his forehead, his wife struggled to fight back tears. "Merchant, we're being given a second chance."

Holding hands, they bowed their heads. The prayer they asked was not for him, but for the family of the young man who would give him a chance at life. Closing his eyes, he realized the shortness of breath that plagued him rested long enough to allow him to pray.

When Shreveport, Louisiana native, Jeremy Shoeford, known as Shoe to his friends, became ill, he thought he was suffering from the flu. Even after resting, he felt extremely fatigued, and in a short passing of time, noticed his stomach was greatly distended. Jaundiced skin and severe itching forced him to seek medical attention. He consulted fifteen doctors, the last a hepatologist, before he was diagnosed with liver disease. Originally told he suffered from Wilson's disease, a rare genetic disorder, further testing showed he had end-stage liver disease. His only hope was a liver transplant, and he was immediately placed on the United Network for Organ Sharing transplant list.

Five months later, his liver enlarged to twice its normal size. A late-night rush to the emergency room soon had him surrounded by a team of doctors. Due to the severity of his condition, he was listed as Status 1 on the transplant list. He held little hope when told the number of people waiting for a new liver was greater than the number of healthy livers available for transplant.

In the early morning hours on May 11, he received the most important phone call of his life. He was told it was possible a liver might be available.

He had prayed for this moment for so long, and on his worst days, had allowed himself to give up. Having suffered for years, his concept of time was forever altered. On those days he cursed his ailing body, his wife would remind him, "God works in mysterious ways, and we should not question His actions, but hold on to faith."

After wrapping his children in his arms and kissing his wife on the cheek, he folded his hands. Together, they gave thanks to his donor and the generous and giving family he left behind.

———

When day turned to night, forty-six-year-old Rudy tossed and turned in the bed he shared with his wife. In recent years, he found guilt had a way of keeping sleep at bay. Behind heavy eyelids, he wept for his father, a bow-legged man who wore thick eyeglasses and a graying beard. Hiding behind closed curtains and locked doors, he continued to grieve. Twice since her passing, they had acknowledged the anniversary of her death with the lighting of Yahrzeit candles and reciting the Kaddish, a prayer for the deceased.

One week after his mother lost her life to renal failure, he was diagnosed with polycystic kidney disease. His father expected the worst outcome for his ailing son. Although Jewish tradition required mirrors to remain covered and faces to go unshaven for ten days during the period of Shiva, he kept the mirrors covered and his face unshaven for two years. Wanting to mourn in private, guests who came to visit were quickly turned away.

Married with three children, he understood the importance of receiving a healthy kidney. When he could no longer work his job as a real estate agent, his wife had taken a job as a receptionist, often leaving their children with her parents when he became too weak to care for them.

When he received the call letting him know it was possible a kidney would be available for transplant, he called his father. Speaking in a gentle voice, he explained that a transplant team would come to Rochester. Remaining silent, his father, an Orthodox Jew, felt conflicted about organ donation.

"Dad, there's a chance I'll be healthy again." Not hearing a response, he continued. "I'll be okay."

"That is all I ask," his father replied.

———

Soon after returning to their home in Chickasaw Gardens after visiting with doctors at Memphis' Le Bonheur Children's Hospital, the parents of five-year-old Luci Woodall, who they lovingly called LuLu, hurried to gather the family together. Hours earlier, they had been told what they waited to hear. It was possible LuLu would be given a cornea.

At age four, she missed weeks of preschool when her vision became distorted and her eyes increasingly sensitive to the classroom's overhead lights. Days before her fifth birthday, she had been diagnosed with keratoconus, a degenerative eye disorder within the cornea that caused it to thin and take on a conical shape.

She did not understand all the excitement until her mother explained the commotion. "There are doctors and an angel in heaven who might help you see again."

In anticipation, she filled a small travel bag with her favorite things to take with her to the hospital. She carefully folded the blanket her grandmother crocheted and gently tucked it into the bag. Hoping her father would have time at the hospital, she packed the book he read to her each night at bedtime. Watching from the door, her mother found it a blessing she was not bothered by the eye shield she wore or the surgical tape that kept it in place.

Up north, on a peninsula known as Locust Point, Jay Wagess worried he would not live to see his seventy-fifth birthday. Growing up along Maryland's coast, he ferried each morning to Sparrow's Point where he worked a ten-hour shift, six days a week, as an industrial laborer. Hefting heavy steel for transportation, he routinely experienced the painful passing of kidney stones. Doubled over and short of breath, he prayed for the guardian angel his mother spoke of when he was a young child to save him. It was during a visit to an emergency room that he was diagnosed with diabetes. Over time, his kidneys began to fail, and within months, he found himself on dialysis and the waiting list for a kidney transplant.

As a transplant candidate, he went through a series of comprehensive tests. When the initial evaluation was complete, he was told the wait might take up to two years. Five years later, he was still making the drive to Baltimore three days a week for the dialysis that now left him physically drained and tired. In that time, he made friends with the center's staff and those, like him, who were in need of a transplant.

Although he lived with chronic kidney failure, he never became discouraged. Every morning before opening his eyes and each evening before they closed, he gave thanks and remained hopeful.

As he and his wife celebrated the upcoming Mother's Day holiday with their children and grandchildren, he received the telephone call from his transplant team letting him know it was possible a suitable donor kidney might be available.

In an idle moment, he found himself thinking of the friends he made at the dialysis center. Recalling most were younger and with small children, a feeling of guilt came over him.

Holding her husband's face in her hands, his wife whispered words meant only for him to hear. "Jay, this is your time. This kidney is being given to you by the angel we've been praying for."

Several states away and hundreds of miles north of Memphis and The Med, twenty-five-year-old Brea McAndray slept comfortably in a dark room on the fifth floor of Omaha's Clarkson Bishop Memorial Hospital. Until now, she could not recall a day when her left eye had been free of pain. Growing up on a cattle ranch along the Platte River, she never questioned the blurred vision in her left eye or its lifeless color. Edging on blindness and uncomfortable in nature's often harsh elements, she preferred to stay indoors. When it was necessary to leave the house, she wore dark sunglasses to protect her sensitive eyes from the gusty winds and blinding sun.

Days earlier, when a corneal ulcer ruptured, she was airlifted to

Clarkson Bishop soon after her own ophthalmologist, who had treated the rare and dangerous infection with ointments, toxic drops, and corneal scrapings, worried he could no longer help her. Upon her arrival, the hospital's renowned ophthalmologist examined her. "To save your eye, you will need a corneal transplant."

CHAPTER 41

The last time Cory's family entered Room 214, loss and acquiescence carried them. Watching the controlled rise and fall of his chest no longer hinted of a miracle, but instead, asked for their acceptance.

Standing close to him, Kirby, Gina, and Jill felt as though an unfair burden had been placed upon them. Although they buried their parents, burying one of their own was unthinkable, until now. Their hearts were hidden in a place foreign to them. He was not supposed to die, not like this, not this young.

Nestled between Gina and Kirby, Jill hated that this day would become a point of reference on her own life's calendar. She did not want to have conversations that began with, "When Cory was alive," or "Before Cory was killed in a biking accident," or "When we decided to let him go." The thought of opening a conversation with any of these words left her feeling angry. Life had cheated him, and in the end, it had also cheated her. He was her family.

Taking his hand, she placed it next to her heart. "My heart breaks for those who never had the opportunity to meet you and it aches for those who were blessed to know and love you. You will never be forgotten. You can rest knowing you made a difference." It pained her to accept that the rest of the chapters of her life would not include him. Before sipping from the glass of water someone had left at his bedside table, she offered it to him. When she placed the plastic straw to his lips, the reality of his injuries suddenly became clear. Putting her finger to his mouth, she traced his lips one last time. Forced to accept she would never again see his smile or hear his laugh tore at her heart. Numbed by the beating in her chest, she searched the space around her for air. In between desperate breaths, she again begged God to reconsider his actions. Fearful of what lay ahead, she fell against his chest. "I'm sorry, Cory. I would give anything to change what happened to you. Please forgive me for not being there for you. Without you, my life will never again be full, but please believe me when I say I will always keep you in my thoughts and close to my heart. I don't want to let you go, but I know it's time. Don't be afraid of what awaits you. The only saving grace in this is knowing Mom and Dad will be waiting for you."

Taking her place next to Jill, Gina thought of the many things death had taken from Cory. Days earlier, before his last ride, he talked about his future and the goals he set not only for his team but also for himself. He was ready to move forward. She laughed when he called himself a *maverick*. He told her he was prepared to sign the divorce papers he had ignored for months and was excited to move on to the next chapter life had waiting for him. "Pain is inevitable and moving on is a choice. Life is good again, Gina," he had said with an enthusiasm she had not heard in months.

Knowing it was time to say good-bye, the mother in her took over. Unlike Jill, she did not rest against Cory. Instead, she pulled a chair next to his bed. "Cory, it's time for you to let go. You're going home now." Her words were heart-felt and sincere, and the tone of her voice was calm and loving. "It's time for you to be with Mom. Sit on her lap and hug her. I wish I could see the look on her face when she wraps you in her arms. You will be the greatest Mother's Day gift she could ever wish for. Let faith guide you. When you hear the angel's harp, search for Dad. If I were a gambler, I would bet my last dollar you will find him strumming his old guitar. I pray when you step through heaven's door, the angels wrap you in their gilded wings. Go, Cory. It's time."

Placing his hand in hers, she was reminded that once the family agreed to organ donation, the machines and monitors supplying oxygen to his body would slowly shut down. She was not aware transplant teams were already underway, making arrangements for transplantation for potential candidates who had already been contacted. Her only thoughts were to tell him she loved him and then allow her heart to let him go. "Cory, I love you more than life itself. I'm so sorry, baby. You will forever be in my heart and my thoughts."

CHAPTER 42

Kirby had not asked, but felt certain Gina and Jill were not emotionally prepared to pack Cory's belongings. Filled with pain and his heart broken, he was not sure he would be able to get through the task he allowed to fall upon him.

Leaving his sisters at The Med, he drove to the apartment complex Cory lovingly called his home. Parking a rented U-Haul in the space where Cory always parked his Jeep, he stared ahead. He asked for strength as he searched the empty space before him. When memories drifted by, he did not have the strength to push them aside.

Several years back, a friend compared Cory to a banyan tree. *"Those people he allows into his heart are eager to wrap him in their arms. Like the tree's twisted roots, they hug to protect him. When he's vulnerable, close friends see his heart and a little bit of the beauty inside. When disappointment broadsides him, he does not ask why. Instead, he looks for a way to adapt."* Knowing the banyan's roots often kill the tree, leaving its core hollow, it was only now he questioned the comparison. Perhaps someday, he would understand. Rubbing at his forehead, he pushed the memory aside.

Twisting the gold band he wore, he recalled his wedding. Ten-years-old and looking polished in a baby blue tuxedo with a white dress shirt so starched the collar pinched his ears, Cory had been his ring bearer. Decades later, when Cory married, he had stood as his best man.

Standing at the front door, the same door Cory faced each time he returned home, he stomped on the woven doormat that failed to live up to its promise. There was nothing welcoming about stepping over the door's threshold, knowing his brother would not be greeting him on the other side. Taking a step back, he kicked the rug aside.

Feeling like an intruder, he struggled to get the silver key the apartment manager had given him into the brass lock. He wanted to ask the manager, a high-strung woman with a no-nonsense attitude and a faint mustache above her lip, to have Cory's belongings packed while his family mourned their loss. Regret's lingering stronghold kept him from throwing Cory's things, along with the rug he turned to stomp on a second time, out to the dumpster.

The last time he helped Cory move was into this apartment. Memories of that day grabbed him, dragging his thoughts in slow motion. He had never seen Cory so excited. Outfitted with new furniture, a set of matching plates, and a three-speed blender, he thought he hit the jackpot. A smile came over his face when he recalled the dinner they shared after the apartment was decorated and new sheets covered the bed. He sent Cory out to get barbecue, a treat he looked forward to each time he visited Memphis. If memory served him, he had been very clear on his order. *"A pulled pork sandwich with coleslaw on the side."* When Cory returned, he was carrying a big bucket of hot wings, a brown bag filled with a variety of hot sauces, and a smile so big it nearly swallowed his face.

Opening the door to Cory's apartment, his eyes flew wide open. At first glance, he thought the apartment had been ransacked. While he considered making a call to the local police, memories of earlier years reminded him that this was how Cory lived. Searching the wall, he was discouraged when a light switch failed to deliver. Moving into the narrow hall, he gave a sigh of relief when his finger flipped a working switch.

A muddied running shoe, its tongue tangled up in the laces, rested in the corner. Its mate was buried under a rolled-up garden hose and a ball of twine. A flyer from a sandwich delivery service and a reminder from the property manager asking Cory to reply if he planned to attend the up-coming Memorial Day picnic, littered the floor. Centered on an exposed brick wall, the Thomas Kinkade painting he won in a raffle hung askew. Worn tube socks blanketed a pile of old running shoes and an empty GU packet clung to the wall. The sleeper sofa was home to unfolded bath tow-els and race shirts left inside out. A black and white Nike flip-flop peeked out from between the cushions. Heat sheets from old swim meets were scattered about on the low coffee table he recognized from his childhood, and a chewed pencil marked a dog-eared page in a recent issue of a swim magazine. Brushing over the wood with the tip of his finger, he traced the table's familiar carvings. He did not have to turn the table on its side to know his initials were carved into its underbelly.

Overhead, a bamboo ceiling fan hummed in rhythm with a low squeak as it struggled to cool the warm room. Stepping over a mound of wet towels, a sandy crunch under his feet reminded him of Cory's weekend at the beach. Impulse made him reach for the sand-filled towels. Holding a damp towel under his nose, he was hit with a wave of memories. Inhaling a cocktail of seawater, chlorine, coconut-scented sunscreen, and a hint of diaper rash cream, he would forever associate the unusual mix with his brother. If Cory had been at his side, he would have teased him until their silliness had them laughing. Unfortunately, alone in the apartment, and without his brother to encourage him, he could not find a reason to laugh.

Wringing his hands and biting at his lip, he fought the urge to run out the door. He had been in the apartment only a few minutes and already the memories were too much for him. He was relieved when the faint sound of a clock's alarm cut through the eerie silence. Wandering through the small space, he was suddenly aware of the sour smell of burnt coffee. As a child, Cory had once complained the smell of fried coffee reminded him of the neighbor's basement. Living down the road from the town's only mortician who ran his business from his home, their father raised an eyebrow. Pushing the memory aside, he hurried into the kitchen. Yanking the cord from the outlet, he placed the glass pot in the sink. Later, after it cooled, he would toss it in the dumpster along with the unwelcomed mat.

Not knowing where or how to begin the process of placing the bits and pieces of Cory's short life into cardboard boxes, he stared at the walls. This had to be a mistake. Cory was too young to die. He had always believed in miracles and maybe, just maybe, Cory would be given one.

Moving about the apartment and stepping into Cory's personal space, he struggled to press on. Nothing about this invasion seemed acceptable. Knowing Cory kept his personal life private and often went to great lengths to guard it, guilt and respect kept him from opening drawers, looking inside closets, and shuffling through a stack of mail Cory had collected from the mailbox but failed to open. What he could not ignore was an open envelope. Next to it, a pen rested on the divorce papers.

Overwhelmed and ready to surrender, he turned to leave. He would rather pay the apartment's monthly rent than pack up remnants of Cory's life only to haul it back to his home in Nashville where it would come to rest in a dark corner of the garage. Cory deserved better.

Passing by the entry hall's closet, he placed his forehead against the door. If he walked out, it was doubtful he would return. This moment would never get easier. Not on this day, months down the road, or in a year's time. He would not leave his sisters to do a job he could not handle. Minutes later, when a clear mind prevailed, he turned the knob on the closet door.

Expecting the small space to be filled with fleece jackets and Memphis Thunder sweatshirts his brother lovingly called his *work uniform*, finding instead Cory's collection of ABBA albums was a stab to his heart. As far back as he could remember, he had teased him about his taste in music. "*Girl stuff,*" he often joked. Sifting through the old album covers, he managed to grin when he noticed that the cover of the group's Christmas souvenir edition was autographed and dated. *Oh, what he would have given to rib his brother at this moment.*

Pushing aside jackets and the trophies Cory refused to present to deserving winners for fear of alienating those who might be left feeling less about themselves, he continued his search. Rummaging through the dark space, he tossed aside race helmets, speed skates, and a stack of Sergio Tacchini tracksuits and warm-ups that soon after the 1980s could be found at garage sales and thrift stores. Reaching the closet's back wall, he eyed his father's guitar case. Taking the guitar from its case, he held it in his hands. Pulling a string, a lifetime of memories rushed at him. Before his mother's surgery, she would gather the children around her when their father reached for Gumbo, the name he pinned on the guitar when a friend flattered him by saying, *"You throw everything you have into your music and it always comes out full of flavor."*

Because his sisters always hurried to take a seat beside their mother, their father usually sat on the floor. When Cory was a toddler, Jill would scoot over, making room for him next to their mother. Crouched on the floor with the guitar in his able hands, their father would relax against the wall, and with a tenderness he seldom displayed, strum the old guitar as though it was an extension of his soul. His strong hands hammered the notes. Sometimes, when the sweet-sounding music he played moved him, he would lock eyes with their mother, but most of the time he would just bow his head, close his eyes, and allow the guitar's seductive poetry to whisk him away, even if only for a short while. While the children listened in silence, exchanging contented smiles, their mother had almost always been brought to tears.

Heavy with an emptiness he had never known before, he longed to laugh with his little brother one last time. If longing made wishes come true, he would want their father to come along for one last ride. Cupping his face with his hands, he cried the tears he held back when his father died. Sliding down the wall, he collapsed into a ball. Holding the skateboard Cory rode to the complex's laundry center, he sobbed for his brother and the pain he undoubtedly suffered. He cried for the loss of not only his father, but for the little time he had with his mother. Rocking back and forth, he shouted into the abyss that once again he had been cheated.

Hearing a tap at the door, he wiped his face on his sleeve. Glancing up, he was relieved to see Gina and Jill. For several minutes, no words were exchanged. What they shared, these three siblings who would forever suffer such an unbearable loss, were images that would forever haunt them and a deluge of tears only they would understand.

"We thought you'd like some company," Gina said. Searching his empty face, she again spoke, only this time there was resignation in her voice. "We are the last of our family."

Jill shook her head. Disbelief kept its hold on her as she slowly surveyed Cory's apartment. "It's difficult to find anything to be grateful for. I'm just glad Dad didn't live long enough to have to bury his son."

"I think when Cory's marriage failed, he lost his compass, and then just as he was finding his way, this happens." Fighting back tears, Gina glanced about the apartment. "Cory got so much satisfaction giving to others what he didn't have. We were the closest he had to a mother. We were his family. Bottom line, Cory never had a mother. You know, I'm beginning to think he left early because he needed to be with her."

Agreeing, Kirby nodded. "In many ways, I think we stepped into the shoes her death left behind."

Pushing her sleeves up to her elbows, Gina scanned the room. "Do you remember that clock I gave Cory? It was bronze with Roman numerals. It used to be on the mantle."

"Was it a wedding gift?" Jill asked, looking to the fireplace. Although she visited many times in recent months, it was only now she questioned the paintings on the wall and the eclectic furniture. Knowing Cory better than anyone, she knew these were not pieces he would have chosen to decorate his home. Her smile did not hide her pain when she recalled the time he tried to convince her a folding chair tucked in a corner was chic and stylish. The next time she visited, she laughed when he tried to convince her a cardboard box was an ottoman. Searching the apartment, she noticed the box and the folding chair had gone missing. "What do you think happened to it? The clock, I mean?"

Coming unhinged, Gina let loose the hurricane in her. "I have a pretty good idea. Anyway, it is what it is. It no longer matters. All of that is history now. We have to pack this apartment. I'll start with the kitchen."

Sweeping a hand through her hair, she turned to Jill. "Are you okay to pack his bedroom?"

Pulling at an empty box, Jill stopped at the bedroom door. "I don't know why, but I always thought something would happen to him. I've had these crazy dreams where snakes were coming for him. I've never understood the dream, but it made me fear for him. Do you remember the time he told us about the beautiful woman dressed all in white who always appeared in his doorway at night? He said she just smiled at him. She never spoke. I think Mom was checking on him."

Gina recalled hearing about the woman in white, and while she reflected on the many times Cory spoke of her, she chose not to respond. Instead, she thought of the close relationship Jill and Cory shared. She had always been jealous, a little envious perhaps, of their special bond. For as long as she could remember, Jill had been Cory's closest friend. They were best buddies. Growing up alongside them and witnessing their interactions, it was easy to understand why her younger siblings were so close. When Jill was in fourth grade and Cory was in kindergarten, Jill convinced him to stay home from school. Three weeks later, their father had been summoned to appear in truancy court. When the court ordered adult supervision, they had to hire a live-in housekeeper. Unable to help care for Jill and Cory, it was one of the few times she regretted moving out of the house at such a young age. She wanted to be a better role model, but life got in the way. She was a young woman with dreams of her own.

Returning to the task before her, she searched the cabinet under the sink. "Something in here smells like burnt rubber and apricots." Pinching her nose, she slammed the door. "I'll clean the refrigerator, too." Holding a garbage bag, she prayed for strength.

———

Alone in Cory's bedroom, Jill brushed her hand over the unmade bed. Stepping out of her slip-on shoes, she eased her way over crumpled blankets to a clearing near the edge. Turning on her side, an imprint on the far pillow let her know where he rested his head in the hours before his accident. Knowing he preferred to sleep in a dark bedroom, her eyes were drawn to the open blinds. She tried desperately to separate the many feelings racing through her mind, but it was the sense of emptiness that refused to budge. Careful not to disturb his pillow, she reached to the floor for one of the matching throw pillows she was surprised to find in his bedroom. Pulling a blanket under her chin, she wondered if she should take his pillow back to Texas.

She had been blessed to have Cory in her life and feared the void his death would leave behind would never be filled. Allowing tears to run down her face, she recalled the time they asked their father for permission to go to the skating rink. When he refused, she had taken matters into her own hands. Waiting quietly, and keeping a watchful eye on her father, she called for a taxi seconds after he had fallen asleep on the couch. Counting coins, she had been excited to find she had enough money in her piggy bank to pay for the driver and the cost of getting into the rink. Separating nickels and dimes into quarter stacks, she squealed when she counted the amount needed to pay the skate rental fees.

Long after they circled the rink forward and backward, they participated in the Hokey Pokey. Turning themselves around, they stopped for a rest when Cory tripped over his skates, kicked and shuffled about to stay upright, and after taking a hit from behind by an unknown speed demon, landed hard on his bottom. After losing in the final round of the limbo contest, the rink's closing competition, she realized she did not have money to pay for a taxi ride home. Given no choice, the rink's manager called their father. A smile swept over her face when she recalled the silent treatment she and Cory had been given during the car ride home.

Curled up in a ball, and resting on an elbow, she surveyed the bedroom. Wrinkled clothes fell from an open drawer, a pool of blue ink coddled a shattered pen, and a stack of paperbacks and yellowed newspapers hugged the wall. A thin layer of dust rested on the windowsill. Inches away from a metal trashcan overflowing with empty water bottles and grocery receipts, plastic wrappers from an energy bar popular among long-distance runners muddled the floor. In the narrow space between the bed and the room's long wall, a canvas satchel rested against an iron bedpost. For a moment, she wondered what it held, but something told her it was filled with swim stuff and wrappers from snacks Cory turned to when enjoying a healthy meal was not possible.

On the mirrored bureau, next to a copy of *Awaken the Olympian Within,* a dog-eared paperback Cory read to page seventy-four and would never read to its best-seller finish, were three pictures. In a frame carved from oak, was a photo of their mother taken during her senior year at Rogersville High School. Her coiffed hair rested inches below her shoulders and the silver necklace around her neck proudly displayed her monogrammed initials. A gilded frame she believed was a recent birthday gift or given at Christmas protected Cory's baby picture. His chubby hands held a blanket a neighbor had made from fabric scraps days before his arrival. Reaching for the last photo, she was again brought to tears. It was his toothless grin that let her know the picture was taken decades earlier when he repeated kindergarten.

Looking at the wall, her chest grew tight. Staring back at her was the Dallas Cowboys poster he treasured. Each time it was taken off a wall, sticky tape tore away at a corner. Fearing she might be sick, she returned to the comfort the unkempt bed provided.

Turning to the bedside table, her heart grew heavy when she recognized the Tag Heuer dive watch that had once belonged to her father. Taking it in her hands, she noticed the numbers on the plastic dial were faded. The worn engraving on the back let her know the timepiece had been purchased soon after they moved to Schooner Bay. Next to it was the Ironman watch she had questioned the nurse about at The Med. Shaking her head, she knew she would not remember to apologize. Beside them was Cory's wallet. Resting against the bed's headboard, she slipped the Ironman watch over her wrist, and with a heaviness she worried would smother her, she pressed the wallet against her hollowed chest. The soft leather was worn and faded, and because Cory had carried it in his back pocket, its shape had taken a comfortable curve. Although uncomfortable about violating his privacy, she longed to see what he held close and carried with him. With unsure hands, she pulled it open.

The corners of his Tennessee driver's license were chewed and the clear laminate had peeled away in three of its four corners. White circles around his eyes and a ghostly strip over the arch of his nose let her know he had been wearing sunglasses in recent days before the picture was taken. Running a fingertip over his picture, she put to memory the color of his eyes, his date of birth, and the poundage he had given to an uncaring clerk with the Department of Motor Vehicles. Careful not to cause further damage, she returned it to its rightful place. Tucked away in another pocket was a frequent customer card from a local copy center and an expired American Express card. Taped to the charge card was a replacement card he had not activated. A third pocket secured his membership card to the YMCA on Walker Avenue. Its expiration date had come and gone. Hidden in the folded cash was an appointment card from the Clip Joint. He was scheduled for a haircut the following Saturday. Wondering if she should cancel the appointment, she placed the card aside. Finding ticket stubs from a Pat Green concert encouraged more tears. He loved country music almost as much as he loved the Cowboys. She was not surprised to find he had saved the concert stubs and the ticket for the Dallas Cowboys game. Recalling the night she picked him up in Plano put a smile on her face. He got a kick out of telling his friends about the time he traveled to Dallas, arrived at the stadium hours before kickoff, and somehow managed to miss the game.

Wiping at tears, she returned the treasures to their final resting place. Brushing her hand over the leather, she placed the wallet on the bedside table.

Dragging from the bed, she made her way into the bathroom, where she came face to face with his bathrobe. Taking the worn robe from the hook, she recalled the day she purchased it for him. She had just arrived in Memphis for a weekend visit when he answered the door wearing a Thunder pullover and boxer shorts. Before lunching at the Blue Cactus, his favorite Mexican restaurant, she insisted upon taking him shopping for a robe. He chuckled when she pointed to his legs. "Your gams may be shapely, but I'm begging you to cover them. They're blinding me. Keep this up and I might have to start calling you Casper." Laughing, he promised to get a suntan. "Robes are for old people," he squawked. He fought the idea of wearing a robe, but once they found a navy one, his favorite color, he was on board.

Placing the robe to her face, she recognized the woodsy scent he often wore. *He loved the outdoors.* Whimpering, she slipped her arms into the robe's three-quarter sleeves and tied the narrow belt around her waist.

Moving to the shower, she stared at the clear, plastic curtain. Invading his personal space made her feel light-headed and uncomfortable. She knew he would hate putting his family through this. A private man who not only kept secrets but also honored them, and preferring to take the high road while turning a blind eye to misguided shortcomings, he would not have wanted his family to walk among the evidence of his last living moments. Catching her breath, she forced her eyes to search the small space.

Pushing the curtain aside, she took a step back. A scummy film circled the tub, and broken bits of soap caked the drain. Hanging from the showerhead, a plastic caddy held a bottle of salon shampoo and a blue and white toothbrush. Pulling at the curtain, she turned her attention to the vanity.

Sifting through an open drawer filled with disposable razors, a used deodorant stick, and a mangled tube of uncapped toothpaste, her eyes were drawn to a wide-handled hairbrush. Tangled in the ball-tipped bristles were strands of red hair. Whimpering, she pulled at the curls. Running the brush through her own hair, she thought of the many times she threatened to tie him to a chair and shave his head. This had been an ongoing routine that always ended with him allowing her to brush the snarls and tangles from his wild mane. It had driven her crazy when he would go weeks without combing his locks.

Tucking the hairbrush into the pocket of the robe, she pulled open the door to the linen closet. There she found a corrugated box tucked in the far corner. Curious what it held, she slid the brown box across the large square tiles to the center of the room. Tearing at the tape, she hurried to glimpse inside. Recognizing the Christmas stocking he made decades earlier in Sunday school, she pulled it from the box. Feeling something deep down in the toe of the red and green felt stocking, she held it to her nose before reaching inside. For a passing moment, she worried a chocolate Santa or a marshmallow nutcracker had gone unfound all these years. Finding Chimpa, she unleashed a wave of tears.

Growing up, the colorful sock toy had been his favorite. She would never forget the time he climbed onto her lap holding Chimpa in his grasp. He smiled up at her and said "mine," confidently declaring it his when she tried to take it from him.

Stroking Chimpa's yarned hair, she felt his presence. Looking up, she searched the mirror for answers. *Would she find them? Probably not.* Like best-kept secrets, the reasons for his death were not hers to know or question, but only to accept. Perhaps later, with the passing of time, she would find answers and be given understanding.

Placing Chimpa on her lap, she returned to the box. This time, looking back at her was Cory's collection of comic books. *Oh, how he loved The Incredible Hulk.* Every Halloween, she and Gina would paint his face with costume makeup they purchased at a five-cent store. Before he escaped into the night on his mission to ward off bad guys and rid homes of sweet treats, they took scissors to old shirts already several sizes too small for his growing body, and pinking shears to the jeans they found at local thrift stores.

On Saturday mornings, oftentimes while eating breakfast, he would sit in the middle of the floor, his eyes glued to a boxy television with a broken dial and rabbit ears, while The Hulk saved the day. He would not move until the credits rolled at the end of the episode.

Placing the worn and yellowed books at her side, she combed through photographs. Searching the pictures, she stopped to appreciate the collection of school pictures his young swimmers had given him over the years. For a moment, she allowed herself to take notice of Silvie and Margo. The first time she met them, he had been coaching the Memphis Tigers. He adored them, and having talked with them at The Med, she could see the feeling was mutual. Holding their school pictures in her grasp, she worried they, too, would never be the same without him.

Setting aside the dozens of Christmas cards she would read later when her heart allowed, she returned to the box. She smiled a little when she found her father's coin collection. He had a pension for finding value in old things. When she was a young girl, she thought he was trying to save money, but later, as she was finding her way in life, she had taken an interest in antiques, especially those pieces that held stories. It was only now she realized she had never spoken with her father of their shared interest.

When she came upon a picture of Cory taken on his wedding day, her chest grew heavy. Standing with the sun behind him, she thought he looked like an angel. Thinking about him now, she prayed he would be given wings made of glitter and gold. "Oh, Cory. I'm so sorry. I stood on the sidelines, too young to understand that the life you were thrown was not one you could handle. Being older didn't make me any wiser. When I think back on our childhood, I'm actually amazed we turned out as well as we did." Unable to continue, she placed the pictures and holiday cards back in the box.

On a shelf in the closet, bath towels were neither folded nor rolled, but shoved into a tight space shared with beach towels and unopened boxes of travel-size soap she gathered he took from hotels when he was away at swim meets. Taking a cologne bottle from the middle shelf, she gave the air a light spritz of Eternity. Thinking of Cory and the monitors hooked up to his lifeless body, she found the cologne's name apropos. Replacing the top, she tucked the bottle into the robe's pocket. Feeling the hairbrush, she returned to the bedside table. With a gentleness the wallet deserved, she placed it in her pocket. Taking the Tag Heuer in her hand, she closed her eyes. Losing her father and baby brother months apart pulled at her heart. Placing her father's timepiece on her wrist, she prayed for help and guidance.

Down the hall, Gina stared at the open refrigerator. Used tissues and a roll of toilet paper sat on her lap. When she offered to clean the refrigerator, she expected to find half-empty jars of spicy mayo, pickles that did not live up to the label's promise, and long-forgotten wilted lettuce leaves—the usual suspects Cory kept in the fridge.

Placing a trashcan at her side, she thought the task would be easy, but opening the door, her attention was immediately drawn to ribeye steaks on a platter. Numb, she held the refrigerator door wide open. Wiping her eyes with toilet paper, she spotted the Weber grill on the apartment's narrow patio. Resting against the rail was an unopened bag of charcoal briquettes. *Two steaks? Was he expecting a guest?* Looking back at the meal he planned to enjoy turned her stomach. Slamming the door, she was surprised to find Jill at her side. Eyeing the robe and its bulging pockets, her face softened. "I had forgotten about that. What's in the pockets?"

"His hairbrush and a bottle of cologne." Jill answered, patting at her side. Holding back tears, she pulled the wallet from the other pocket. "I want to keep this."

Nodding, she turned back to the refrigerator. "He was marinating steaks for dinner."

"Steaks? As in more than one?"

Opening the door a second time, she pointed to the seasoned ribeyes. "He was expecting company." Reaching for a carton of milk, she glanced at the expiration date stamped on the plastic lid. *May 10, 2005.* Angered by the coincidence, she clenched her teeth as she slammed the carton into the garbage.

Finding a recipe for grilled salmon taped to the wall sent Jill into a rage. "This was no accident. He had taken the first step into his new life and was not planning just one meal, but two. Someone wanted him gone."

Surprised by her sister's outburst, Gina threw her hands in the air. "What are you suggesting? That Cory was murdered?"

"It's not out of the realm of possibilities, you know. Think about it, Gina. He had this great team. He had everything to live for. Maybe a coach was jealous and decided to have him taken out. Or maybe it was about money."

"That's insane." Turning to a stack of mail, she tore open an envelope. "He had four hundred and eleven dollars in his bank account. And nine cents, if you include the change."

"We know people have been killed for far less."

Pressing her back against the counter, Gina crossed her arms over her chest. "Cory was not murdered. What happened to him was an accident."

Falling into a seat at the table, Jill fanned her hands on the table. "I can't do this, pack his apartment, I mean. It's too personal..." her voice faded.

Pulling a chair from the table, she sat down next to her. "I remember when Cory begged to ride Space Mountain, the high-speed roller coaster at Magic Kingdom." Recalling his excitement as he waited in the long line brought a smile to her face. "Mike and I had taken the kids earlier in the day, and all Cory talked about was coming back later that night to ride Space Mountain. All day long it was Space Mountain this, Space Mountain that. He drove us crazy." Finding the memory funny, she paused for a moment. "You know, it feels good to smile."

Having heard the story many times before, Jill joined in the laugh. Melancholy was cut short when she shared a story from decades before. "He was hardly the daredevil. Even when he was just a little kid, he played it safe." Recalling the time she dared him to let go of the bike's handlebars put a lump in her throat. Losing control of the bike, he had flown over the handlebars and into the ditch. When he crawled up to the road, his face was as raw as hamburger meat. Lowering her head, she wished his last fall had been blessed with a similar outcome.

Hearing his sisters reminisce, Kirby joined them in the kitchen. "I heard you mention Space Mountain. He was what? Twelve years old?"

Searching her memory, Gina tilted her head. "Maybe thirteen. He was at that awkward stage. His arms and legs were growing faster than his brain could keep up. I remember the line for the ride wrapped around the corner and edged up to the concession stand. It was a good thing he was too excited to eat." Reclined in the chair, she repeated the story she shared many times before.

"There was a posted sign that let you let know the expected wait time was over two hours, and along the way, there were opportunities to exit the line. As with most rides, the line moved at a snail's pace. Mike kept asking Cory if he thought the wait was worth it or if he wanted to jump on an exit to go to a different ride, but he was dead-set on riding Space Mountain. *'Are you sure, Cory? I hear it's pretty scary,'* Mike had asked over and over. *'I'm sure, Mike. It's Space Mountain.'* Each time an exit presented itself, Mike would again ask if he wanted to come back another time, and each time his answer was the same. *'We're almost there!'* Hours later, when they finally reached the top, Cory suddenly had a change of heart. Standing high on the platform and looking at the ground below, he worried he would fall to his death. The thrill of riding Space Mountain was replaced with fear. When he turned to make his escape, Mike grabbed at the collar of his shirt. I was watching from the ground and I knew he was scared. He was screaming at the top of his lungs. Mike told me later that Cory was so terrified he closed his eyes and hid his face in his lap. The next day Mike had bruises all over him."

Together, as only siblings could, they laughed at the story they were sure to always remember. Visiting the past, if only for a few minutes, allowed them to escape the truth and move away from their pain. In their hearts, they knew if Cory had been with them, either in arm's reach or a phone call away, he would have laughed along with them.

Moving to the living room, they continued to share their favorite memories.

"I will never forget his first triathlon. It was the summer before his senior year of high school. Dad had accepted the job in the Virgin Islands, working for the same builder who hired him after Mom died. Cory didn't want to return to St. Croix or remain in Memphis. He wanted to go back to Halfway, the town that always welcomed and embraced him."

It was easy to recall Cory's conversation with their father. *"I don't know what will bring me fortune and fame, but I'm pretty certain I won't find it in plywood and sheet rock."* Returning to Halfway, old friends invited him to stay at their home. In exchange, he was expected to help with the daily chores on the family's farm.

Growing quiet, Kirby recalled the summer Cory came to live with him in California. Immediately after graduation, he decided he was not ready for college. Taking a sojourn, he promised their father he would pursue college the following year. In the interim, he moved to San Diego. Arriving by bus with all of his worldly possessions in a backpack, he was eager to explore the coastal city. Needing transportation, he used the little money he had to buy a Schwinn Le Tour bike he found at a consignment shop.

Admiring the coastline as he biked his way around the area, he found life in San Diego exciting and refreshing. In place of dairy farms, fields of corn, and miles of unpaved roads, he saw cyclists. He learned the sleek bikes they rode were racing bikes designed for the sport of triathlon. It did not take long for him to grow envious of the racers outfitted in team gear and the camaraderie and fellowship they displayed and seemed to enjoy. Riding his bike to a nearby library, Cory read everything he could get his hands on about the swim, bike, and run sport, and soon realized San Diego was the mecca for multi-sport training.

In the early morning hours, about the time Kirby left for work, Cory would take to the streets. Learning the city, he rode the wide streets, some heavily traveled and others without stop signs or signals, stopping only to eat the peanut butter sandwich he packed before leaving the house. On a morning when he joined a group of serious cyclists, he struggled to keep up, but determination kept him in the pack. Riding single file, he was careful to stay out of drafting zones. When he needed to overtake a slowing cyclist, he passed on the left. The leader of the chain gang, a term he learned from a fellow enthusiast, was a climber. Leaving the pack, he picked up speed each time they encountered an incline. When the cyclists stopped for a water break, he recognized Mark Allen, a respected Ironman he read about in several of the magazines the library offered. Overhearing Mark's plan for the next day's ride, he locked the time and location in his memory. At that moment, what he wanted more than anything, was to train with these elite athletes. *"A fraternity of friends,"* he called them. When he learned they were gearing up for a triathlon, he wanted to give it a try. Filling out his race entry at a bike shop he passed each morning, he was motivated to get into shape.

The following weeks had him in hard-core training. Needing help with his technique, he joined the university's master swim program. When he was not coughing up pool water, he was holding onto the navy and gold ropes. Worried he would hold the others back, the coach gave him his own lane. Logging hundreds of miles on the bike, he did not feel it was necessary to include running in his training schedule. He was confident his strong legs would carry him through the triathlon's run portion.

Soon, he excelled in the early-morning bike rides. Keeping in pace with Mark Allen, he soon met Dave Scott and Paula Newby-Fraser, tri-athletes who not only pioneered the sport but also earned their living competing in triathlons all over the map.

The morning of the event had him feeling well rested and ready to compete. Having witnessed the results of his dedication and hard work, Kirby was excited to watch the triathlon, especially the first wave that placed the most talented athletes out in front.

The triathlon's first leg was a 200-meter swim. Recognizing his brother by the race bib he wore, Kirby cheered from the sidelines. Hearing his name, Cory turned and gave a fist pump in the air. When he entered the water, everyone was surprised to see he was swimming the dog paddle. Concerned he would drown, race officials in kayaks flanked alongside, escorting him through the swim portion. It did not worry him that he was the last swimmer out of the water, because he knew he would make up for lost time in the bike and run portions.

Now, telling the story to Gina and Jill, Kirby fell into a belly laugh. "By the time Cory was on the bike, the asphalt was so hot it burned the rubber off his tires." He would never forget the look of panic on Cory's face, or that he never stopped to blink, as he rode in on bent rims.

Recalling another biking accident that put him in the hospital, Jill placed a hand over her heart. "I remember Cory's triathlon in Lemoore, California. The force from a passing truck blew him off his bike. Poor kid was covered with road rash."

While their thoughts turned to him at The Med and the injuries he suffered, the room grew silent. There would never come a time when they would find humor in this accident. Although the words never escaped her lips, Gina believed God had not intended for his actions to leave behind a pain the passing of time would never heal. She wanted to believe God needed Cory in heaven, and although he was no longer present, his life did not stop on that long stretch of open road. The pain was still too fresh to understand what it was they were to accept. Her only thought was that God's timing had been premature. Calling Cory home at a time when he was ready to embrace the future was unfair.

Resting on the sofa, Kirby again thought back to his wedding. The only other time he had seen Cory in a suit was at his own wedding. Tears ran down his cheeks when he realized the last time Cory would wear a suit would be for his own funeral. Depressed by the thought, he welcomed Jill's interruption.

"You know, mom died at thirty-five, too. I remember she had to wear socks all the time. Their similarities don't end there. At age thirty-five, they both suffered a fatal brain injury in the month of May, days away from Mother's Day."

Giving it some thought, Gina found a reason to smile. "Perhaps that was always the plan."

In a faint voice, Jill spoke up. "I think we should bury him between them. Between mom and dad."

Recalling the space between their parent's final resting place, Gina agreed. "He would want that. He would be home." The thought of Cory reuniting with their parents brought a smile to her face. "You know, he would want us to speak as though he were here with us. Imagine his pain if he were to hear us skirt around him and the life he lived. The truth is, he will always be with us. Anything less would tear at his tender heart. He would want us to speak of him, mention his name, talk of his fiery ringlets, and laugh at the silliness he etched in our lives. We should live as though we expect him to walk through the door, pull a chair from the table, and laugh with us as we share precious stories of the short time we were given with him. We must promise to never allow the passing of time to take him from us." Grabbing a tissue, she wiped at her face. "Cory's life isn't over—he's just waiting for us to catch up."

Moved by his sister's words, Kirby knew only to nod in agreement. "You two should head back to the hospital. I'll take care of things here."

"Are you sure? There's still a lot to do."

His heart ached with a pain he feared would never go away, but he was stronger than his sisters. "I'll take everything home with me. We can go through his things later."

Turning away, he cleared his throat. "We're expected to meet with the transplant coordinator first thing in the morning. After that, we'll need to begin making funeral arrangements."

CHAPTER 43

Resting at his home in Halle Plantation, Bob Compton withdrew from the world. Retreating to the home's guest room, he begged for Cory's accident to be a nightmare. Window shades were drawn and lights were lowered. Clutching his cell phone, he buried his face in the pillow. Afraid to miss a call from Cory, he turned the phone's volume to its loudest setting.

Cory had been more than a friend. He was like a brother. In their brief time together, he had encouraged him to be a better man. When Cory pulled him off the sofa and away from the computer, he showed him a world he wanted to be a part of. Watching Cory coach, he wanted to be a part of his team.

He could not deny he had done well at Harvard, or that he had given his best to Sofamor Danek. As the group's president and CEO, he had been richly rewarded, but Cory opened his eyes to what was important at the very core of one's existence—living life. He pushed him to do better and be better. He taught him physical discipline and proper nutrition. Within minutes of meeting him, he knew Cory was a man of honor. Learning of his early years, he admired and respected his determination.

Thinking back upon his own life and what he hoped to leave as his legacy, his thoughts turned to Cory. Speaking his name aloud, he promised his friend he would find a way to honor him.

CHAPTER 44

The only light in the room, other than the sliver the small window offered, came from matching candlestick lamps. The walls were the color of rosemary, and blue and gold tasseled pillows and a floral throw added a splash of color to the room's two-piece sectional. A glass coffee table separated the taupe sectional from matching wingback chairs, whose tapestry fabric complemented the sectional's box edge pillows. The room's framed art looked like it belonged in a villa overlooking Italy's famed and picturesque Amalfi Coast. Painted in oils by artists whose names were difficult to pronounce, the rugged coastlines, cascading bougainvillea, and yachts anchored in the Mediterranean's serene waters were meant to provide a calming atmosphere when decisions regarding loved ones were discussed and decided.

The first to enter the room, Kirby moved to a chair near the window. Leaning back against the tufted fabric, he pressed his legs against the low table. Holding hands, Gina and Jill hugged the sectional's wide corner.

The donor coordinator took a seat in the empty chair and offered her condolences. "I want you to know this moment is often the most difficult and painful part of letting go. While God holds one hand, you are holding the other. I believe in the weeks, months, and years to come, you'll find comfort in knowing you and Cory chose to give the most unselfish gift—the gift of life."

Pulling away from Gina, Jill folded her hands in her lap. "I'm not ready for this."

Uncrossing her legs, Gina shifted about. "We are so torn. They tell us he's already gone, but we see him and his chest rising and falling." She looked to Kirby and Jill for affirmation. "We don't want to agree to anything if there is a chance—even the slightest—Cory will pull through this. He's the baby of the family. This isn't a decision we want to make in error."

"I don't want to believe that he is already gone," Jill whimpered into a tissue.

Finding it his time to speak, Kirby lowered his eyes to the floor. "I'm unsure about donating his heart, and I think Jill is torn about donating his eyes."

Sensitive to their concerns, the coordinator, the same woman who met with them soon after Cory had been admitted to the trauma unit, spoke in a nurturing voice. "I want to tell you the story of a man I met last year at the Transplant Games." She was referring to the festival that provides an opportunity for transplant recipients and living donors to compete in athletic events. It also celebrates the lives of organ donors. "He was a freshman in high school when a science experiment exploded inches from his face. His corneas were severely damaged. Accepting it as his fate, it never angered him that he lost the gift of sight. Living as a blind man, he graduated from college, married his high-school sweetheart, and welcomed four children into their family. When his wife of thirty years read an article about us in their local newspaper, she urged him to visit an ophthalmologist. Eight months later, he saw his wife and children for the first time. Days before the games, this man celebrated his sixtieth birthday." Reaching across the table, the young woman offered Jill a tissue, who hearing the story, was brought to tears. "More than 47,000 corneas were transplanted last year and the waiting list is far greater."

Lowering their heads, Cory's family sat in silence. Although their hearts were filled with pain, the tears they cried were moving toward acceptance. Turning to his sisters, Kirby knew they, like him, had arrived at a decision. "Losing Cory leaves a void in our lives, but in time, we believe—and we have to hope—we will find comfort in knowing that through his gifts, others will be given the chance to live healthier lives." Looking to Jill, he continued. "And others will be given the gift of sight."

Sitting tall and taking Jill's hand, Gina cleared her throat. "Just as he had in life, Cory continues to give. We only stay on this earth until we accomplish what God put us here to do. Cory made a difference, and in giving hope to others, I know he is allowed a place in heaven. I think I speak for all of us when I say we are, and continue to be, so proud of him."

CHAPTER 45

In the early morning hours, on Sunday, May 15, 2005, long before they were expected at Cory's memorial service, his family rode in silence in a black limousine provided for their travel. Kirby wore a dark suit and white button-down shirt, and Gina was dressed in a fitted jacket and an A-line skirt she purchased months earlier before attending their father's funeral. Dressed conservatively in a black dress, Jill played with the strand of black pearls that once belonged to their mother.

Traveling along Houston Levee, their hearts were heavy and their minds and bodies empty. The mood was sober, and as expected, tears were plentiful. The day ahead promised to be long and trying, and although they fought them, they were often given reasons to question their faith. They had been in full agreement when they decided that on this morning they would mourn their loss in private.

Turning onto Raleigh Lagrange, each tried to imagine what it must have been like for Cory when he traveled along this road minutes before his life ended. Looking through the tinted windows, they were certain he noticed the budding tulips and the blossoming crepe myrtle trees in the road's wide median. Crossing over a narrow bridge, they wondered if he had stopped to admire the small creek flowing beneath.

Eyeing a convenience store up ahead, Gina asked the driver to pull over. "I'll be just a minute," she promised as she exited the car. Minutes later, when she returned, she was carrying a large paper bag. Before Kirby could question the timing of her purchase, she offered him a Bud Light tall boy, Cory's favorite beer. "I have one for Cory, too."

Inside a white, picket fence, a tall, wooden cross displayed Cory's name along with painted images of a swimmer, cyclist, and runner, the three sports of triathlon. A Thunder sweatshirt fell from a post and a framed picture of Cory taken during a recent bike ride rested against it. Red roses framed a poster of the Dallas Cowboys while the ground was carpeted with cards and letters visitors to the site of the accident left behind. Someone placed a bag of popcorn, a treat he often enjoyed during morning swim practice, at the foot of the cross.

Twisting the aluminum caps, they raised the bottles in the air. Together, they toasted their little brother and the legacy he would surely leave behind.

With unsteady hands, Gina sipped from the dark bottle. "Cory, you always looked for the positive, not just in life, but in everyone you met and in everything you did. I have no doubt you will soon be coaching heaven's swim team. From now on, I will believe every falling raindrop is a splash from heaven's pool. Each time I reach for an umbrella or see a trickle down the window, I will imagine you and the angels are playing a game of sharks and minnows." She then turned her face to the sky. "I'm not the best swimmer, but I hope you'll save a spot for me on your team."

Following Gina's lead, Jill lifted the bottle to her lips. "You were the best little brother anyone could ever ask for. I'm going to miss laughing with you, the long talks I was hoping we would continue to share, and every minute of every day, I'm going to miss your smile. I love you, Cory."

When it came his time to speak, Kirby shook his head. "I'm missing you, Cory. When you are reunited with Mom and Dad, hug them for me. Until I see you again, you take care of yourself."

Standing under the morning sun on the very spot where he lost his life and theirs were forever changed, his family locked hands. The prayers they asked were given in silence. Believing the time had come to join his friends at the memorial service, Gina took one last sip before placing the bottle inside the fence. "This one's for you, Cory."

Their limousine arrived at St. George's High School just as members of Thunder Racing, and those who wished to join in the Ride in Silence, began to trickle in. Considerate of his family, television crews and news reporters kept their distance. In recognition and to show their respect, the school's flag waved at half-staff.

Fragrant magnolias cut from branches in full bloom, and blue and silver balloons, the colors of the Dallas Cowboys, filled the school's gymnasium. *Come to the River,* a Christian gospel he requested months earlier for his father's funeral, played while mourners gathered.

Unscathed, his bike rested near the podium. Heart-shaped balloons floated above the curved handlebars, and strands of blue and yellow forget-me-nots fell in an easy cascade from the frame. As the room grew silent, Jeff Buckley's version of *Hallelujah* played in the background.

Asking those who gathered to open their hearts and thank God for every day, Reverend Barkley Thompson gave the homily celebrating Cory's life.

"It is one thing to have touched a life or a few lives, it is another to have the ability to draw together for good such a different and varied group of people…I wonder if Cory knew the number of lives he touched…I'll bet he didn't. Few of us rarely do. Many people go through life with the feeling that fate or the world or God has something big in store for them. I feel sure you all know what I'm talking about because I had that feeling as far back as middle school. I'm here to tell you that feeling is true, and you should hold on to it. God is at work in every one of your lives in amazing and even earth-changing ways. The problem is too many of us spend too much of our time trying to figure out what grand thing we're supposed to do in this life. We spend so much time we miss those small occasions of grace every day to touch the lives of those around us. Cory never fell into this trap. By everyone's account, he lived every day fully and never became so caught up in a future plan that he forgot the swimmer, or the runner, or the triathlete, or the student in need right in front of him. His simple yet profound way of living for a brief span of thirty-five years enacted the grace of God in more lives than most people would affect in three times as long. You all are about to leave this place for another summer, and I beg you to take this message with you. Plan for the future. Think grand thoughts? Absolutely, but remember Cory. Talk about him with your friends, your teachers, your parents. Remember this gym. Do good. Touch people's lives. Thank God every day."

School president, William Taylor, was next to take the podium. "His death leaves a void in this community that cannot be filled. In time, though, many happy memories of his passionate commitment to swimming, St. George's Independent School, the Memphis Thunder Aquatic Club, and most importantly, the young people with whom he worked will begin to assuage our pain and sadness."

Letting go of her sister's hand, Katie Siegal made her way to the podium. Sharing her favorite memories of the brief time she shared with Cory, laughter soon filled the gymnasium. The stories were new to many and familiar to most. When she laughed, his friends and family laughed along with her. Her chosen words made it easy to imagine him and what he meant to her. Those times when her voice cracked or she paused to dry a tear, the room grew silent. Cradled between her parents, Lori sobbed into her mother's shoulder.

Lesley Brainard and Keith Anderson shared entertaining stories, but also spoke of the void his absence left in their hearts and with the team. A video remembrance honoring his interrupted life played on a large screen above the podium. Lastly, everyone joined together to recite The Lord's Prayer.

After the closing prayer, Kirby went in search of Doug Ruddle. Finding him in the building's outer foyer, he placed in his hands the green bike helmet Cory often wore when they rode together. "I know Cory would want you to have this."

Accepting the helmet, Doug wrapped Kirby in his arms. "I'm going to miss him so much."

"I understand, my friend. I already do," Kirby said, giving a longing look around the gym. "His sense of humor was legendary. He always kept us laughing." As Kirby turned to step away, an elderly man reached for his arm.

"I had the privilege of knowing your brother. He coached my daughters. He was not just a man who loved his team and the thrill of the sport, he was a hero to many, and family to all. There is a kinship in this room. He will be missed."

Wandering through the crowd, Jill was approached by a man whose face was familiar, but whose name remained on the tip of her tongue.

"I want to offer my condolences to you and your family. I rode with Cory a couple of times and I just wanted you to know he had tremendous respect and a deep love for you. He was so proud of you."

Moved by this man, a friend to Cory and a stranger to her, she returned a smile and an easy nod. "Thank you. He was a gentle and giving person. It was easy to love him." Hearing her name, she turned to find a man with wet eyes at her side.

"I just want to share with you a conversation I had with Cory when we were in Florida. It was one of those days when he opened up about his childhood. He spoke of your mother's injuries, moving to Halfway when your father remarried, and of the time he left you and Cory behind when he took off to Alaska for three months."

"We were lucky to have each other," she said, wiping tears with a handkerchief the stranger offered.

"When Cory spoke of your father, he always said kind words. He spoke of you and how you took him under your own delicate and fragile wings. Those were words he used. He credited you for making sure he had food to eat, clothes on his back, and other than that stunt you pulled in grade school, made sure he went to school. He loved you so much."

Fighting back tears, she placed a hand over her heart. "Cory was a man with generous promises. At an early age, he built his life on two pillars— his love of family and what you see here today. He asked so little in return." Waving her hands out wide in front of her, she swept the room with her eyes. "This was his dream—his crowning achievement. Looking around this gymnasium at the number of friends gathered here today, I'm in awe of the many people whose lives he touched. Many would describe him as shy, and that may be true, but even in those times he purposefully chose to be silent, he had a way of reaching people. He was a fair and honest man. When it came to these kids, he didn't just coach them, he served as a role model and a mentor. The stories they've shared in passing days will remain in my heart. To his friends, Cory was fun and caring, and always a loyal and trusted confidante. To me, Cory was, and will always be, my baby brother."

When Gina arrived at her sister's side, a woman whose eyes showed evidence of the tears she cried, stepped forth to offer her condolences. "I'm so sorry. Words seem so empty at a time like this. Cory was such a dear friend. I know he is up in heaven with a winning smile on his sweet face ready for the next journey God has planned for him. I'm hoping you find comfort in knowing he is now, once again, one of God's angels."

———

On the far side of the gym, a young man grieved along with Cory's family and friends. Like those gathered around him, he wished he could erase the events on that fateful day. Each time he traveled Raleigh Lagrange Road, images of Cory's smile, along with his broken body, continued to haunt him. Relieved to go unnoticed, he made his exit.

———

Weeks later, Cory's family gathered in Rogersville. Standing before his grave, Jill recited the words engraved upon the large tombstone nestled between their parent's graves. "Love is not about who you live with, it's about who you can't live without."

When she could not go on, Kirby continued for her. "Beloved son, brother, uncle, and friend."

CHAPTER 46

Driving along St. George's tree-lined roads, Coach Keith rolled up to the curb in front of the school's Agape Chapel. Staring at the glass doors, it occurred to him that in his hurry to help Cory coach Thunder, he had never taken the time to appreciate the small building's beauty. To the left of the entry was a young evergreen. Its branches had spread wide, and looking at it through untrained eyes, he believed the young tree was thriving in its new environment. Several feet to the east of the chapel's painted downspouts were mature sycamores he was certain the building's architect took great measures to protect.

Eager to have a look inside the campus' small chapel, he threw the truck into park and released his seatbelt. Reaching for the keys, his eyes fell on the passenger seat. An open box overflowed with the black "Swim Strong–Cory Horton" bracelets he would later pass out at practice. Stepping from the truck, he made his way up the walk.

Peeking through the window, he came to understand why Cory's memorial service had taken place in the school's gymnasium. Although it was spacious, the fellowship hall was not large enough to accommodate the hundreds of friends who gathered to honor his life and offer their condolences to his family. Placing his hand on the door's brass handle, he lowered his head. Snippets of conversations he had with him regarding the swim team, his own future, and what he had planned for the years ahead, raced through his mind. When Cory shared with him that Thunder would grow into something bigger and better, he had foolishly called his friend a dreamer. Knowing Cory's dream would have to continue without him was too much for him to accept. Pulling his hand from the door, he returned to his truck.

Driving to the far side of the school's campus, habit made him search the parking lot for Cory's white Jeep. The apple on his car tag had always made it easy to identify. Finding the back lot empty, he prayed his good friend would soon arrive. Staying true to his routine, he pulled into his usual space and cut the engine. Whipping his sunglasses from his face, he tossed them on the dash.

Laboring along the sidewalk, he struggled with each step. His breathing was shallow, and when he reached the building, his heart threatened to jump out of his chest. In his attempts to unlock the door, he twice dropped the keys. Struggling to turn the lock, he cursed in anger as he kicked at the door. When he was finally able to enter the center, he thought he would be sick. Looking past the pool to Cory's office, he was surprised to see the room in lights. Picking up his pace, he hurried across the deck. As he approached the door, he called out Cory's name. Finding the room empty, he took a seat on the floor, and rubbing at his temples, followed his mind through recent events.

When he was asked to speak at Cory's memorial service, the events leading up to that moment seemed surreal. *Cory couldn't be gone. He had so much going for him. He had a team who thought he hung the moon and friends who were always encouraging him to be a better athlete.* In his eyes, life was living through Cory.

Glancing up at his desk, he did not have to open the top drawer to know it held a plastic container filled with sour punch straws, a generous supply of Tootsie Pops, and a jar of homemade peanut butter a parent of one of his swimmers had made for him. The slim drawer, which Cory lovingly called *"a flea market of surprises,"* was home to permanent markers, dull pencils, and a sandwich bag filled with rescued buttons, pencil erasers, and key chains he found on the deck. Searching his memory, he could not recall a single time anyone had asked to search the center's lost and found. Curious about the bottom drawer, he pulled at the double-screw brass handle.

Knowing Cory kept his personal life private, he was surprised to find an envelope of old photos of his family. There were several black and white pictures the backsides identified as Cory's mother, candid pictures of his siblings running in a grassy field, and a collection of love letters and flirty cards he recalled watching him toss into the trash. Reading the fortune Cory saved from a cookie, a confused smile claimed his face. He found the cookie's fortune, "*the best is yet to come*," both painful and knowing. Having seen enough, he closed the drawer and turned out the lights.

Keeping a watchful eye on the door, and stopping occasionally to look out into the parking lot, he filled the vacant time by sweeping the pool deck, posting drills on the dry-erase board, and because the kids always enjoyed a change in their routine, dragging the resistance ropes to the edge of the pool. When he finished, he searched the deck. Two essential elements were missing—Coach Cory and his team.

Taking a seat midway up the bleachers, he stared at the pool. He found the filter's constant swoosh deafening. For the third time in fifteen minutes, he glanced at the large clock at the far end of the pool. Practice was supposed to have started forty minutes earlier. Although his time with Thunder was brief, he could not recall a single time a swimmer had been late to practice. "*It's just as easy to be early as it is to be late,*" Cory had often reminded his team. Having heard these words before, he wondered who coined the phrase. Seeing that it had worked in Cory's favor, the quote's origin did not matter.

Always arriving suited up and ready to go, Cory's team would rush the deck, eager to tell him about their day and ask him about his. If time permitted, he always allowed the kids to play a game of Marco Polo, Sharks and Minnows, or Mighty Water Ducks, a favorite among the older swimmers. Quacking like ducks, they dove for the coins he tossed in the deep end. Passing over the nickels, dimes, and pennies, they would race to claim the quarters. Knowing he could never replace his friend, he brushed a heavy hand through his hair. Hearing footsteps, he was happy to see Lesley pass through the door. "What brings you out here?"

Walking the quiet deck and taking a seat in the row below him, Lesley pulled a notebook from her bag. "When I saw your truck all alone in the parking lot, I figured you'd want some company. I have to tell you, I feared this would happen. Truthfully, I'm not surprised. I had a hard time coming out here. I can't begin to imagine how the kids must be feeling. For many of them, Cory was their first and only coach. I'm always amazed when I am reminded these kids had other options. We have four competitive teams in the city and two in the county. Still, they followed him from pool to pool. For them, it was not about having a home base, hosting a meet, or having their names lit up in lights. Cory made them feel proud of their achievements. They didn't have to claim the fastest time, win every event they entered, or set a new record. Each time they returned to Cory after finishing an event, all they asked was for him to confirm with a checkmark to the cheek they had given their best. Not once did he ask more from them. I believe they would have followed him to the end of the earth. Looking around at this empty space makes me sad for them. There were times I stood back and watched the interaction between Cory and all these kids who wanted nothing more than for him to validate their existence. So many times, I wanted to be a part of it. I'd leave here wondering how he always managed to make each swimmer feel like they helped to hold up the team. In his eyes, it wasn't about the individual performance, but working together as a team."

Keith took a deep breath and stretched his legs out in front of him. "Lesley, I don't think they're coming back."

"That crossed my mind, too." Flipping open a notebook, she nodded in agreement. Handing a black and white spiral notebook to him, she hoped she had found a solution. "I prepared a letter you might consider sending to the parents. I worked on it late last night, so there are typos and misspelled words, but I think we should send an email and drop a copy in the mail. By the way, are you going to the Excel meet?"

"I was planning on it, but looking around the deck, it doesn't appear I have a team to take."

"Well, if you decide to go, and you need help, I have a friend I can call." In the lower corner of the letter, she scribbled a name and telephone number. "His name is Phillip." Letting the silence drag, Lesley placed her hand on his shoulder. "Are you going to be okay?"

"Yeah. Maybe not today or tomorrow, or in the coming weeks, but eventually. I'm telling you, Lesley, this is not something I want to get used to. I'm missing him. It takes all I have to get out of bed in the morning."

"I understand. I miss him, too. I'm fortunate to have my family. They keep me grounded. Listen, I'm going to get my ride in. If you're still here when I get back, I'll stop in. Hang in there. Remember, you're not alone in this."

Turning his shoulders, he looked into Lesley's eyes. "Promise me you'll be careful out there."

Exchanging a hug, they agreed that now, after Cory's accident, those words had taken on new meaning. They would forever remain with them.

Jumping from the bleachers, he bee-lined to Cory's office, stepped around boxes filled with old heat sheets, swim caps, and team suits, and fell into his swivel chair. Taking the cell phone from his pocket, he pulled the team's roster from the drawer. Starting from the top of the list, he telephoned his team.

By noon, he had spoken with the parents of thirty-two of the team's 133 members. The questions he asked were answered, but only after a noticeable and awkward pause. Many parents shared with him that their child swam because Cory made each practice fun, adding that with vacation from school underway, their children were looking forward to enjoying time with friends. Others spoke openly about their child's depression and withdrawal.

Scratching a line through the last name on the roster, he balled up the list and tossed it into the trash. Only two swimmers promised to see him in the coming days. Walking out to his truck, he questioned not only his future but also Thunder's.

CHAPTER 47

On May 22, 2005, seven days after Cory's memorial service, his friends and family gathered in Millington for the Memphis in May Triathlon, an event Cory trained for and planned to attend. On this day, his friends rode in his honor. Before the start of the race, heads lowered in a moment of silence. Hundreds of athletes wore black armbands honoring his life, and many wore race belts with his picture pinned to their bibs. Pictures of him were posted throughout the course.

Memphis Thunder swimmer, Taylor Flynn, whom Cory coached for eight years, swam the first leg of a mixed relay team honoring his life. His friend and training buddy, David Carl Jones, biked the middle leg, and Mark Newman, who trained with him for fifteen years, finished out the event in the running portion.

Just as Lesley crossed over the finish line, Cory's picture fell from her bib to the ground. Later, when she spoke of this with her friends, a feeling of warmth embraced her. "This was one of the most tangible inspiring moments from God I have ever experienced." Believing he carried her through the race, which turned out to be her best time for that distance, she looked up to the heavens and smiled. "I believe Cory was telling me it's time to let go."

Five days later, on May 27, 2005, seventeen days after Cory's accident, several Thunder members, including Lindsey Brackens, competed in the Excel Stars and Stripes Long Course Meet in Versailles, Kentucky. Swimming in lane six, she struggled through the 50-free, her first event. As she pushed through the water, she could not put aside thoughts of Cory. Losing focus, she added time to the event she was expected to win. Hours later, she was disappointed with her time in the 100-free. Days before his accident, Cory talked with her about the meet. *"You'll do great, Sparky. I bet you will swim a personal best."*

When it was time to swim the 200-free, Coach Keith pulled her aside. "Lindsey, this is your strongest event. Cory might not be standing here with us today, but I know in my heart he is watching over you. If there is paper in heaven, you can bet that once you enter the water, he'll be waving it in the air."

Standing in her assigned lane, she closed her eyes. Missing Cory, she reached for his belief in her. Stepping onto the block, a wide smile owned her face. In a whispered voice, she dedicated the event. "This is for you, Coach Cory."

Watching from the deck, her teammates cheered. Walking alongside her lane, Coach Keith swept the air with an open hand. When she made her flip turn, his thoughts turned to Cory. Taking his place as second in command, he could not bring himself to wave the heat sheet in the air or brush it alongside his leg. Instead, he hoped that calling out her name would be enough to push her to the finish.

Hitting the touch pad, she whipped off her goggles and turned to the scoreboard—2:12.16. She had bettered her time from the 2:13.32 she swam at Nashville's NAC Summer Sizzler.

Later, when asked about the meet, she opened up about missing Cory. "I'll never forget that meet because it was right after Cory's death. I remember talking to my teammates about everything, leaning on each other for support. Keith Anderson and Phillip Wood were our two coaches for the meet and they did a great job helping us prepare for the swimming aspect despite our broken hearts. I remember Cory's brother stopped by the pool...they looked just alike. I remember breaking down in tears because all I wanted was for Cory to get me ready for my race, draw on my face a *mark of excellence,* and call me Sparky one more time. His fun twist on meets made them so much more than a competition. It was about bonding and enjoying the company, as well. The meet was probably the most difficult meet and it had nothing to do with the competition in the pool. It had everything to do with missing the man who taught me so much about the love of swimming and how to have fun at the same time."

CHAPTER 48

In the days following Cory's memorial service, Memphis Thunder Racing organized and hosted Cycle for Safety, a cycling event to bring attention and awareness to safe cycling and to help educate the cycling community and the public. The fifty-four-mile ride traveled along Houston Levee and Raleigh Lagrange Road, the road Cory last biked, and past his memorial site. The donation-only proceeds went to purchase "Share the Road" and bike caution signs to be placed along well-traveled bike routes in Germantown and neighboring Collierville.

In late September, four months after Cory's accident, plans were underway to design "Share the Road" specialty license plates. Communicating by phone, the Internet, and email, Cory's siblings, along with many of his friends, took to the task. Bob was the first to offer his support. "Count me in. This is my way of honoring my good friend and his love of cycling."

"We need to create public awareness. My goal is to reduce the number of cyclist and driver accidents. Cory would like this," Kirby added.

Responding to a group email, Jill expressed her concerns. "Public awareness and education are paramount. I'm sure Cory would be proud just knowing we are doing something to help the sport he loved the most. Our goal is to bridge motorists and cyclists."

Within the year, his friends and family displayed the new license plates on their personal vehicles.

Left to right:
David Jones, Billy Tune, Cindy Ashe, Curt Ogle, Lesley Brainard,
Chuk Bible, John Brainard, Lloyd Crawford, Damie Roberts,
Andi Johnson, Greg Anyan, Robert Bannon, David McDaniel,
Renee Humphries, Lane Purser, Doug Ruddle, Russ Lewis
Photo courtesy of Lesley Brainard

CHAPTER 49

The Mercers struggles were just beginning. Closing the door to her bedroom, Silvie begged for privacy. No longer interested in swimming, she sought comfort in food. Binging on salted chips, buttered croissants, and leftover dinners her parents carried home from popular Italian eateries, she put on weight. Discouraged by the mirror's reflection, she pulled the truth-teller from the wall and slid it under the bed. When she was not moping about the house, her days were spent hiding under heavy blankets.

Having been told in advance her presence was required at dinner, she came to the table dressed in short-sleeve and ankle-length flannel pajamas she had outgrown years earlier and bunny slippers she carried down from the attic hours after Cory was taken to the hospital.

Taking a seat next to Delia Mercer, her grandmother, she rested in a chair with her feet tucked under her bottom and her elbows spread out on the table. When she thought no one was looking, she bit at her nails and spit to the floor the bits of skin she thought would go unnoticed. Looking at her now, no one would believe she grew up in a home where manners were not only taught but also practiced, and rules were never broken but followed.

"I know you don't see it, Silvie, but God has a plan for all of us. His plan for you is not the one He has for your parents, me, or for Cory. I know you feel cheated that he was called to heaven at such a young age, but it is not for us to question God's timing."

Biting at a stubborn skin tag near her nail, Silvie remained focused on her plate. "I miss him, Grandma. Every second of every single day. In the small numbered boxes on my brain's calendar, Cory shared time and space he expected me to honor. It's not swim practice if I show up and he's not there. It's not fair that he was taken from me."

"I know you miss him, my sweet angel, and that's normal." Cupping her chin in her hand, Delia placed a kiss on her forehead. "For what it's worth, I'm missing you."

Wrapped in her grandmother's arms, she cried the tears she tried to bury under anger. Wiping them away, she asked to be excused.

Closing the door to her bedroom, she pulled the mirror from under her bed. In her reflection, she saw a child drowning in sorrow. Taking a step back, her heart grew angry when she was forced to accept she was alone in her misery. No one was rushing to offer comforting words to ease her pain, or, in taking her hand, promising that all of the anger and loneliness she fought would fade away. Reaching for a strength she knew her family had come to expect from her, she corrected her posture, steadied uncertain nerves, and forcing a smile, displayed the deep dimples in her cheeks. Before escaping her sanctuary, she took a brush through her unwashed hair and secured her long locks with a beaded headband. Adding a touch of rouge to her cheeks and a thin layer of gloss to her lips, she painted a hint of life into her forced smile.

Minutes later, when she returned to the dining room, she hoped her mood would appear lighthearted. The black and white Thunder sweatshirt she wore was frayed. Its collar had been cut away months earlier when she thought the tight and narrow opening was on a mission to choke her. Resting inches above her ankles and missing several links in the zipper, her old jeans were torn and tattered. Before taking a seat, she caught a sneeze in her elbow. Picking up the scent of the hard pack of slim cigarettes she smoked earlier in the day, she turned away from the hug her grandmother offered.

"If it's alright, I'd like to say grace." Turning to her father, a man who always displayed a smile in his effort to avoid conflict, she took his hurried nod as permission to proceed. Closing her eyes, she folded her hands together.

"Oh, Heavenly Father, we thank you for your many blessings. I want to give thanks for those people you place in our lives and in our hearts. As you already know, I cannot begin to understand why you took Cory from me, but it's not for me to question." Pausing, she looked to her grandmother. Accepting her unspoken approval, she continued. "My heart is heavy without him." This time, when she paused, it was to wipe her nose on the dinner napkin her mother had ironed earlier in the day. "Cory, if you can hear me, I hope when I get to heaven you'll let me be on your team. Oh, and for those seated around me, I also give thanks for this dinner. Amen."

Long after dinner dishes were washed and put away, and her grandmother had driven her Seville from the curb, she returned to her sanctuary. Turning the lock on the bedroom door, she plopped down on the bed. The words she had spoken to pacify her family were neither heartfelt nor genuine. When she asked to say grace, it had been her intent to scream angry words and challenge anyone within earshot, including God. It was only because her aging grandmother, a woman of strong faith, was present, that she hooked a leash on her angry tongue.

Sliding from the bed to the carpeted floor, her hands grew sweaty and her broken heart raced. Unplugging the bedside lamp, she pulled open the closet door. Committed to her mission, she no longer needed a light to guide her. She fumbled about in the closet until she found the random and odd-shaped key chains she, like many of her Thunder teammates, had collected over the years. Although she played along with her friends when adding to her collection, she found the trend of attaching key chains to her swim bag boring and a waste of money.

Staring at the Speedo bag, her mind went back in time. Recalling the afternoon she came home from school and found it on the kitchen table, she broke into tears. Her name, first and last, was written in calligraphy below a threatening bolt. Proud to be on Cory's team, she carried the blue bag to daily practice and every swim meet. Looking at it now, she saw its flaws. Threads had pulled away, and stuffed with rubber bands, the mesh side pocket was a tangled mess. Once oblivious to the smell of chlorine, the bag's bleachy odor now made her queasy. Revisiting the past was not the reason she pulled the bag from the dark corner of her closet. She wanted what was hidden inside.

Reaching into the bag, she placed the prescription bottles in a straight line. Weeks earlier, during a night when sleep had kept its distance, she used a permanent marker, similar to the one Cory carried in his pocket, to number the plastic bottles in the order she would swallow them. Now, hearing *Collide*, a Howie Day song, play on the radio, she broke down in tears. Listening to each word, she could not help but think of Cory and his accident. He was the best, and he had fallen.

The neighbor next door, a man whose day job labeled him an orthopedic surgeon, prescribed oxycodone tablets weeks earlier when her father dislocated his shoulder after falling from a ladder. The label on the second bottle had been scratched off, but she was sure the peach-colored pills belonged to her mother. Overhearing snippets of her mother's late-night whispers behind closed doors, she believed the pills had something to do with dolls in a valley.

Until Cory's accident, she enjoyed life. Swimming filled her days, and although she had little free time to spend with friends, she lived her life with no regrets. Cory had seen promise in her and that was all she needed. She was born to loving parents who always had her best interests at heart. Of course, there were occasions when swim meets took priority over a family vacation or a holiday when they wanted to escape for a weekend, but like her, they too understood there were sacrifices and compromises made if she were to swim her way to the Olympics.

Resting against the bed's wrought iron post, memories of Cory continued. The first time she met him, he shook her hand, and after repeating his name, he asked hers. Polite and self-assured, she responded, "Silvie. Silvie Mercer."

"Nice to meet you, Hi-Ho Silver," Cory responded. She readily accepted the name that from that day forward he would always call her. Burying her face in a pillow, she came to accept that so much had changed since those early days at Tigers. A strong-willed child, she did not always get in the pool when he asked. Ignoring her stubborn nature, he would cruise the deck, sneak up behind her, and while her teammates watched on, toss her into the pool's deep end. Recalling the many times he threw Margo into the pool had her missing his silliness.

A smile crossed her face when she thought back to the day he raced into practice with a smile on his face and a skip in his step. Waving a paper bag in the air and dangling car keys for all to see, he shouted for all those near to hear. *"I won the McDonald's challenge!"* Eager to share in his excitement, everyone rushed to gather around him. Clapping their hands, they shot questions at him. "What was the challenge? What did you win?"

Knowing they were hooked and hanging on his every word, he had played it up. "I had to eat two all-beef patties, special sauce, lettuce, cheese, pickles, and onions on a sesame seed bun!" Looking back at him, their faces showed admiration and envy. Still waving the keys in the air, he continued. *"And I won a Mustang convertible!"* When he laughed at their gullible innocence, they knew only to laugh along with him.

"Where is it?" Silvie asked, searching the parking lot.

"I ate it."

"You ate a car?"

"No, silly. I ate a Big Mac."

Having been her coach for more than a decade, she wished she had taken the time to thank him. She wanted him to know she appreciated him, not only as a coach but also as her friend and mentor. He had a way of telling stories, even those he made up, just to get a laugh. Thinking about it now, she wondered if perhaps he needed the lighthearted moment more than his listeners.

Grabbing the pill bottles, she crept into the bathroom, closed the door, and turned the lock. Standing at the sink, she cringed at the stranger in the mirror. Full-faced, puffy-eyed, and skin so pale it was blinding, she doubted he would recognize her. Embarrassed by her appearance, she turned away.

Placing the bottles on the marble vanity, she struggled to remove the childproof lids. Drowning in grief and fueled by anger and disappointment, she damned the day of his accident. She had come to hate the words she heard others use to describe his death. Coming at them with all teeth showing, she barked words she doubted they would understand. *"An accident is when you spill milk all over the table, or when the cat snags your favorite sweater. It's not when your coach is killed while riding his bike along an isolated stretch of road."*

She cringed each time she heard, *"It'll be okay, it was an accident."* Those were the words her mother had always said reassuringly when it was easier to disguise a misfire than to proclaim loudly that her day had been ruined. Moving forward without Cory was not going to be okay. His *accident* could not be fixed. He was gone. Falling to her knees, she called out his name.

CHAPTER 50

When she was not busy with her granddaughter, Gina spent much of her time in her backyard. Sitting on the deck with her toes touching the water, she read the pages of the latest novel, sipped her favorite pinot noir, and helped her husband prepare dinners they would later throw on the grill. One evening, soon after dinner, she and her husband hurried to rescue a small turtle that had fallen into the pool's deep end. Weak and bleeding from under his shell, the turtle was unable to move. Given its injuries, she worried it would not survive through the night.

Her granddaughter, Allison, made a warm bed for the injured turtle in her playhouse. Flipping a box top, she layered the bottom with grass clippings, small pebbles, and twigs she gathered from the garden. Until it was time for her to go back to her home, Allison stayed with the turtle, petting and talking to him, and although it did not eat the lettuce she offered, she reminded him he needed to eat. Knowing Cory would have done the same thing put a smile on her face.

Later that afternoon, she received a call from Debra, a close friend. Sitting on her porch swing hundreds of miles away, Debra's thoughts had drifted to Cory when a turtle crossed in front of her. "Cory would stop in the middle of a race to rescue a wayward turtle."

The following morning, when she made her way out the back door, she was surprised to find the turtle inside the screened porch. It was then she recalled an afternoon when she and Cory were driving in the car. Spotting a turtle in the middle of the road, he begged her to stop the car. Because he never had a speeding ticket, and having been ticketed for driving below the posted speed, he was incessantly teased that the turtle moved about as fast as he drove. Pulling off to the shoulder, she watched as he raced into the street, scooped up the turtle, and dodging oncoming traffic, placed it in the tall grasses a safe distance from the road.

CHAPTER 51

On November 28, 2005, six months after Cory's accident, Katie's sister, Lori Siegal, passed away. "Someone said to me after she died that Cory would have taken Lori's death hard, so maybe it was all part of God's plan that he was taken before her and was there to greet her in heaven," Katie reflected. "It was an unimaginable year to lose two of the most influential people in my life within six months of each other, so I take some comfort in the fact that they are together."

Lori had been the first self-elected advocate for the Down Syndrome Association of the Mid-South Board and was later elected to the National Down Syndrome Association Board. Born with Down syndrome and a heart defect, Lori always struggled with physical movement and fatigue. Her huge personality made up for her petite size.

"She was very smart, hilarious and quick-witted…she lit up a room," she shared. "Cory never treated Lori differently, and as much as she would have loved to have been a swimmer for him, she had to settle for being a cheerleader on the sidelines. She was my biggest cheerleader."

Obsessed with *I Love Lucy*, Lori often quoted lines from her favorite episodes. Katie has a tattoo on her wrist that is a heart with a checkmark in it. "The heart symbolizes Lori's love and literal obsession with *I love*

Lucy. The checkmark signifies Cory's 'mark of excellence' he used to draw on our cheeks after a good swim during meets. I am so proud of it and it is a constant reminder of Cory and Lori. I hope I can live a life even close to the ones they lived...always inspiring others, happy, and giving one-hundred-percent in everything."

CHAPTER 52

Holed up in her bedroom, Jill continued in her struggle to regain some sense of normalcy. When she grew tired of the sleepless nights, tossing and turning and wrestling in her nightmares with the memories of Cory in the days following his accident, she finally gave into her battles with insomnia. It was easier to accept the lack of sleep than continue a losing fight. On the few occasions she managed to drift into a deep sleep, the screams she cried from recurring nightmares woke the house and left her crying into a pillow she repeatedly fisted in her sleep. Deteriorating under stress, she tried to bury thoughts of his accident, his apartment, and those final days watching him lie in wait under a layer of starched sheets only to learn the prayers she asked would go unanswered. Shielding her eyes from daybreak, she wanted only to have all of her yesterdays returned to her. In those rare moments of lucidity, she worried she was going insane.

Instead of suffering from a loss of appetite, which her therapist warned might happen, she turned to food for comfort. A touch to the phone had Chinese food delivered to the door. When she grew tired of General Taos chicken, she turned to moo shu pork and steamed rice. When this no longer appealed to her, she ordered pizza from the restaurant around the corner. Placing an order, she reminded the waitress she liked her pepperoni pizza blanketed with extra cheese. Dining took place above the blankets, and because guilt still managed to seep into her thoughts, away from open windows. She did not want to be the talk of the neighborhood. Although her stomach was full, her heart remained empty. Alone in her darkness, and preferring to stay in bed, she propped pillows behind her head and kept the television's remote control at her side. Most of her days were spent watching basic cable and *Dr. Phil*. Hearing the program's invited guests air their difficulties and disputes to the host of the popular afternoon program, she screamed at the television. Her voice grew louder when families with troubled teens failed to appreciate that, unlike Cory, they were still among the living. One guest had her so upset, she threw a pillow at the screen.

By December, she gained forty pounds. Depressed and overweight, the thought of decorating a Christmas tree, wrapping packages, and listening to holiday carols had her feeling anxious. It was still too soon to celebrate. It took all she had to muddle through the Thanksgiving holiday. *Oh, and what a disaster that was.* The turkey she served remained frozen in the middle, trays of buttered rolls were turned to ash, and when asked about dessert, she shamefully admitted to having eaten the pumpkin pie.

In the early morning hours when the house was quiet and the children were away at school, her thoughts turned to the days ahead and what was expected of her. Shopping for gifts was out of the question. Staring out the window at the falling snow, she thought the flakes looked wetter, the dreary sky a little grayer, and looking at the dark and lifeless trees against the dulled sky sent a shiver through her. Turning away, she realized it was not Christmas she dreaded, but Cory's birthday. Feeling an ache in her heart, she was reminded he would not want her to mourn his death, but instead, celebrate his life and begin to live her own again. Glancing at his picture on the bedside table, his smile assured her she was right. The time had come to move on.

Throwing on a sweatshirt and old warm-up pants she took from her husband's closet, she made her way through the house. Passing by the boys' rooms, she noticed their beds were made, bureau drawers were closed—something that almost never happened—and the floors were clear of everything except tennis shoes and sports magazines. It was comforting to see they were adjusting. She doubted those words had been used in any conversation when used to describe her.

Drawn to the guest room, she crossed over the hardwood floor to the bed. Pushing aside the decorative pillows, she brushed away a falling tear. It had been weeks since she held the pillow she carried from Cory's apartment. The imprint, now smooth and no longer recognizable, had been replaced with a scent the passing of time leaves behind. Arranging the pillows as she found them, she shuffled from the room. Stepping into the kitchen, she inhaled the familiar scent of peppermint, a sweet treat she began adding to her morning coffee days after returning home from Cory's memorial service. Reaching for a mug, she eyed the sink. Finding it empty, she wondered who had washed the dishes.

Taking a seat at the table, she stared out the window. Sipping her coffee, she watched the neighbor across the road sweep the newly fallen snow off his porch. His wife, a woman she met some time ago at a progressive party her street hosted, held Chowder, their Cavalier King Charles spaniel, on her hip like a teething toddler. Word at last month's Thursday night Bunco was Chowder had won the Noble Paws Prize, an award for completing a six-week obedience training class. She could not recall having ever seen the lapdog move about on its own four legs. Another neighbor was busy framing his front door with holiday lights. Just as she turned to look away, she caught sight of a catering van. Placing her elbows on the table, she rested her chin on steepled fingers. Watching life continue around her made her realize she was missing it. Feeling a sense of calm come over her, what suddenly mattered was that she let go of the past, and embrace and attack her future with renewed hope.

Dragging the garbage can from under the sink, she tore through the pantry like a village pillager. Emptying its shelves of bags of chips, boxes of cookies, and the chocolate-covered graham crackers she ate by the dozen, she began to feel like her old self again.

Grabbing scissors, she tore at a package she received weeks earlier.

Left on her front porch, there was no return address in the corner, and she had not been asked to sign for its delivery. Tossing foam packing peanuts to the floor, she was surprised to find the box filled with Christmas ornaments she recalled having seen on Cory's tree the previous year. Taking a gold angel from wrinkled tissue paper, she was surprised to find it solid and heavy. Turning it over, a smile softened her face. Cory had scribbled his name on the backside of its gilded wing. With the tip of her finger, she followed the feathered curves. Putting it aside, she reached for a red and white ornament. The ceramic candy cane had a small chip, but she did not mind. What mattered was his signature on a bend near the arched curve. There were seven Santa ornaments, all handmade from blown glass. Recognizing an ornament from her childhood, she laughed aloud. Wearing a helmet of thick black hair, his plastic body painted green, she was thankful The Hulk had survived all these years.

Sipping her coffee, her mind cleared and her closed heart began to open. Looking out the window, she found the sky brighter than it had been in months. Shaking her head, she apologized for having wasted so much time. She rushed to the bathroom, ran a brush through her hair, and then raced out the door. She had been given a reason to celebrate.

Standing ten feet tall, the Fraser fir was the tallest tree the farm offered. Jill paid an additional twenty dollars to have it delivered and set up within the hour. Glancing at the Tag Heuer watch she wore on her wrist, she hoped she had time to visit two more shops before returning home.

Later, when she returned home and her packages begged for her to follow through on the promises she made in the store's busy aisles, she raced up the stairs. The old milk crates she carried from the attic held ornaments she collected over the years. In the mix were several ornaments she purchased as keepsakes from vacation resorts and points of interest travel guides suggested she visit. There were family heirlooms, including those she made in her own childhood, and those she found among her father's belongings soon after his death. A smaller crate held the ornaments her children had made in Sunday school and throughout their elementary years.

Pulling at faded tissue, she placed the delicate ornaments on the dining room table. Stepping back, she examined the tree's many branches, each meant to hold a trinket from her past. Unlike previous Christmases, decorating the tree would not be as simple as placing a glass ball here or a felt mitten there. This year's tree would tell a story. Its branches would hold and display precious memories.

As the minutes ticked away, she hummed along with the music on the radio. Hearing *White Christmas,* a holiday favorite, she looked to the window. Until now, she had been unaware the snow had stopped falling. Recalling Christmases long ago—the many snowballs Cory had lovingly thrown at her and those times he stood on top of a mound of recently plowed snow declaring to his kingdom below he was King of the Mountain—warmed her heart and encouraged her eyes to cry more tears. Breaking a forlorn smile, she remembered the mornings he traipsed through mud and slush in worn-out sneakers in his hurry to catch the bus to school. She could not recall a single time he complained.

When she was satisfied the tree was *almost* finished, she turned her attention to the shopping bag and the collection of ornaments spread out on the table. Taking a must-have treasure from the bag, she held the bicycle ornament as she searched the tree for the *perfect* branch. Earlier, when she spotted a monkey ornament at the Christmas Store, a small boutique offering Old English Santa ornaments, small collections of golf, tennis and baseball hangings for the sport enthusiast, and replicas of vintage cars, she remembered Chimpa, Cory's sock monkey. She had to have it. It, too, now had a place on the tree. The last ornament to grace the fir was a framed picture of Cory. Capturing him with a smile on his face, it was taken the previous Christmas, five months before his accident and only months after losing their father. Holding the bronze ornament in her open hand, she brushed her fingers over the frame. "Merry Christmas, Cory."

Foregoing their traditional family gathering, Gina and Mike, and their daughters, along with Kirby and his family, decided on a spur of the moment to celebrate in the mountains. As they backed out of Gina's driveway, she stepped out to gather the afternoon's delivery of bills, holiday cards, and flyers from the mailbox. Glancing at a small package, she recognized Jill's handwriting. In her rush, she tossed the mail onto the backseat and the box into her purse. "I'll get to it later," she promised.

The log cabin they rented was a stone's throw from Columbus, Georgia, in nearby Warm Springs. Nestled near a small stream, Pine Mountain Inn offered the solitude they needed for their first Christmas without Cory. In the early mornings, they rode horses along the Roosevelt State Park's many trails, and when time allowed, hiked the paths the resort's guide recommended.

Reaching for the spirit of Christmas, Gina suggested they put up a tree. "The girls can help decorate."

Thankful she remembered to pack their Christmas stockings, she carefully hung them on the fireplace mantel. The artificial tree was decorated with ornaments they found at a local boutique. Placing strands of silver tinsel on the branches, she suddenly remembered the package from Jill.

Seated on the edge of the sofa, with her daughters at her side and Kirby an arm's reach away, she unwrapped the small box. Curious to see what the gold tissue held, she tore at the paper. When she saw Cory's face, her eyes flooded with tears. Recalling the picture had been taken the previous year when the family celebrated together, she was grateful Jill thought to preserve it in an ornament. Cupping the ornament in her hands, she hurried to place the treasured gift on the tree. Placing an ornament addressed to Kirby in his out-stretched hand, she let go a whimper when he placed a kiss on the gold frame.

Photo Courtesy of Jill Horton Carpenter

CHAPTER 53

In 2004, the first year the Donate Life Rose Parade float made its way along the rose-lined streets of Pasadena, California, it was seen by almost one million parade attendees and nearly double that number of people worldwide. In 2013, almost nine years after Cory's accident, his family received a telephone call letting them know he had been selected to be an honoree on the 2014 Donate Life float.

In mid-December, weeks before the Rose Parade, Cory's siblings and friends, together with teachers and students, gathered at St. George's Independent School, along with Randa Lipman, Mid-South Transplant Foundation's community outreach manager, to decorate the floragraph that would later become part of Donate Life's *Light Up the World* parade float. Commemorative buttons were presented at the door. Tables were set up in the gymnasium and bowls were filled with colorful seeds to finish Cory's floragraph, which was designed from the same picture Jill placed on her tree the first Christmas following his accident. Like most floragraphs, Cory's allowed those who wished to participate in the opportunity to finish the personal details friends, family, and loved ones are encouraged to complete. In his case, they were also allowed to add the finishing details to his shirt. After placing the final seeds on the floragraph, his family posed for pictures and answered questions presented by local television and newspaper reporters. Jill and Kirby were presented roses dedicated in Cory's honor. Following a closing prayer, Addison Janz, a Memphis Thunder member and St. George's student, who had the privilege of training under Cory, shared a song he had written in Cory's honor.

Before the day ended, Cory's floragraph was on a plane to California where it would later be placed on the float alongside the floragraphs of the float's other honorees. With the parade just weeks away, Jill and Gina decided they would travel to Pasadena to represent his family.

In the early morning hours of Wednesday, January 1, 2014, Cory's sisters sat with their cameras ready and a box of tissues nearby. The welcome packet they received included programs, schedules, and picture buttons. They were presented with a framed poster of Cory's float. As the Donate Life float made its approach, they stood tall. When the colorful float of lanterns came to rest in front of them, their thoughts turned to the organs he donated. *Was his strong and giving heart still beating? Were his kidneys functioning? Did his liver continue to carry out its purpose?* The most painful question they asked brought them to tears. *Are his eyes watching this parade?*

Searching the red and purple lantern, they pointed to his floragraph. Below his smiling face was a bed of purple and gold irises. Steadying their hands, they snapped pictures on their cell phones they would later send to Kirby. Taking photos of the floragraph, their hearts were overwhelmed with pride.

Miles away, Merchant, who sat wrapped in a parka and wearing gloves to protect his hands from the cold, was fishing the pond when he heard his wife call out his name.

"The parade is starting," she shouted before turning to hurry back inside.

Paddling to the bank, Merchant pulled the small boat out of the water before gathering his thermos and cooler. It did not matter that he had not had a single bite. His time on the water was no longer about catching fish, but enjoying life. The cardiologist he visited every six months told him his heart was strong, and once he reached a healthy weight, his future was promising. In his eyes, he believed every day held promise. Stepping out of his galoshes, he took a seat in the old La-Z-Boy. Reclining, he repeated the words he spoke every morning. "Thank you, Lord, for giving that young man's heart to me." When the Donate Life float appeared, he placed a hand over his beating heart.

—

Shoe and his wife were eating breakfast at their home in Shreveport, Louisiana, when the television caught their attention. Watching in silence as colorful floats traveled through Pasadena, they gave thanks. They remained glued to their chairs, waiting to see the Donate Life float. Years after he received Cory's healthy liver, Shoe felt it was his time to give back. He volunteered at the Organ Donor Network, and at age 54, attended the Transplant Games, where he competed in track, cycling, and swimming. He had no way of knowing those three sports were Cory's favorite activities. In 2008, he attended the World Transplant Games in Pittsburgh.

—

Six years after his transplant, Jay Wagess lost his life when the car he was riding in veered into oncoming traffic. At age eighty, he honored Cory's memory when he donated tissue.

—

Two years after his kidney transplant, Rudy returned to his job as a real estate agent. Months after his transplant, his father requested his own organs be used for transplant. Suffering a fatal heart attack, he donated his corneas, pancreas, and both kidneys.

—

Resting in a room at Mercy General Hospital, thirty-four-year-old Brea McAndray hoped her husband remembered to set the television's recorder before leaving the house. Since her corneal transplant in 2005, she never missed the Rose Parade. Holding her newborn daughter in her arms, she shared the story of the man who gave her the gift of sight.

—

Watching the parade from her home in Memphis, LuLu Woodall's eyes grew wide and her young heart warmed when the *Light Up the World* float took center stage. Giving her mother's hand a gentle squeeze, they gave thanks for the gift LuLu's donor had given her.

Years after her daughter's corneal transplant, Mrs. Woodall read the many articles the newspaper printed about Cory and the swim team he left behind. Recognizing his face on the float's floragraph, she whispered a prayer for him and the family he left behind. Turning to her daughter, she gave a grateful smile.

Jill Horton Carpenter and Kirby Horton

Seated: Kirby Horton, Jill Horton Carpenter,
Matthew Horton, Jennifer Horton
Standing: Bari Horton, Bill Carpenter, Christopher
Carpenter, Josh Carpenter, Jacob Lindsey

Donate Life's *Light Up the World* float

Jill Horton Carpenter and Gina Horton Cheatham
Photos Courtesy of Ruth L. Lovell, M. Div., CT of
the Mid-South Transplant Foundation

CHAPTER 54

On Saturday, May 10, 2014, five months after the 2014 Rose Parade, on another anniversary when they were reminded Cory was taken from them far too soon, his family gathered in Memphis. Making their way along Raleigh Lagrange's winding road, Kirby, Gina, and Jill rode the same route Cory had ridden on that fateful day so long ago. The white shirts they wore displayed Thunder's logo on the front. Cory's floragraph owned the back.

Catching a glimpse of a slender creek along the road's edge, Gina wondered if, on his final ride, Cory noticed it, too. Hearing a lark sing out overhead, she received her answer.

Enjoying the wind at her face, Jill inhaled the sweet fragrance of blooming oleander trees. She recalled a time, decades earlier, when Cory floated mature magnolias he broke off a neighbor's tree in her swimming pool. Recalling his contagious laugh, a smile came over her. *"A swimming pool is nothing but a big ole giant vase,"* he playfully insisted. His convincing smile had her laughing along with his silliness.

In the weeks following his accident, she found herself calling his cell phone. She had taken comfort in hearing his voice when unanswered calls went to the phone's voicemail. On the first birthday following his accident, she attempted to celebrate his life with a cake she ordered from a local bakery. Shaped like the star of Texas, it was decorated with silver, navy, and white icing. While wishing him the happiest of birthdays, the pain in her heart turned to resentment. Staring at the cake through teary eyes, she thought the five-point star looked like a soiled puzzle piece. Stepping outside, she hurled the cake across the yard, smashing it against an innocent fence. On this day, nine years since his death, she finally found the reminiscing healing.

Keeping a short distance behind Jill, Gina leisurely pedaled a bike she purchased for the ride. Nowhere near the skilled cyclist Cory had been, she kept a firm grip on the hi-cruiser handlebars. Taking in the fresh air May in Memphis offered, she questioned why she had never taken to biking. Enveloped in nature's pure beauty, she came to share Cory's passion. With her heart finally at peace, she recalled a conversation they shared long ago. "*Why do you coach?*" she asked. There was no hesitation in his answer. "*It's all about the kids.*" A coach herself, Gina agreed. When she asked how he dealt with the parents, he turned serious. "*I never forget I'm coaching the most precious thing in their lives—their child.*"

Easing her grip, Gina thought about his childhood. Through coaching, she believed he received from the kids what he never had. He found satisfaction in giving to his team what he always wanted, and surely needed. Surrounding himself with young people who looked to him for structure and discipline, he created his own little family.

Taking advantage of the silence, Kirby thought of the many times in recent years he telephoned his sisters. Their silence reminded him that he and Cory shared a similar voice. Before Cory was taken from them, they took turns confusing their sisters with messages they left on their answering machines. Pretending to be Kirby, Cory talked about Jennifer and Matthew, Kirby's children, their activities at school, and the latest happenings in Nashville. Enjoying the game, Kirby left messages about swim practice, the records his team broke, and Memphis' newest barbecue joints. They were so in sync with each other's lives, Gina and Jill never grew wise to their playful misconduct.

Riding these winding roads, it was difficult to not get flashes of Cory's last seconds when his bike slid out from under him. *Did he panic? Did he feel the pain of his injuries?* It took all he had to push these questions from his mind, and in some small way, he thought because he was riding the bike Cory had ridden his last day on earth, his brother was watching over him.

Much like the afternoon he packed Cory's apartment, the mood turned somber when he reflected back upon his own wedding day. Recalling Cory's low comb-over, he let go a grin. More than once, Cory had been called Opie. It was years later while watching an episode of *The Andy Griffith Show*, Cory finally understood the reason for his nickname.

It was nearly two months after Cory's accident, and almost a year since their father died, when he once again was reminded how much Cory meant not only to his family but also to thousands of others. It was a Sunday morning when he stopped at a local coffee shop after church service. Given his father had always called on Sunday mornings, and now that Cory was absent in his life, he found the day difficult and challenging. This particular Sunday had him missing Cory more than in recent days. Just about the time he was ready to give into the tears he struggled to hold back, he felt a hand on his shoulder.

Exchanging a handshake and a hug with a young man who often rode with Cory, he learned the triathlete and his teammates were returning from the Sunfish triathlon, an annual event Cory once enjoyed. Before parting, the young man, whose name he had forgotten, shared with him that he knew a guy who knew the man who received Cory's liver. On those days, when he allowed his thoughts to turn dark and empty, he worried about these agonizing moments. It was not yet noon and he had already been saddled with painful memories. A few days later, he received a phone call from the liver recipient. In their brief conversation, it was easy to hear he was a humble and gracious man. More than once, he repeated how thankful he was for the chance at life Cory had given him.

Focused on the road, his smile turned flat. Up ahead was the site of Cory's accident, the place where he took his final breath. The enclosed area, constructed by close friends the day they learned Cory was taken off support, was decorated with floral arrangements and notes visitors left behind. A Memphis Thunder sweatshirt hugged the small cross that bore Cory's name. A Thunder Racing jersey hung from the white picket fence. Standing several feet away, a *Share the Road* sign held his eye. At this moment, he had never been more proud of his baby brother.

Waiting for Jill and Gina to catch up, he stopped along the road's edge. As his sisters cycled toward him, a ray of sun danced through the trees. In the distance, a church bell rang. Gathering together, Cory's family held hands. The smiles they exchanged were wistful and heartfelt. Accepting the closure the moment intended, their hearts quickened. The time had come to turn back.

Taking to the open road, they pedaled side by side. Reaching into his pocket, Kirby retrieved the small urn he accepted from Gina at the start of the ride. Appreciating the warm wind at his face, the citrus scent of orange blossoms, and the knowing nods he received from his sisters, he removed the urn's pewter lid. Riding under a clear sky, Gina, Jill, and Kirby smiled when a gentle breeze caught Cory's ashes.

Photo Courtesy of Lesley Brainard, Memphis Thunder Racing

CHAPTER 55

It was on a Friday morning when Jill parked her car in a metered space along Dallas' McKinney Avenue. Needing caffeine, she darted into a coffee shop. Five pounds away from her goal weight, she waved away the cream cheese and raisin Danish the clerk suggested, and foregoing an added sweetener, ordered her coffee black. With a skip in her step, she made her way to an outside patio. Placing two quarters in the clerk's outstretched hand, she grabbed a newspaper along the way. Placing the world news, comics, and local insert aside, she turned to the restaurant reviews. She agreed with the critic's opinion on several of the restaurants she, too, had visited. Nothing was worse than a hot meal served at room temperature, receiving a well-done filet when ordered rare, or asking an uninformed waiter about the menu. When the writer criticized the long wait at a new establishment, she disagreed. A dinner she enjoyed there was well worth the wait.

When she reached for the sports section, her eyes were drawn to the picture on the cover. Posing in a swimsuit, a young girl held a trophy. Thinking of Cory, she turned to the story.

Only fourteen, LuLu Woodall has taken the swimming world by storm. A native of Memphis, she does not let a corneal transplant keep her out of the water. She continued reading as a chill came over her. When she read the girl's transplant had taken place on May 12, 2005, she threw a hand to her face. While the café's patrons watched on, she began to tremble. *Was it possible this young girl had received one of Cory's eyes?*

Thinking back to those days at The Med, her stomach snaked into a twisted knot. It was only now she remembered the child who wore sunglasses. Turning back to the picture of LuLu Woodall, she looked into her eyes, and believing they were once the windows to Cory's soul, she was brought to tears. Sweeping up the paper, she hurried to her car.

Weeks later, when she made a visit to Rogersville, LuLu Woodall continued to weigh on her mind. Carrying a blanket in her arms, she walked along the newly cut grass, now muddied after three days of rain and brief periods of intermittent sun. Pausing to brush hardened dirt from her spiky heels, she continued along the northern edge of the county's oldest cemetery. Arriving at the cornerstone, she stepped onto the Horton's family plot.

Dabbing at her nose, she placed a red rose on her mother's grave. Turning to her father's final resting place, she gave a gentle nod. Kneeling at Cory's headstone, she could not help but feel she had been cheated. Blowing a kiss in his direction, she bowed her head. "My Dear God, I pray you brought them together in your loving kingdom. Please let them know they are never forgotten, and that each and every day, they are missed far more than my simple words can say. Please continue to hold them in your loving arms."

She spread the blanket on the ground and sat with her legs at her side. Turning the pages of the book she had taken from Cory's apartment, she paused to exchange a smile. When it was first suggested that his picture be placed on the granite marker, she rejected the idea. Looking at him now, she was thankful she had been outnumbered in the final vote. "I believe you left off on page seventy-four." Stopping occasionally to share her thoughts about the inspirational book, she read aloud until it was time to say goodbye.

She allowed the cemetery's silence to comfort her. Turning to her mother's grave, it saddened her she could no longer remember the touch of her skin, the smell of her hair, or the voice she once found comforting. It had been difficult saying goodbye to her father, but those memories of him she kept close to her heart continued to be vivid and uplifting. Recalling his laugh, she chuckled. When her father fell into a deep belly laugh, his tummy rolled like an ocean's wave. His hands, once strong and able, softened in later years. His thick hair thinned with age, and the dark spots he once lovingly called freckles became badges of honor he earned along the way.

Turning her thoughts to Cory, she begged for only good memories to embrace her. Closing her eyes, she recalled the time he hopped onboard a Greyhound bus destined for California. His pockets were empty, but his heart was filled with promise. Just as she had then, she envied his innocence. When her thoughts began to drift to the days following his accident, she spoke of her children and their recent accomplishments. "You'd be so proud of them, Cory."

Recalling a recent visit to a shopping mall, she hurried to share a story. "I thought I saw you the other day. I was walking behind a man. He was about your height. He stopped several times to study the store windows. When he inquired about the goods a kiosk vendor offered, I was suddenly drawn to his red hair. My heart skipped a little when I saw that his shoulders were pushed back and that he walked with a slight rise in his step. As I grew closer, a lump hugged my throat when I noticed he was wearing khaki shorts. It wasn't until he turned in my direction that I realized I had called out your name."

She inhaled the sweet fragrance from a nearby rose garden. "I saw a picture of LuLu Woodall. Oh, Cory, I was such a mess...not wanting to believe what I was seeing. There was a story about her in the newspaper. She's a swimmer. Can you believe it? Her coach said she moves through the water like a hungry shark." Thinking back to the many times she stood on the pool deck while Cory cheered his team to the finish, she knew he would have enjoyed coaching this young woman. "You did a great thing, Cory. And all those times I find I'm still so angry about everything, I'm guided toward a different path, one where I'm reminded of how proud I am of you."

Staring at his headstone, her throat tightened. "I didn't want to give any part of you to anyone. I couldn't imagine losing more of you, if that makes any sense. I will say, though, and then I have to get going, when I saw that young girl and read she was living her life to its fullest, I wanted to shout at the top of my lungs that you, my baby brother, played a part in it." Placing her fingers to her lips, she blew three kisses up to the heavens. "Take care of each other. I love each of you with all my heart."

CHAPTER 56

In 2005, shortly after Cory lost his life, Memphis Thunder Racing held its first Kids Triathlon in his memory. In attendance were nearly 200 participants from seventeen cities and five states. Traveling from his family's home in Texas, Joshua Carpenter, Jill's son and Cory's nephew, competed in the junior division. The course was lined with blue, white, and silver balloons, and a barbecue picnic followed the awards ceremony. A health fair set up near the picnic area provided brochures on cycle safety and awareness, proper nutrition, and sports programs aimed at introducing young athletes to the sport.

Now an annual event held at the Compton Aquatic Center at St. George's Collierville campus, the triathlon's junior division includes ages seven through ten, and a senior division for ages eleven through fourteen. The event also includes a relay division. The Cory Horton Sportsmanship Award is given based upon community nominations.

CHAPTER 57

In losing Cory, Silvie lost a part of her. Looking back at the moment she raced from The Med, refusing to accept his death, she survived the days ahead by turning her back to miracles, hope, and her faith in something greater. In the days following his accident, she was made aware of his arrangement with her parents. All those things he had seen in her died with him.

In her time of pain and darkness, when quitting life appeared to be the only answer, memories of her days with him passed before her eyes so fast she struggled to keep up.

A decade later, the memories were still painful, but her heart had grown a little stronger. Now, when her thoughts turned to him, she understood how fortunate and blessed she had been to have him in her life. Recalling his infectious laugh, a smile broke out across her face every time.

Stepping into the assistant coaching position Cory once held, she hoped he would be proud of her.

Each afternoon, when she made her way to the student recreation center on Echles Road, her thoughts turned to him. Like many of her Thunder teammates, she had not returned to swimming—until now.

Surrounded by the team's guppies, she opened practice with a cheer. *We are the guppies, and we're here to swim. When Coach Cory speaks, we zip our lips and listen to him.* When the children asked about Cory, she raised her face to the heavens. "He's the angels' favorite swim coach."

EPILOGUE

During his short life, Cory Scott Horton touched the lives of many people, including family, friends, swim team participants, and many others. Hopefully, this book presents an accurate picture in honoring his life.

Any omission of events and facts are not purposeful. The challenging task of incorporating the vast amounts of information from those who shared both insight and quotes was, at times, overwhelming. If I have offended anyone, I ask for your understanding and forgiveness.

As a writer, my intent was not to cover his life in detail. That, of course, is an impossible task. From the beginning, my objective was to write a book capturing the true essence of his being—the value of serving others rather than oneself. This selfless desire to make others feel better about themselves and to develop their innate potential is what made him such a tremendous mentor and friend to the young and the old.

Cory's siblings provided information about his early childhood and their family life. I am forever grateful for their input. I also wish to thank Jill Horton Carpenter for personally meeting with me. She provided ongoing support by answering questions and filling in the gaps.

A special word of thanks goes to Donate Life America, Mid-South Transplant Foundation, and Explore Transplant. I cannot thank these organizations enough for their input and support.

Through his organ donations, Cory's legacy lives on with a new team. How apropos that a man who gave so much of himself while living is also giving of himself after his departure.

Today, a replica of Cory's bike rests high among the trees on the Collierville campus of St. George's Independent School. Below it, a plaque honors his life. "*In Memory of Cory Horton, St. George's Director of Aquatics, 2000-2005. This bike hangs high against a background of pool and sky as a symbol of Cory's perseverance, charisma, ability to motivate, and his commitment to promoting his students' best efforts. Let us take a moment now and then to remember Coach Cory and to use his memory as an example to try harder, never quit, stay positive, be kind to all, and always seek the best within us and others.*"

In writing *Thunder's Glory*, I reached out to Gina Horton Cheatham, Jill Horton Carpenter, and Kirby Horton. They answered a myriad of questions, some more painful and difficult than others, and several that returned their thoughts to May 10, 2005, the day that forever changed their lives. I also asked members of Memphis Thunder Aquatic Club and Cory's close friends to share their memories.

"Cory, not a day goes by that you are not in my thoughts. You are missed beyond words. I love you and will always be your 'Hurricane.'" — Gina Horton Cheatham

"Cory, it has taken me many years to learn to live in a world without you in it. I love you and miss you every day." — Jill Horton Carpenter

"Cory was a very special person. He brought out the best in everyone by encouraging and challenging them. He was a wonderful role model and led by example." — Kirby Horton

"The essence of transplantation:

"I was told I had two weeks to live. I had chronic liver failure from Hepatitis B, which I contracted in the operating room while practicing orthopedic surgery. I had been sick for the previous three years and now found myself at the end of the line. My only hope was that a liver could be found that would perhaps save my life. A thirty-year-old South Texas housewife had a bleeding aneurysm, and died, but before she died, she made a commitment to be an organ donor. Just as the decision Cory Horton made, my donor gave me the gift of life. The miracle of transplantation is to be so sick and then to be so well. This was twenty-eight years ago. I've had my forty-ninth wedding anniversary, experienced the love of eight grandchildren, and have had the opportunity to help thousands of people as a physician, all the things I would have missed. We met my donor's family and they told us they were so happy for us, knowing their daughter was still alive, doing things for other people. This is the very essence of transplantation.

"Donate Life Texas, the organization which maintains a registration list of people who have made the decision to donate if the circumstance arises, was instrumental in this process. Each state has such an organization to ensure needed organs may be placed to patients in need.

"Needless to say, I will be forever grateful for my gift of life. Cory made such a gift, and his gift to others will ensure his memory will be alive for many years to come." — Phil Berry MD, Past President, Texas Medical Association, liver recipient

"Some of my favorite memories are from EMCC—playing foosball before practice, and when the greyhound fell in the pool, and the bubble always deflating. I also remember all the bike rides we would do in the summer." — Patricia Black, MTAC member

"Whenever I hear Howie Day's *Collide*, I think of Cory. It came out right about the time Cory died, and the verse that goes, 'Even the best fall down sometimes. Even the wrong words seem to rhyme. Out of the doubt that fills my mind, I somehow find you and I collide,' will always make me think of him. For the longest time, I cried when I heard the song. Cory fell, and when he fell, a part of me fell with him. Today, when the song comes across the radio, I smile. Cory fell, but I'm standing stronger and taller today because I knew him." — Sarah Kramer, MTAC member

"Cory used to give high-fives, not unusual for a coach, but his were different. His were *earned*. When my tiny palms met his larger ones, I knew I'd done well. Maybe I shattered my time or crushed the girl next to me. Who cares? I didn't, so long as he fived me. One other thing. Spit. Yes, spit. Cory was a prankster par excellence. He was particularly proficient in the Wet Willie (a prank whereby an assailant moistens one of his fingers with saliva, quietly sneaks up behind a victim, and inserts the finger into the victim's ear hole). The first day I met Cory, he willied me. Rather than cringe with disgust, I surveyed his dampened finger with interest and asked matter-of-factly: Is there saliva on that? Cory roared with delight. Why that tickled him so I'll never know." — Chelsea Michta, MTAC member

"Cory was family—kind of like an older brother, I guess. Frustrating and ridiculous at times, but always my role model. Cory taught me the importance of self-discipline and hard work. Cory taught me the importance of confidence. Cory taught me the importance of timelines (I'm still working on this one). Most importantly, Cory taught me the importance of a smile. There are too many memories to recall, but there isn't one memory I have that does not end in us laughing. We lost Cory too young, but he played a critical role in forming the person I am today and I will be forever thankful for him and grateful for the time we got to share." — Ryan Weaver, MTAC member

"I love that you are writing a book about Cory; it's an amazing way to remember him. Because of Cory, I am the person I am today. He has been with me every step of my life, whether it has to do with swimming or not. He was not only my coach, but also a great friend and person for thirteen years of my life. When I was younger, he would have to throw me into the pool because I was too stubborn to get in the water. While not much has changed from that except the fact he no longer has to throw me in, he has still taught me so much about life and how not to care about the little things in life. There are too many memories and lessons that I have learned from Cory that it would fill up at least fifty pages, if not many more. For me, this serves as a letter to thank him for everything he has given me throughout our time together, and I just want him to know that I appreciate it all even if I never showed it. Cory, I love you more than anything else in the world, and I am going to miss you so much! Thanks for everything again, and I dedicate to you all of my swimming success." — Margo McCawley, MTAC member

"Cory parked his Jeep at my house when he went out biking, so he would not have to climb the hill up to Raleigh LaGrange. We talked the morning of his accident...just small talk. He was so happy to go out and ride. I told him to be safe, and he smiled and waved as he rode down my drive. He never came back." — Kathleen Fortner Clark, parent of MTAC members, Caitlin and Chris

Kathleen wrote the following after Cory's memorial service:

"Because of Cory, I have happier, more self-confident children, have wonderful memories, have more gray hair, will always love redheads, will never be annoyed by bikers on the road, am working out again, and will encourage my children to remember to strive for excellence."

"I think one of my favorite things about Cory was that he made swimming fun. For example, on the Fourth of July, we did about ten or so 400s (16 laps each). Despite the long distance, he made the sets interesting and we felt like we were having fun the entire time. He called them "Firecracker 400s" and gave us candy whenever we completed a set. At practice, he was always joking around with us, cheering us on, and making us laugh. I never felt like I was going to a boring swim practice, but rather that I was hanging out with friends and swimming for fun. Cory was definitely the reason why I loved swimming and stayed with the sport for as long as I did." — Aska Arnautovic, MTAC member

"Who knew this curly red head would change my life? Cory founded Memphis Thunder Aquatic Club in 1997 with only one swimmer, Margo McCawley. Little did he know that this would turn into a nationally ranked swim team. The swim team grew larger and went on to train at the East Memphis Catholic Club. There were now sixty swimmers. In this pool, Cory taught us life lessons, such as how to restore a pool bubble and where to go when there is a tornado while you are swimming. Swimming for Coach Cory had its advantages and disadvantages. During 'cool downs,' he had us scrubbing the algae from the pool. He laughed each time he called Alex Kaltenborn and me the 'love birds'...he called me eli-ANA. I chased him around the pool deck singing Blondie's song, *One Way or Another*...he'd laugh. The disadvantages? Wet willies and falling for his 'dog jaw' prank. The best advantage was learning I was capable of more than I thought, and even when I wanted to give up, he never let me quit. Cory not only encouraged my comedic behavior, he played along with it."— Sophie Eliana Kramer, MTAC member

"I wonder why my swim coach had to die. They say the best die last but this was far from true. Cory Horton changed hundreds of people's lives in more ways than he will ever know. Most kids dreaded going to any sporting practice their parents forced them into, but with Cory as a coach, practice never seemed like practice. If everyone had Cory's carefree outlook on life, this world would be a much happier place. The thing I admired most about Cory was how he made every single one of his swimmers feel like they were the next Michael Phelps. You never felt defeated after a bad race. If someone asked me to pick my favorite memory of Cory, I honestly would not be able to tell you. Whether it is the obscure nicknames, adventure races, cheese fries, camping trips, or just a normal day of practice, every time we were with Cory we never left without a smile on our faces. You would think after so many years it would get easier to write or talk about Cory, but the impact he left on my life is irreversible. I know you're looking down on us with your fiery red hair, laughing at all the shenanigans we get ourselves into nowadays. I just want to thank you, Cory, from the bottom of my heart for helping shape my elementary and middle school days for the better. You will never know how much you and your constant attempt at cheesy jokes meant to your entire fellow MTAC swimmers. Love, Mad Madison Mucus May Membrane." — Maddie McMillan, MTAC member

"Cory. He was Cory, himself, unpretentious, goofy, disorganized (he said that) with his heart in the right place—1000% for the kids. As a parent, I knew he had my child's best interest at heart—always—not just when she did well, but always. He knew what to say to her when she did poorly and what to say when she excelled. Usually, it was what he did not say, that meant the most. I think about him often. I am grateful that she had the privilege of training under him. He cared and that is what ultimately counts." — Cristina Michta, parent of MTAC member, Chelsea Michta

"Cory was so special to me. He inspired me to be confident in myself, not just swimming ability, but everything in life. He had an incredible ability to encourage us both lovingly and sternly. He made us laugh, whether it was by giving us wet willies or speaking in funny voices. One special time I remember was when Cory rode to a swim meet with my mom and me. We listened to Tim McGraw the whole way, sang loudly to *My Next Thirty Years*, and talked the whole time. Cory was full of life, and he made such an impact on my life and so many people's lives." — Mary Jensen Nease, MTAC member

"One of my favorite memories was doing relays at Ridgeway with sour straws." — Chris Clark, MTAC member

"Cory was a goofball. He always liked to kid around whether it was with his bee stings behind the arm, the wet willies, or making fun of you for wearing a camouflage swimsuit and claiming that he can't see you talking to him, but he could hear you (yes, that was me). Cory always made practice fun no matter what we were doing, but he was also serious about it. He taught me a lot about working hard, never giving up, and showing me a passion for the sport of swimming even when days were rough. Cory never wanted you to quit. He always wanted you to push through when it was hard because pushing through hard workouts only made you better, and that's what he wanted for us, to be better and not give up. I think this is why I call myself a 'grinder' to this day—I just push through. I would like to share two stories that I still remember to this day. It was at one of my first few swim meets on Thunder and Cory wanted us to come talk to him after every race. Well, I had a race I was not proud of because I did not have a good time. I was upset at myself so I did not want to go talk to Cory after it because I didn't want to hear what he had to say. The next huddle we had as a group (I believe it was around relay time) he mentioned that we needed to make sure we talk to him after every race and sure enough, I was called out for not doing that very thing he had asked from us. This shows that Cory cared about everyone and their races. He wanted us to come talk to him whether it was a good race or not. He wanted to talk about it so we could fix what was wrong or concentrate on what was right, all because he wanted us to be better and be the best. My second story was when we were building the pool at St. George's School and we were swimming in an above-ground pool, for the time being, that was only two lanes. One day, I was swimming in the left lane (closer to the trees) and there was a snake in my lane. Panicked, I switched lanes because I hate snakes and was afraid to swim next to it. I got caught and Cory asked, 'Kirby, what are you doing in the other lane?' I replied, 'There is a snake in that lane.' He came back with, 'I don't care. Don't bother it and it won't bother you, now move back over.' With fear and anxiety running through my mind and across my face, I did what he said and swam with the snake. Thinking back on it now, I probably did the fastest flip turns in my life during that practice!" — Kirby Rhodes, MTAC member

"Cory was the person, the elite athlete person, who always ran back on the course to cheer for the rest of us. That is his legacy...a talent beyond measure with a huge, gracious, encouraging heart." — Angela Redden

"I can still see his smiling, freckled face and his mop of red hair as he joked with his swimmers. He was infectious—so happy and vibrant. I don't recall him ever getting angry or yelling. He was always positive and upbeat." — Bruce S. Kramer, parent of MTAC members, Sarah and Sophie Kramer

"His death leaves a void in this community that cannot be filled. In time, though, many happy memories of his passionate commitment to swimming, St. George's Independent School, the Memphis Thunder Aquatic Club and, most importantly, the young people with whom he worked will begin to assuage our pain and sadness." — William Taylor, School President, St. George's Independent School

"I have so many great memories…checkmarks of excellence…his willingness to try so many different things to make us faster (getting a massage service to come every week, buying motivational CDs). Just the time he spent talking to us about life. Strangely, I enjoyed the time I was injured, because I got to ride the bike on the deck of the pool while Cory coached. While everyone was swimming, we chatted, and it was really fun for me. I look back on that time and am grateful that I had it with him. One of the last times I talked with him was at the University Club at a country club swim meet. I was very burned out on swimming and he knew it, so we just talked as he coached. It's a great memory." — Grace Jensen Knight, MTAC member

"There was this one Saturday morning practice and I was told, along with a few others my age, while most got out of the water for dry land, that we were going to finish the day with six 1650s (miles). My mouth dropped. We had already done so much swimming (I was probably ten), how could we do six? When we had a fifty left in the mile, Cory would hold up a kickboard to let me know we were almost done with that one. I got faster each mile, because Cory kept telling me I was 'tough as nails' and that was the morning he came up with the nickname, 'Sparky.' He told me I had so much energy and was going to be one of the best in the country. That man made me believe in myself more than anyone ever has and I truly believe it's because of him that I had any amount of success. He pushed everyone to believe they could do anything they wanted. He always reminded us he would never give us a set that we couldn't handle." — Lindsey Brackens, MTAC member

"Coaches don't always practice what they preach. It was the spring of 1995, and it was time to get into shape. It had been about three years since Cory competed in anything. Food was tasting good and watching WWF wrestling was better than getting out on the road to run and bike. Cory had a great idea one night after watching wrestling. 'Why don't I try the Bay Swim in Pensacola, Florida?' I looked at him and told him, 'You're getting fat...maybe you can float across the bay.' It was a long swim across the bay, and I honestly thought he was crazy for even considering it. There were four weeks until the swim, and Cory was determined to prove me wrong. He left at four o'clock each morning to go to swim practice. He informed me that he was swimming before practice, and everything was on track for him to complete that bay swim. Cory started to eat better, too. No more frozen pizzas. Red beans and rice was the carbs and protein for Cory now. Each day I would give him a hard time about it. I told him he would never be able to swim across the bay in Pensacola. I told him he was basically going to be fish bait and the sharks were going to have a nice dinner. Cory just looked at me and said, 'Shut up!' Yep, that was me, the true motivator. The four weeks quickly flew by, and it was time to drive down to Pensacola. We took my wife's car because Cory's car had not been driven in over two years. We got down to Pensacola in great spirits. Cory was excited, and also confident that everything was going to go well. We went out for the pre-race dinner. Cory was determined and excited about the next morning. We woke early the morning of the race and drove Cory down to the bay. Hundreds of swimmers were in the water warming up for the race. Not Cory. He was just stretching and walking around. I asked him why he wasn't out there warming up. He said, 'I'm saving my energy.'

The blow horn sounded a five-minute warning until race time. Cory went over to the water, got wet, and started to get ready. Five minutes later, the horn sounded, and Cory took off. We got in the car and drove to the finish line. We waited and waited. Swimmers started to come in after an hour or so. We kept thinking Cory should be done in the next fifteen minutes. Another thirty minutes went by…and still no Cory. Then, we started to see some older swimmers come in. I actually did begin to wonder if he was eaten by a shark. A little while later, we saw Cory. We cheered loudly for him. As he staggered out of the water and up the beach, I told him, 'Well, you made it!' His reply? 'Yeah…get me a towel. I gotta rest.' We got some fluids in him and a towel, which he spread out on the beach and collapsed on. When I asked Cory what was wrong, he told me that he had to stop nine times to hang on the ropes to rest. We laughed and teased Cory about almost being eaten by a shark the rest of the weekend. He had the worst sunburn from that swim. We lazed around the rest of that day and the next. He was so sunburned one of his friends suggested he use some of their stuff to help ease the pain. He took it and smeared it all over his face. He was truly a sight to be seen with his red hair and white gunk all over his face. We looked at the tube of white stuff…it was Desitin. We laughed so hard and told him he was smearing diaper ointment all over himself. Cory was a good-natured person and shrugged it off. It didn't bother him. I think he was willing to try anything that would ease his discomfort. For Cory, that race was his wake-up call. He decided to get himself back into shape and begin (to) truly start competing again.

Cory was a great guy, best friend, and Great Teacher. I have seen his ups and downs with forming Thunder and also getting back into shape after a long layoff. We had a big picture for Thunder, making it one of the top swim clubs but also Tri clubs and distance running clubs in the USA. Cory had a vision but also a passion for giving back to the sport. But I think Cory has done more with his death than Thunder would have done. Giving his organs to another person is unselfish and he is a true hero. This is what he was all about…always giving." — Bill Hoffman

"I was never the best swimmer. I'll admit to that. My talents lay in my academics, theater, and singing. Cory knew that, and always encouraged me. My favorite memory of Cory occurred one day before practice at World Overcomers. I was incredibly nervous, because I was auditioning for a school play that week. Cory noticed that I was distracted, and asked me what was wrong. When I told him that I was nervous about the auditions, he smiled at me and had me come back into the office with him and a couple of my teammates. He sat down at his desk, and he asked me to sing my audition piece for him. I was so surprised. I knew he was very supportive of my other endeavors besides swimming, but I had never really thought he would want to hear me sing. I did, and I felt much more confident afterward with his applause and approval. I never forgot that day. A year and a half later, I was once again auditioning for a play and had practiced my number for Cory the week before the auditions. Little did I know that the next week, he would be gone. I held it together during my audition and did my very best; because I knew he wouldn't want me to fall apart then. I dedicated that performance to him when it was time to open the show, and I know Cory has had a front row seat at every performance I've done since." — Caitlin Clark, MTAC member

"Remembering May, 12, 2005...the ringing of the phone with the tragic news forever will be imprinted on my mind and heart. I recall a blur of emotions, anxious and sad; gatherings of athletes, sitting on the floor at the memorial service at St. George's High School gym, a drive out to Rossville where "it" happened. Because for everyone, it was unbelievable, surreal, just not possible to have lost someone so talented, so young, so loved. Now in the summer of 2015, walking the boardwalk on the campus of St. George's High School in the misty early morning hours with my husband, David, by my side, we stop and reflect on "trying harder, never quitting, staying positive, showing kindness to all, and to always seek the best within us and others." Cory's memory is forever honored by the students and faculty with those beautiful words in a peaceful, verdant space where his bike is suspended between statuesque, sun-kissed trees in a "background of pool and sky." Cory's Life Mattered. — Denise Burnett Stewart

"Because of Cory I...

"...have learned that when you put a simple ballpoint pen checkmark on a child's face and call it a 'mark of excellence,' that child can swim faster and their confidence will soar.

"...have learned that a 'bee sting' is fun and a sign of affection, that being called 'ugly' is a good thing, and that having a kickboard thrown at you is an honor.

"...that you don't have to have a mean bone in your body, or even know how to be harsh, to make children listen to you, respect you, and work hard to please you.

"...have seen that you only have to be kind, loving, understanding, and funny to make kids want to come every day and swim a couple of miles and work harder than they ever have for anything in their lives.

"...know that you don't have to be related to someone by blood to be family.

"...will have a footprint on my heart that will last forever. We will never forget you. We love you, and always will." — LeeAnn Wahlen, parent of MTAC member, Kristen Wahlen

"Cory had an influence on me unlike any other. His upbeat attitude and infectious smile were never-ending, even in times when he was faced with the most adversity. He loved working with the kids and encouraging adults to get the most out of themselves. We used to ride together and he always made sure I ran first to get me tired. It took me a while to figure that one out, but when I did he just smiled. With my running and swimming background, Cory encouraged me to try the sport of triathlon. He never let up on me. I never did triathlons while he was still with us, but did years later and always hope he is happy with my performances. Cory also helped my daughter, Katherine, learn to swim. One day in the pool, she was swimming all over the lane. Cory made her stop to ask her if she needed a map so she could swim straight. Just so typical of Cory. I only hope my life can have the impact on people that Cory's had on so many. There isn't a negative memory or feeling in my heart when thinking of my old friend. I knew him from the early '90s when he lived with Bill Hoffman in 'hobo heaven,' and always enjoyed his company and friendship." — Mark Newman

"My first swim tryout is an experience I will never forget, thanks to Coach Cory. I was nine-years-old and determined to make an impression with my newfound swim skills. To my surprise, it was not the kind of impression I had been planning. As I entered the pool, Cory told me, "Okay, let's see what you got." I fiercely put on my goggles and started to swim what I thought was a flawless freestyle out and back. Once I was back to the wall, I looked up at Cory in anticipation of a compliment such as, "Whoa. That was awesome!" Instead, Cory's witty and comical response was, "Gee, Katherine, do you need a map of the pool?" I didn't understand at first, but then realized I had arbitrarily swum all over the place, in every direction. This was one of the first times I had ever learned to laugh at myself. Afterward, he graciously taught me how to use the lines at the bottom of the pool in order to swim straight. Now, over fifteen years later, every time I swim laps and look down at those stripes I am reminded of Coach Cory, his sharp sense of humor, and to swim in a straight line." — Katherine Newman, MTAC member

"Thinking back to my days spent swimming for Cory, I can honestly say that he inspired us all to work hard, regardless of the situation, which is something I've carried with me throughout my life. When I started swimming at Thunder, we were in a tiny, moldy pool (which we spent plenty of time writing our names at the bottom when we thought he wasn't looking). It was far from glamorous, but the day I tried out for the team, I told my mom that this was where I absolutely wanted to be. Our pool wasn't the biggest or cleanest, but Cory taught us that we didn't need any of that to swim fast. In the winter, our outdoor pool was covered only by an unheated bubble that was so foggy that you couldn't see someone ten feet in front of you, and in the summer, we switched to an equally as small country club pool that was so cold we all turned blue. On top of that, his practices were hard, sometimes nearly impossible, but I still asked to come early and stay late nearly every day because he made working hard fun. Cory's job wasn't over when practice was over. He enjoyed being around us even outside of practice. Cory would judge our pike competitions before and after practice, watch us 'ice skate' (more like shuffle) on the frozen baby pool outside in the winter, play foosball with us in the game room (sometimes with a cheese puff if we couldn't find the ball), and, as soon as some of us starting showing an interest in triathlons, he would take us for long bike rides on top of our normal practices. There was something about the atmosphere he created that made you proud to be there. We wore our sore muscles and frozen toes as a badge of honor. Cory helped us to believe that if we could succeed in these conditions, there was nothing we couldn't do." — Miranda Kaltenborn, MTAC member

"It's a hard lesson to learn that life can be taken away in an instant, especially a life that was so vibrant and energetic. I found myself questioning why bad things happen to good people and thinking about things I should have said or done differently. With time though, the anger, the questions, and even the tears fade, and now I focus on all the good memories. The last time I cried in front of Cory, he had his hand on my back pushing me home after he got us lost on a bike ride to Shelby Forest. He decided that since it was ninety degrees outside, we should take his short cut to get home faster, but soon, we were lost in a really bad neighborhood outside of Memphis. Our seventy-mile bike ride ended up over a hundred miles. From then on, I knew to be weary of Cory's sense of direction, but I also knew he would have done anything to make sure I was home safely. My relationship with Cory began when I was eight years old, and I could never have imagined the impact he would have on my life. I will never forget the first time I met him, he was instantly my idol. I don't know what it was about him, maybe his red hair, his kind nature, or even just his huge smile, but I was fascinated by him. When I started swimming for Cory two years later, I knew I would never have any other coach. He taught me to have fun, set goals, and dream big. When Cory started Memphis Thunder, I knew right away I wanted to continue swimming for him. I called Cory that night and told him I wanted to be on his team. He was so excited and told me I was the first member of his team. When Cory started his team, he had five swimmers and no pool. We swam an entire summer either in the basement of an old building downtown or in a backyard lap pool. Yet, we were really good. We were good because Cory pushed us to work hard, he motivated us to be the best swimmers and people that we could be, and he encouraged us every step of the way. Cory dedicated his life to his team; he was so selfless that he would not even save any money to buy himself a new car. Cory drove the ugliest, dirtiest, most run down little red car. It was pretty horrendous to even look at, but the real fun started when I was privileged enough to ride to school in it after morning practices. As I held the falling ceiling above my head and sat on top of piles of stuff, Cory would slowly make his way to my school. I was so embarrassed that he drove me to school in that car that I would make him drop me off far out of anyone's sight, and then I would sprint from the car to the building. Cory did not care that his car was broken down or that we did not have our own pool. Cory was just happy he had his team, and he did everything he could to make sure that we were the best swimmers and people we could possibly be. Those were the reasons we loved Cory so much. He was such a simple guy on the outside, but he had an innate ability to change people's lives for the better. I'll never forget the year we biked over 3,000 miles together, the time my sister serenaded him with Shania Twain songs, or that he lacked any fashion sense which was especially noticed on a mostly female team. I'll also never forget that a few weeks before Cory passed away, he told me that he was going to really focus on his passions in life: his family and friends, coaching, and training for triathlons. Cory's zeal for life was contagious and spread throughout every one of those aspects of his life. I have to remind myself often to live a little more like Cory, and it is that example and role model that I am forever thankful for. Cory was more than just a coach and training partner to me and hundreds of other people. Cory was a mentor and best friend." — Katie Siegal Griffin, MTAC member

"Working and coaching with Cory was a lot of fun. Some of the mornings at Ridgeway I think we had as much fun talking and joking with each other as the kids did swimming. He was usually in the mood to tease the kids and he would let them have fun until it was time to be serious. You knew when it was time to work and he expected the kids to work hard… Cory was not much for deadlines and paperwork, but always expected everyone to arrive on time to practice. Things always had a way of working out, even if it seemed our entries would not be there on time for the meet, or we didn't know what pool we would be in next. This was frustrating at times. I would think of all sorts of things to say to him and how I was going to approach him with a particular concern, and then I would see him and I usually softened quite a bit because I could never really be upset with Cory. Every month or so, I would have to remind him that I had not received a paycheck. He would ask how much he owed me, and then usually get it to me fairly quickly. He was not driven by money or recognition, and coached because he enjoyed it and was good at it. He was also very trusting. He was a big kid himself and once he started really training again he did not want to miss those bike rides for anything. He would plan his training around the swim practice schedules, and I think some of the teaching at St. George's cramped his style a little because he was not as free with his time as he had been previously. He enjoyed the coaching a lot more than the teaching. When we started Thunder Racing Triathlon Team, I found out, even more than I already knew, how good a 'salesman' Cory was. He could talk about his ideas and I often wondered how he was going to achieve some of his dreams, but somehow, he got others to believe and have similar dreams. When Thunder Racing really took off, he definitely wanted the name to get out there and he wanted us to beat all of the other local teams, and everyone else for that matter. This was really exciting for all of us, especially when we did. We were so proud to have the beginners and the elite on the same team and this is why Thunder has really grown over the past few years. It is a dream for everyone, and the main thing is we have fun with the sport of triathlon and achieve our goals in the process. One of the last times I ran with Cory was to warm up for the Dash n' Splash at the University of Memphis…he chose to do a relay with Margo instead of doing it as an individual for himself. This was probably her last time to do this race, and he wanted her to do it because she had never missed it and she didn't want to do the whole thing herself. Anyway, I thought that it was so unselfish for him to do this as a relay when he could have possibly won the event on his own since he was in really good shape. Once again, he was not there for the recognition. This is just one example of how he lived his life. I was blessed to be able to coach alongside Cory with Memphis Thunder Aquatic Club and there was never a dull moment. From my 'interview' which consisted of breakfast at Perkins in which we chatted about everything from swimming, to triathlon, to common friends we knew, we knew we had to work together. It was a match made in heaven and we looked forward to seeing each other on the pool deck every day. The pool deck ranged from St. George's to Ridgeway to World Overcomers to the blow up pool at St. George's, but Cory would not give up on his team and we did what we had to do to help those kids become better swimmers. He would let me bring my young girls to practice while we coached and he would always find time to make everyone feel special. He had a talent for being a friend, and also a coach that could be respected. He could pick up my girls and act like he was going to throw them in the pool and turn around the next moment and critique someone's stroke. He was full of life and lived life to the fullest. Cory didn't care about money or worldly possessions. His car was a mess and he didn't care. He cared about people. He would do anything for his swimmers and he poured his life and his love into his team that he built. Cory was special and he touched every life that crossed his path. I was one of the lucky ones that can say he was a great friend. My life has been changed because of my close friendship with Cory and I will always miss his smile, and the pool deck will never be the same without him." — Lesley Brainard, friend and Co-Founder, Memphis Thunder Racing

"There is a special and very strong bond you get with other endurance athletes who you spend many hours training and racing with and who become close friends. It comes from having this crazy drive to push yourself to the limits of your capability, which requires tons of focused and often painful effort, and then looking around to see that someone else *"enjoys"* the same thing. It comes down to the incredible, deep sense of accomplishment and self-fulfillment that comes first from just being willing to make the effort, and second, when you have a performance or fitness peak to be proud of, by whatever measure you have. As Andrew Talansky, Pro Cyclist with Garmin Racing, said, 'All the pain, suffering, crashing, and sickness is worth that one moment of reward.' I've often said it is a blessing and a curse to have such passions, and I know so well what is going on in my fellow athletes' heads regarding all of this. It is a great and funny group to spend time with. And you REALLY come to know who has a special, deep, and sincere kindness and interest in others doing well. I can tell you that doing a 100-mile training ride in Memphis heat teaches you a lot about someone you're with. Cory was EVERYTHING a fine person could be. I promise you, I know. And thank you to all the others that have given me the same special bond of friendship." — Jimmy Reed

"Cory was someone I admired. It always amazed me how hard he worked when we were out training. Cory was an inspiration to all the young kids that he coached. He was always able to motivate them to do more than they thought they could do." — Walt Rider, Owner of Rider Performance Cycles

"I was fortunate to get to know Cory through a mutual interest in the sport of triathlon. So many good memories of him. He had the best sense of humor that spilled over into the sport we loved so much, including the last weekend before his accident. He spent it competing in the Panama City Beach Half Ironman along with a beach house full of his friends. I was there and haven't had so many belly laughs in my entire life. From bodysurfing the day we got there to watching him fill his grocery cart full enough to feed a small family of four. That was a special weekend for me that I will never forget. On the day of his accident, which was only one day after returning from the beach, he called me for the recipe for a dish that I had fixed for everyone at the beach house that weekend and said he was going for a ride and then fix that same dish afterward. It's hard to think about it because of the pain of missing Cory, but I like to think back to those great times and as I sit here and write about him, I see vividly his face and it makes me smile. Miss you, Cory."— Doug Ruddle

"TENNESSEE'S swimming community is in mourning after the death of Cory Horton, the owner of the Memphis Thunder Aquatic Club and the coach of St. George's Episcopal High School. Horton passed away last Thursday, after being involved in a cycling accident on Tuesday. He was 35 years old.

"According to newspaper reports, Horton was riding his bike around noon on Tuesday when he began to be passed by a tractor towing a piece of land-leveling equipment. A motorist behind the tractor said that Horton's bike began to wobble as the land-leveler passed and Horton fell under the rear wheels of the equipment.

"On Sunday, a memorial service was held at St. George's, where hundreds gathered to celebrate the life of Horton. Prior to the memorial service, about 100 individuals took part in a bike ride to St. George's that honored Horton. Recently, Horton had returned to triathlon competition." — Swimming World/Sports Publications, Swimming World News, May 16, 2005

"Because of Cory, I...

"Realized you never outgrow skateboarding.

"Learned that the skateboard is the preferred method of transportation while carrying a bag of laundry in one hand and a bag of popcorn in the other from the apartment to the laundry room...and back.

"Learned that a bag of microwave popcorn contains all the major food groups and that it is not just for breakfast anymore.

"Realized that some people cannot help but smile whenever they see a familiar face regardless of the situation…and that smile will brighten the recipient's day.

"Learned that a stroke of a pen on a child's face means as much as any hug or spoken words ever have.

"Realized that children will try harder because of mutual love and respect than fear of failure.

"Learned that you can be a softy and tough at the same time and that it can be done quietly.

"Realized that having Starburst thrown at you while swimming is 'cool.'

"That being told, 'My favorite time of day is when you leave' is a good thing.

"Realized that I could not have found a better mentor and role model for my child than Cory Horton. You will be dearly missed." — David Wahlen, parent of MTAC member, Kristen Wahlen

"Cory and I spent many hours on the bike, in the pool or out running on the road. Quite honestly, most of the stories I would tell are hilarious to me, but probably not very funny to anyone who wasn't there. He could put a smile on your face on your worst day. He was selfless, and was always ready to help. I'm not sure Cory even knew how to put himself first. His smile was contagious. His face would beam in the presence of his swimmers and friends. I'm so thankful for my lack of swimming ability. Without that, I would never have met Cory. We were introduced one evening at the gym through a mutual friend. We set up a few nights of "lessons." Cory would be all dressed and ready to go out, but first he'd be on the pool deck giving me instructions and trying to help me swim. Always putting others first! Those nights turned into seriously early swim practices at St. George's before the school would open. We had some great race road trips, small bike wrecks, relationship conversations, and just plain ole good times. Cory and I were riding, swimming, running buddies back in the day. He taught me how to ride

and swim (and race, really) and I got him back into running. He was one of the best friends I've ever had. There is not a day that goes by that I don't think about him and that smile. Every time we would go for a ride, if there was a turtle in the middle of the road, Cory would stop and move it to the side. Goes to show you how big his heart was. This time last year, I went for a run. Right before the run I was thinking, 'If you're around Cory, it'd be great to know.' So I went for my run and in the middle of the street, in the middle of a busy neighborhood, there was a turtle! I picked him up and put him on the side of the road. I cried and laughed the whole way home. One story about his kind heart...we were riding out in Lakeland...I called a right-hand turn late...we ran into each other. He went down...I somehow stayed up. We continued to finish our ride. About a week later, I found out he broke his thumb in the fall. He didn't want to tell me...I guess he didn't want to make me feel bad. His accident was on Tuesday...we had planned to ride on Friday, three days later. He was going to wait on me to ride because I couldn't go with the main group on Saturday. He sent an email, 'I'll wait for you. It's not safe to ride alone.' I wish he had waited. I only knew Cory for four years, but he left a lasting impression on my life that will never leave me...I'm honored to have known Cory. I'm not sure we'll ever understand why he was taken, but heaven gained a tremendous soul. I feel as if we have an incredible guardian angel watching over us. I'll see him again one day...hopefully swimming, riding and running thru heaven's clouds."
— Debra Valas Bevard

On the first anniversary of Cory's accident, Memphis Hightailers Bicycle Club, a nonprofit cycling club founded in 1962, hosted an event in his memory. With a starting line at St. George's Collierville campus, the Cory Horton Ride for Safety offered a twenty-five and fifty-mile ride. Cory's friends and fellow riders decorated the course with posters of Cory, and participants opened the ride with a moment of silence. A five-mile fun ride followed the events, along with a silent auction and a raffle that included a Specialized mountain bike.

On January 1, 2014, almost nine years after donating his organs for transplant, Cory was honored at the Rose Parade in Pasadena, California, along with 80 honorees, each with their own unique gift of life stories. Ranging in age from 14 hours, 58 minutes to 73 years, they earned a place on the "Gift of Life" team. Donate Life's float, *Light Up the World,* celebrated their gifts in the parade.

In total, the float's 81 honorees had saved the lives of more than 1,487 people. Donations included 37 beating hearts, 93 functioning kidneys, 43 healthy livers, 82 corneas, 1,139 bone and tissue donations, 8 heart valves, 30 lungs, and 17 pancreases. In addition, skin was donated to the New York Fire Fighters Skin Bank, organ and tissue samples were given for SIDS research, and eyes and organs were gifted for research to find new ways to treat and cure diseases.

Among the honorees were Annie Rachel Ahern, Oklahoma's first infant newborn organ donor, and Cheryl Denelli Righter whose family chose Carmen Blandin Tarleton to be the recipient of Cheryl's face after she suffered a stroke.

On February 27, 2010, 65-year-old Robert Sills of Thornville, Ohio, suffered a brain aneurysm. He donated both corneas and 179 tissue grafts, which helped better the lives of more than 180 people.

ACKNOWLEDGMENTS

I give a heartfelt "thank you" to music artist Pat Green and to Dr. Phil Berry for believing in *Thunder's Glory* and taking time out of your schedules to hear Cory's story.

A special thank you to my husband, Jim Staley, for believing in me and calling me a gifted writer. Your never-ending love and support continues to amaze me.

Thank you, Sarah and Sophie, for your continued belief in my dreams and supporting *Thunder's Glory* each time I reached out to you for clarification and facts. Thank you for your time, devotion, and for reading excerpts even when your hearts could not handle it.

I also thank my personal assistant, TinkerBella Staley, for always being at my side. It would be a blessing if one day you would learn to type.

A special thank you is given to Denise Burnett Stewart and Bryan Randolph Burnett, both of Memphis, Tennessee, for the cover photograph. They offered several amazing pictures. I believe the chosen one is perfect.

I also wish to thank Ruth L. Lovell, M. Div., CT of the Mid-South Transplant Foundation, for providing pictures of Cory's floragraph and Donate Life's Rose Parade float, *Light Up the World*.

A special thanks to Randa Lipman, Mid-South Transplant Foundation's Community Outreach Manager, for answering my many questions.

I wish to thank Addison Janz for allowing me to include *Cory*, your original song.

Thank you, Bruce Kramer, the father of my children, for providing advice and legal counsel. Please accept my apologies for those late-night telephone calls.

I give special thanks to the Reverend Barkley Thompson. On Sunday, May 15, 2005, he led us in opening prayer at Cory's memorial service. When I asked to include the sermon he gave at St. George's Independent School, he did not hesitate in his response.

Thank you, Lesley Brainard, co-founder of Memphis Thunder Racing, for providing photographs of Cory's memorial site, Share the Road signs, and the racing team he will always be a part of.

I also thank George Lapides for answering questions regarding "I Beat Lapides," the famed bumper sticker; Swimming World/Sports Publications, Swimming World News for allowing me to include their press release; and William Taylor, School President, St. George's Independent School, for permitting me to include the touching words he offered when Cory was taken from us.

I also thank my editors, Sheila Steiger and Lauren Shriver, for their professional editing expertise and their never-ending patience.

I also wish to thank Bryan Stewart, executive director of Explore Transplant, chairman of the Donate Life Rose Parade Float Committee, and past board member of Donate Life America and Donate Life California, for providing not only the names but also the stories of those who were honored along with Cory on the *Light Up the World* float.

Donations to Donate Life America can be made by visiting www. donatelifeamerica@donatelife.net or by mailing your contribution to the following address:

Donate Life America
701 East Byrd Street, 16th Floor
Richmond, VA 23219

From the bottom of my heart, I thank Gina, Jill, and Kirby for sharing your memories of Cory. In those moments when we shared a laugh, I'm certain Cory laughed along with us. When we revisited the painful memories, I believe he offered strength and guidance.

CORY

By Addison Janz

He was a man of many different dreams.
He taught us how to live if life had thrown us some bad days.
He was a man of many personalities.
And his name was Cory.
Oh yeah, his name was Cory.

He was a swim coach and a teacher guy.
He wouldn't care if he had found some way to fly.
He had a big heart that cared for me and you.
He wore high socks with sandals and shoes.
And his name was Cory,
Oh yeah, his name was Cory.

He was a young man who lived so many dreams.
His sense of fashion wasn't very keen.
He got to room with the best cyclist of all.
He loved country music that said the word y'all.
And his name was Cory,
Oh yeah, his name was Cory.

He was on his bike and had a serious fall.
The terrible news was spread around to all.
He was in the hospital and they knew he couldn't live.
He donated his organs and that's the last thing he did.
And his name was Cory,
Oh yeah, his name was Cory.

His body may be dead but here's the truth-
His spirit's still alive and his spirit's full of youth.
He is up in heaven teaching God how to swim
And he's teaching everybody in heaven how to win.
And his name was Cory,
Oh yeah, his name was Cory.

Made in the USA
San Bernardino, CA
05 January 2016